THE BATTLE AGAINST THE LUDDITES

Other books by Paul L. Dawson

The Battle against Slavery (2022)

A Potted History of Wakefield (2022)

The Art of Keith Rocco: Napoleon's Last Army (2021, with Keith Rocco)

Napoleon's Peninsular War: From Vimeiro to Corunna 1808–1809 (2020)

Wakefield at Work (2020)

Napoleon's Waterloo Army (2020)

Battle for Paris (2019)

Wakefield A to Z: People and Places (2019)

Uniform and Equipment of the Imperial Guard: Vol. 2, Foot Troops (2019)

Uniform and Equipment of the Imperial Guard: Vol. 1, Mounted Troops (2019)

Waterloo: The Truth at Last (2017)

Napoleon and Grouchy (2017)

Marshal Ney at Quatre Bras (2017)

Crippled Splendour: Napoleon's Cavalry in the Napoleonic Wars (2016)

Napoleon's Gods: The Grenadiers à Cheval 1812–1815 (2017)

Secret Wakefield (2015)

Pas de Charge! Napoleon's Cavalry in the Waterloo Campaign (2015)

Changing Wakefield (2015)

Charge the Guns! Allied Cavalry in the Waterloo Campaign (2015)

Boots & Saddles: Horses and Riders of Wellington's Army (2014)

Au Galop! Horse and Rider of Napoleon's Army (2013)

French Artillery of 1824 (2008)

Napoleonic Artillery (2008)

'Excavations at 40-42 Broad Street, Sheffield' (2007)

Wakefield Memories (2005)

Wakefield Revisited (2003)

'West Parade Methodist Church' in *Aspects of Wakefield*: Vol. 2 (ed. Kate Taylor, 1999)

THE BATTLE AGAINST THE LUDDITES

UNREST IN THE INDUSTRIAL
REVOLUTION DURING THE
NAPOLEONIC WARS

PAUL L. DAWSON

FRONTLINE
BOOKS

First published in Great Britain in 2023 by
Pen & Sword Frontline Books
An imprint of
Pen & Sword Books Ltd
Yorkshire – Philadelphia

Copyright © Paul L. Dawson 2023

ISBN 978-1-39905-240-5

The right of Paul L. Dawson to be identified as the author of this work has been asserted by him in accordance with the Copyright, Designs and Patents Act 1988.

A CIP catalogue record for this book is
available from the British Library.

All rights reserved. No part of this book may be reproduced or transmitted in any form or by any means, electronic or mechanical, including photocopying, recording or by any information storage and retrieval system, without permission from the Publisher in writing.

Typeset by Lapiz Digital
Printed and bound by CPI UK

Pen & Sword Books Limited incorporates the imprints of Atlas, Archaeology, Aviation, Discovery, Family History, Fiction, History, Maritime, Military, Military Classics, Politics, Select, Transport, True Crime, Air World, Frontline Books, Leo Cooper, Remember When, Seaforth Publishing, The Praetorian Press, Wharncliffe Local History, Wharncliffe Transport, Wharncliffe True Crime, White Owl and After the Battle.

For a complete list of Pen & Sword titles please contact:

PEN & SWORD BOOKS LIMITED
47 Church Street, Barnsley, South Yorkshire, S70 2AS, England
E-mail: enquiries@pen-and-sword.co.uk
Website: www.pen-and-sword.co.uk

or

PEN AND SWORD BOOKS
1950 Lawrence Rd, Havertown, PA 19083, USA
E-mail: Uspen-and-sword@casematepublishers.com
Website: www.penandswordbooks.com

To Sally Fairweather

Thank you for your unstinting help to travel to archives across England, Ireland, Scotland and France to enable me to write my books over the last fifteen years. Without your help, guidance and friendship, my work would be diminished.

CONTENTS

List of Illustrations ix
Acknowledgements xi
Opening Words xiii

Chapter 1	**The Eighteenth-Century Woollen Industry** 1
	Resistance to mechanisation 8
Chapter 2	**Community and Tradition** 12
	Milnes, Heywood & Co. 13
	Change and decay 15
	Community 17
Chapter 3	**Enclosure** 21
	Jacobinism 25
	Religion 26
	Comment 28
Chapter 4	**First Stirrings of Discontent** 30
Chapter 5	**Combination** 37
Chapter 6	**Luddites Arise** 44
	Every man out 49
Chapter 7	**Political Agitation** 54
	Fighting trade unionism 56
	Electioneering 57
Chapter 8	**Economic Warfare** 61
	Peace petitions 64
	Lancashire 64
	Leeds 66
Chapter 9	**Fermenting Revolution** 73
	Nottinghamshire outrages 74
	Ludd and Yorkshire 78
Chapter 10	**Yorkshire Machine Breaking** 83

Chapter 11	**Yorkshire Climax**	95
	Rawfolds Mill	98
Chapter 12	**Cottonopolis**	105
	Orders in Council	108
Chapter 13	**Food Riots**	110
Chapter 14	**The Revolutionaries**	120
	Enter Napoleon?	123
Chapter 15	**The Revolution Begins**	128
	The death of Spencer Perceval	132
Chapter 16	**Arming the Revolution**	136
	The Crown strikes back	149
Chapter 17	**Arms Raids Continue**	152
Chapter 18	**Lady Ludd**	160
Chapter 19	**Death and Burial**	173
Chapter 20	**Conclusion**	184

Notes 191
Sources and Bibliography 207
Index 211

LIST OF ILLUSTRATIONS

1. George Walker toured Yorkshire in 1814, drawing scenes from everyday life. Here we see croppers at work with their shears.

2. Spinning fleece into yarn was a traditional craft carried out at home by women, as we see here.

3. Once cloth had been cropped, the surface was checked for defects on a burtling table, and small holes sewn closed before the cloth was pressed. The men on the left of the image are working at the burtling table.

4. Lengths of cloth were sold at the cloth hall. Leeds at one time boasted three halls, two of which still stand; Huddersfield had one, which no longer stands; Wakefield had two, of which one partly remains; and Halifax had the magnificent Piece Hall. On the image, we see the interior of the Leeds Coloured Cloth Hall.

5. Cloth was taken to and from the hall by clothiers, who carried their wares on packhorses, as George Walker shows here.

6. Bean Ing Mill in Leeds was one of the first and largest factories in Yorkshire, depicted by George Walker, with ubiquitous child labourers heading off to work.

7. Georgian threshing machines were substantial pieces of equipment built into barns. They took away seasonal work form hundreds of families and were the target for destruction by Luddites.

8. Replacing the spinning wheel in the home was the spinning jenny. Its adoption had caused riots in the early 1770s. By 1812, many homes had these simple machines rather than a spinning wheel to make yarn.

9. A carding machine: a machine that processed raw fleece into a web that was passed onto a slubbing machine, which drew the web into slubs, which were then spun into yarn. The adoption of these machines had provoked community outrage in the 1780s.

10. The target of the Luddites' fury was the gig-mill, a machine that used plates of teasels to raise the nap of the woven cloth. The machine would complete in a day what a skilled man had previously been able to undertake in a week.

11. The shearing frame, patented in Sheffield in 1787, replaced the skilled cropper with a machine. These machines were the target of retribution by the men rendered economically obsolescent by their adoption.

12. A slubbing machine processed webs of fleece into slubs, which were then sent to spinners to produce yarn.

13. Benjamin Gott: Leeds industrialist and bitter opponent of the Luddites.

14. Robert Bakewell, Unitarian cloth merchant and champion of the domestic system, the leading voice for making peace with Napoleon across the West Riding in 1801 and 1807–8. His business was destroyed by the trading conditions occasioned by the Napoleonic Wars. A friend of Thomas Jefferson, he was outspoken in his support for French Revolutionary principles, for which he was gaoled in 1793.

15. Milnsbridge House, home of Magistrate Joseph Radcliffe. Now semi-derelict, the house is one of the few buildings that remain today with a direct link to Luddism.

16. The Dumb Steeple at Mirfield. Originally positioned on higher ground, this was a rallying point for the Luddite attacks at Rawfolds Mill.

ACKNOWLEDGEMENTS

I must start by thanking all those who have encouraged my return to studying this topic. The Covid-19 epidemic closed off the world of archive research in France and in the UK, and forced me to return to a long-dormant piece of study. The digitisation of records by the National Archives at Kew, and making these free to download, allowed me to reimmerse myself in early nineteenth-century West Yorkshire to study the tumultuous year of 1812.

My much-missed friend and co-religionist John Goodchild must be thanked for instilling in me a fascination for all things Unitarian and History. His infectious interest in and insatiable appetite for learning about the West Riding woollen trade, and the role Westgate Chapel members played in the world, has been eloquently passed on to me through our twenty-five years of friendship. This study is the tip of the iceberg on a much overdue reassessment of the woollen trade of the West Riding during the eighteenth century and earlier.

I must also thank David Glover of Halifax Antiquarian Society for his critical comments on Halifax Luddism, as well as Claire Pickering of Wakefield Library for permission to quote the Tomlinson diaries. I must also thank staff of Barnsley Local Studies and Archives, Leeds City Library, Sheffield City Archives and Oldham Local Studies for permission to quote from archive holdings.

OPENING WORDS

The Industrial Revolution was a defining moment in the history of Britain.

In many senses, it was a genuine revolution, fought at gunpoint between two groups of people: those whose lives would benefit from sweeping away the medieval practices and customs that had bound society together in a moral economy since Tudor England, and those who fought to defend their centuries-old way of life. Those seeking to defend their community and tradition, we know today as Luddites. Traditional history presents the Luddites as mindless vandals smashing machines, who stood in the way of progress, capitalism and the modern world. The Luddites did not stand in the way of machines: they stood against factories and mass unemployment; they stood for workers' rights and for the right to have a say in how society was governed. It is undeniable that the Luddites represented a resurgence in underground Jacobinism that had lain dormant since the Despard conspiracy of 1799–1802, discussed at length in *Fight Napoleon at Home*, by the same author.

Despard has been 'written off' as a 'mad man' and Luddism relegated to machine breaking and nothing more. Edward Royle, in his book *Revolutionary Britannia?*, argues that no national network of underground radicalism existed, nor was there any threat from Ireland or France.[1] Malcom Thomis goes further, implying that the British spy network was 'wild and imaginative' and 'unbelievable'[2] – a view shared by John Dinwiddy.[3] Perhaps this stems from a narrow, Anglocentric view of the period, divorced from the wider world, especially Ireland and France. The effect of the Napoleonic Wars on the home front has been studied consistently from English archives, and Luddism has been the focus of an exceptionally narrow aspect of research concentrating on machine breaking alone. This has failed to explore the claims made by the Luddites themselves that they were to be aided by France in support of Ireland as part of a nationwide movement. Luddism had wider political aims and motivations than machine breaking; these desired socio-economic-political reform, and found support from the French state, thanks to an underground network of informants linking Yorkshire to Paris. The Luddite movement of 1811–12 had remarkable similarities to the United Englishmen and its West Riding derivative, the Black Lamp. Arguably, the selfsame men and women of 1802 were involved in Luddism in all its forms a decade later. I would argue that the Luddite disturbances marked a decisive sea change in the relationship between the 'mob' and the authorities.

Indeed, it is fair to say that the revolutionary element of both the Industrial Revolution and the revolutionary intent of the people has been downplayed consistently since the events took place: it is almost as if a national consensus has been agreed upon to forget how close revolution came to the British Crown. *Battling the Luddites* is, in essence, a continuation of my previous book, *Fighting Napoleon at Home*. Many of the same themes and main actors in the drama appear in the fight against Luddism, political reform and revolution. The tensions that led to Despard exploded into Luddism.

To try to paper over the cracks in society, Crown propaganda, through print, cartoon and sermon delivered in the Parish church or Methodist chapel, told the masses: 'We are fighting for the survival of our culture!' Henry Addington (later Viscount Sidmouth) as prime minister deliberately propagated this message to create a sense of purpose and nationhood, to rally the people behind the Crown. He and his ministers hoped that rallying the people to '*La Patrie en danger*' would end the discontent on the home front that had blighted the previous decade. Historians J.E. Cookson[4] and Linda Colley have called this 'national defence patriotism'.[5] This phenomenon brought together both Whigs and Tories as well as Anglicans, Methodists and other dissenting groups such as Unitarians and Catholics; the latter two had been persecuted for hundreds of years, and following the events of the past decade, were displaying all the virtues of being 'good little loyalists' to end persecution. Both faiths were still illegal as the nineteenth century dawned.

Yet deep divisions remained just below the surface.

Chapter 1

THE EIGHTEENTH-CENTURY WOOLLEN INDUSTRY

As Britain went to war against Napoleon's France in 1803, Henry Addington led a broken and divided country: the previous fifteen years had seen riots and protests on the streets in a battle of ideology about ideas of Britishness. On one side stood the supporters of Charles James Fox and anti-war liberals who wanted to bring about constitutional reform and to extend the electoral franchise following the ideals of Major John Cartwright, Francis Burdett and others. Upholding the counterview that reform was bad and the state had to stamp out ideas of reform and French Revolutionary principles at home and abroad were the Tories, led by Henry Addington , William Pitt and many others of the same ilk. The nation was also divided on grounds of religion: either you were a loyalist Anglican, or a Dissenter – Catholics, Unitarians, Independent, Baptist – who were second-class citizens in their own country, with Methodists occupying a middle ground between Anglican loyalist Toryism and Dissent. The Wesley brothers were, after all, good Anglicans, and the various 'brands' of Methodism had yet to shape their own unique identity. The Methodist New Connexion of Alexander Kilham formed in the 1790s were known as 'Thom Paine Methodists' for their radical views and support of the ideals of the French Revolution.

Divided on the grounds of politics, religion and loyalty to the Crown, the divisions were further exacerbated by poverty, homelessness and famine. The Tories believed that any restriction and legislation on market forces was a bad thing, and libertarian or *laissez-faire* economics was the way forward: they understood that the 'money men' had the right to change the economy to suit their own needs and ends to maximise profit. The working class were becoming 'things' and not 'people', to work on a highly regulated pattern in factories to watch over machines. The rich, largely insulated from the everyday realities of an economy in decline, built the large Georgian country houses we now flock to see as tourists, filled them with the latest Chippendale furniture and bought the must-have artworks. At the same time, the urban and rural poor were experiencing the greatest collapse in living standards for more than 150 years, since the dark days of the English Civil War. The poor became poorer. The rich became richer by investing in the flourishing slave trade and slave-based economy as well as in the expanding cotton and woollen markets benefitting from the trade boom following the ending of the American Revolutionary War. This saw the introduction of increasing mechanisation and the beginning of an end to a working-class community that had flourished since the mid-sixteenth century. Rapid industrial change brought new stresses. A good analogy would be with the 1980s in England – the era of Thatcherism, where the rich got very wealthy indeed, and working-class communities across the north of England were destroyed. The end of coal mining, steel production and shipbuilding resulted in a decade or more of industrial discontent and societal anger not seen since Luddism. Exactly the same forces that drove the 1980s' miners' strike and the brutal oppression at Orgreave drove the working class in the 1790s; a multiplicity of factors led to the development of Luddism, as with the conflict between trade unions and the state in the 1980s.

To understand the divisions that resulted in the explosion of violence in 1811 and 1812 known as Luddism, we have to chart the economic factors that led to the situation, particularly in Yorkshire – the epicentre of Luddism.

The West Riding economy, as in the west of England, was dominated by the woollen trade. In the West Riding, a cartel of a few families controlled the merchanting side of the trade. At the close of the eighteenth century, the dominant family were the Milnes of Wakefield, who controlled over 50 per cent of the trade.[1] By far the largest demographic of those engaged in the woollen trade were the independent clothiers. From the 1770s, it became apparent that this community would decide the political direction of the county between Whig and Tory. In order to understand the Luddites' grievances, we have to consider the economic world in which they lived. Historians favour the term 'protoindustrialisation' to describe the form of industrial organisation that emerged in the sixteenth century. Initially, the word was associated with cottage industries located in the countryside. In spite of opposition from the urban guilds, rural residents were performing many industrial tasks. Agricultural labour did not occupy the peasantry for the entire year, and spare time, if such a concept existed, was put to such activities as spinning wool, or weaving and washing cloth. Peasants usually received lower remuneration for their work than did urban artisans. Protoindustrialisation gave rural residents supplementary income, which conferred a certain immunity from harvest failures. It also enabled them to marry younger and rear larger families, and prepared them, socially and psychologically, for eventual industrialisation. The efforts of urban guilds to limit rural work enjoyed only limited success; in England, for example, the restrictions seem rarely to have been enforced. Cottage industries certainly existed in the Middle Ages, but the economic expansion of the sixteenth and seventeenth centuries diffused them over much larger areas of the European countryside, perhaps most visibly in England and western Germany. In the woollen textile industry, for example, processes were highly specialised and scattered across the country, centred on domestic manufacturing carried out in the homes of workers.

In the traditional woollen industry, master clothiers, croppers or finishers could only take on two apprentices: this primarily controlled both wages and the labour market. This conflicted with the vision for the woollen trade set by factory owners like Benjamin Gott and Thomas Lloyd. Commenting on the woollen trade in the West Riding, Daniel Defoe said in 1724:

> The nearer we came to Halifax, we found the houses thicker, and the villages greater. The sides of hills, which were very steep, were spread with houses; for the land being divided into small enclosures, that is to say, from two acres to six or seven acres each, seldom more; every three or four pieces of land had a house belonging to it.
>
> Their business is the clothing trade. Each clothier must keep a horse, perhaps two, to fetch and carry for the use of his manufacture, to fetch home his wool and his provisions from the market, to carry his yarn to the spinners, his manufacture to the fulling mill, and, when finished, to the market to be sold.
>
> Among the manufacturers' houses are likewise scattered an infinite number of cottages or small dwellings, in which dwell the workmen which are employed, the women and children of whom, are always busy carding, spinning, etc. so that no hands being unemployed all can gain their bread, even from the youngest to the ancient; anyone above four years old works.[2]

This manner of organising manufactures is known as the 'putting-out system', an awkward translation of the German *Verlagssystem*.

The key to its operation was the entrepreneur, who purchased the raw materials, distributed them among the working families, passed the semi-finished products from one artisan to another, and marketed the finished products.

The production of cloth began with shearing sheep of their fleece. Wakefield, by the end of the eighteenth century, was de facto capital of the West Riding. From the Middle Ages, the trade in raw fleece was a major contributor to the economic development of the town. The sale of fleece off the sheep's back resulted in the establishment of the raw wool market, which was held in Westgate, in front of the house that belonged to John Burton, on the site of the modern-day Picture House Cinema. In his will, dated 1753, Burton refers to the house, as well as the nearby wool shops and wool market. He also lists the tolls and profits arising from the market. Burton was a man of considerable property.

Wool-staplers bought the fleece at specific fleece markets, or bought the fleece directly from the farmer. The sale of fleece was highly lucrative. The Unitarian Harper Soulby laid out Wakefield's Cheapside in 1806 to provide two spacious houses, one for himself and another for his brother, and developed the road as warehousing for wool-staplers. On King Street, Joseph Jackson built a huge four-storey warehouse in which to store wool. Titus Salt was an apprentice here.

The process of transforming a fleece into woollen cloth was as follows: After shearing, the fleece was washed – an activity that required running water and a prodigious amount of soap to remove the grease. Many becks and rivulets in the West Riding became heavily polluted due to the discharge of dirty, soapy water, which would often flow downstream to dye works or fulling mills. After washing, the fleece had to be carded – brushing it to separate the fibres. Carding was usually done by children. This involved using hand-carders to remove and untangle the short fibres from the mass. Hand-carders were essentially wooden blocks fitted with handles and covered with short metal spikes. The spikes were angled and set in leather. The fibres were worked between the spikes and, by reversing the carders, scraped off in rolls (cardings), about 12 inches long and just under an inch thick. Then a comb was used to make the fibres parallel. In Wakefield, one such concern was managed by the Lumb family of Silcoates. Richard Lumb was a wealthy wool-stapler who operated a combined dye works and wool-breaking yard. He bought fleeces from Norfolk and Suffolk and transported them back to his warehouse in Wakefield. Here the fleece was graded by quality and then carded into six or seven different qualities, before being sent out to spinners as piecework. The yarn was then collected from the spinners, which was dyed prior to being used to weave broadcloth or worsteds.[3] The proceeds from this business allowed Richard's nephew, Thomas Lumb, to build a steam-powered mill at Silcoates, completed in 1794, to card, scribble, wash, spin and dye yarn.

This process was frequently carried out by young girls. If these girls had not got married at a young age, it was believed that they would remain unmarried all their life – hence the term 'spinster' today. The spinsters spun the carded fleece into yarn. The process of carding, cleaning and spinning fleece into yarn was the first part of cloth production to be mechanised. By 1780, Jonathan Akroyd of Halifax employed perhaps 1,000 women on piecework, solely for the spinning of carded wool. It was reckoned it took a year to spin sufficient fleece to make 160lb of yarn.[4] Once it had been spun, the thread was then passed on to weavers to make it into cloth – one family of weavers were the Shuttleworths of Outwood. The finished products were returned to the employers for payment on a piecework or wage basis.

Each of these processes took place in separate cottages. Spinning was regarded as a job for women whilst weaving was seen as a man's job. If an artisan did not work in his own home, he might work in a small workshop. In the seventeenth and eighteenth centuries, such was the division of labour that many entrepreneurs concentrated solely on the processing of fleece yarn or the production of cloth, which was sold in the West Riding at the vast piece halls of Huddersfield, Halifax and Leeds. The woven cloth was sold to merchants called clothiers who visited the villages with their trains of packhorses. These men became the first capitalists. The finishing of the cloth was left to others, the great cloth merchants. They employed specialist croppers, finishers and dyers. Wakefield was the regional centre for such work. It was urban entrepreneurs, like the Milnes family of Wakefield (who by 1783 controlled over 50 per cent of the white cloth trade of Yorkshire)[5] that coordinated the efforts of the rural workers and marketed their finished products. They engaged with over 200 separate clothiers, weavers and spinners, creating lines of patronage across the West Riding from Saddleworth, where they bought cloth, to Dodworth, near Barnsley, from where they bought spun yarn to weave into cloth.[6]

Despite the production of yarn and weaving being largely rural, certain processes – usually the most highly skilled and the most remunerative – were centred in urban areas: cloth finishing and dyeing was such a skilled activity and was centred in Wakefield for a large proportion of the West Riding, in the Calder and Aire valleys.

The urban centre was also the distribution point for the finished cloth for sale to merchants.

What was so good about the domestic system? The artisans involved could work at their own speed while at home or near their own home. Children working in the system received better treatment than they would in the factory system. As women usually worked at home, someone was always there to look after the children. Conditions of work were better as windows could be open, people worked at their own speed and rested when they needed to. Meals could be taken when needed. As people worked for themselves, they could take a pride in what they did. Tension in the workplace was minimal as the family worked as a unit. The best home-produced goods were of a quality that, at first, machine-made goods could not match.

However, the domestic system did have a number of major weaknesses. The production was very slow and, as we shall see, was restricted to certain times of year. A better and faster system of production was needed. The complete process of production spread across several cottages, so time was lost as materials were taken from cottage to cottage as one stage progressed to the next. The utilisation of water to drive manufacturing processes was developing and producers in small cottages could not possibly take advantage of this source of power. The image of working in quaint country cottages giving producers a quality (if not well-paid) lifestyle is simply not a correct one. Defoe witnessed children as young as 4 working in the domestic system. Also, the waste material that gathered around these cottages did nothing to enhance the quality of life for those who lived there.

Mechanisation and centralisation of trades was a logical next step in the development of the woollen trade given logistical difficulties and costs in transporting the cloth to the cloth halls and from the halls to be dyed and finished before being sold. This was in addition to the need to improve the time it took to organise the purchasing of fleece and production of yarn. It is therefore apparent that before the Industrial Revolution, the small-scale nature of the many manufacturing activities limited any growth in productivity or output. It required a total transformation of the woollen trade.

However, mechanisation meant the end of a centuries-old way of life. The Industrial Revolution, like the French Revolution, brought about decades of animosity and, at times, open warfare between both sides of the debate. Unlike in France, where the Revolution lasted no more than a decade, England's Revolution resulted in, perhaps, fifty years of tension between the haves and the have-nots in society.

The ramifications of the Industrial or English Revolution of 1775 to 1832 were as long-lasting and important as in France, yet the story of those on the losing side, the Luddites, has largely been ignored. It was here in the battleground of the working class that nascent democratic idealism was fought for and, ultimately, despite virulent opposition, won out with the various Reform Acts of the mid to late nineteenth century. The disparity in attitudes of the rule makers and the rule takers, and of who could be admitted into the rule-making class, resulted in a long-running dispute that only ended with the formation of the first working-class government of Ramsey MacDonald in the 1920s.

Master clothiers were well aware of their own autonomy and of their collective strength as independent clothiers. They owned their own business, produced their own cloth and employed their own scribblers, carders and spinners. They had erected cloth halls in Leeds, Halifax, Huddersfield and Wakefield as opulent signs of their wealth and power in the West Riding. Any visitor to the Piece Hall in Halifax becomes immediately aware of the scale of the historical woollen trade in the West Riding and the wealth it generated. Between 1765 and 1773, the production of broadcloth in the West Riding doubled, driven by access to markets in America as well as by Yorkshire taking over business from the West Country. Recession returned in 1774, further hampered by the American War: the amount of broadcloth milled reduced from 120,000 lengths in 1773 to 87,000 in the following year.[7] From the end of the American War, the economy boomed: the West Riding woollen trade experienced an unheralded era of constant expansion, which allowed the wealthiest to invest in mechanisation: this allowed an increase in production speed and reduction in labour costs. Indeed, we note that between 1788 and 1800, production of broadcloth in the West Riding increased 105 per cent compared to levels of business up to 1788. From 1782, the production of broadcloths had grown year on year. The trade in worsteds had grown steadily, increasing 28 per cent from 1788 to 1800. This increase in trade allowed merchants to invest capital into mechanisation.[8] Indeed, the lengths of broadcloth milled from 1783 to 1800 doubled, which meant that Yorkshire accounted for at least 60 per cent of the total English output of broadcloth, of which 90 per cent went to export.[9] In 1796, £952 worth of goods went to Germany, £1,047 to Portugal, £670 to Africa and £2,525 to America: the woollen trade was almost exclusively reliant on exports. Any disturbance to the trade would spell disaster for many master clothiers and merchants.[10] To meet demand, and to speed up cloth production, merchants and manufacturers sought new ways to feed the market. As technical innovations continued to develop, manufacturing machinery became larger and more expensive to purchase and maintain, which could only be financed by a handful of wealthy industrialists who had the fiscal resources capable of investing in these new technologies. This situation prompted the emergence of the familiar factory system and signalled the end for many traditional modes of production.

Resistance to mechanisation

In popular imagination, Luddism occurred just once in 1812. Not so. It had a much longer history than heretofore supposed.

As previously discussed, the first process in the production of cloth was carding the wool fleece before it could be spun into yarn on a traditional spinning wheel. Carding was the process whereby the fleece was teased out and cleaned using large wooden brushes with closely packed iron bristles, very much like a modern-day Velcro cleaning brush, to produce a continuous web or sliver suitable for processing. As with carding, spinning was traditionally the employ of women and children. The capacity of yarn production depended on the number of wheels at work as well as available light in which to work. Traditional weavers' cottages had large third-floor windows to provide as much natural light as possible to allow a long working day, and to illuminate the workplace at no cost, as candles and oil lamps were expensive. Hand spinning of yarn created a bottleneck in production, thus to increase production, the 'spinning jenny' was developed.

The spinning jenny first appeared in 1769, in Lancashire. The early jennies were designed to be powered by women and children working in the home. As they developed into larger apparatuses, with more spindles, they became the preserve of men operators; hence, wool spinning gradually became a male domain and within a generation, they became master workmen. The nature of the domestic system required the clothiers to buy finished yarn from the master spinners: the quicker production methods, and being able to produce more yarn than ever before, resulted in masters purchasing several jennies and establishing embryonic factories for the production of yarn. The adoption of the jenny, or slubbing machine, in the West Riding does not seem to have occasioned the same degree of anger as in Lancashire.

On 14 June 1769, a number of workmen who were anxious about competition and the lower price of yarn being produced smashed jennies in a riot that has remained famous in Lancashire. About fifty men and women, armed with cudgels and hammers, smashed five machines at Turton. In the days that followed, a jenny was smashed in Bolton, while another machine was destroyed at Bury.[11] In 1776, the West Country experienced widespread sabotage of almost every form of machinery associated with the woollen industry: spinning jennies and carding machines were smashed. Three years later, a mob around Blackburn demolished every carding engine and all jennies that used more than twenty-four spindles. Calling themselves Luddites, the mob demolished other machines utilising water or horsepower. The same year, the water frames at Richard Arkwright's works at Chorley were destroyed simultaneously with those at several recently established cotton mills. Machine-breaking episodes in Lancashire and the midlands flared up from 1778 to 1780. In the West Country, the introduction of the flying shuttle sparked riots at Trowbridge in 1785 and 1792. Joseph Brookhouse's attempt to utilise Arkwright's techniques to mechanise the spinning of worsted yarn provoked a violent response in Leicester. In 1792, Manchester witnessed an attack on a factory containing twenty-four of Edmund Cartwright's power looms, and the factory was eventually burnt down by outraged handloom weavers.[12]

After the adoption of the jenny in the spinners' homes, the next process to be mechanised in the West Riding was scribbling and carding. This time-consuming and dirty job was mechanised in 1775 when Joseph Arkwright patented the first scribbling/carding machine. This machine prepared the fleece for spinning into yarn: scribbling was hand-carding writ large, and was traditionally carried out by hand. The processed fleece was now passed through a 'slubbing billy' before being spun into yarn on a jenny rather than a traditional spinning wheel. The slubbing billy was a machine for putting a twist into freshly carded wool so that it could be spun. It was used to process partly spun wool, or 'rovings', from the piecing machine into a leaner yarn. The mechanisation of this trade did not result in violence, although the mechanisation of the next stage of cloth production did.

Scribbling and carding machines needed to be run by steam or water power: fulling mills were traditionally powered by waterwheels, and by the early 1780s were becoming steam powered. It was easy enough for the miller to erect carding and slubbing machines in the attic spaces of his mill. Carding is a mechanical process that disentangles, cleans and intermixes fibres to produce a continuous web or sliver suitable for subsequent processing. This is achieved by passing the fibres between differentially moving surfaces covered with card clothing (like Velcro brushes joined together on a moving belt). The process breaks up locks (knots) and unorganised clumps of fibre and then aligns the individual fibres to be parallel with each other. In preparing wool fibre for spinning, carding is the step that comes after teasing. With wool, two carding machines were used: the first, the scribbler, opened and mixed the fibres, the second, the condenser, mixed and formed the web.[13]

One of the first mechanised mills for cleaning and processing fleece was established in 1781 by Ebenezer Aldred in Wakefield. Aldred's mill was one of just six such concerns in the West Riding established since 1774.[14] By 1780, at least 100 fulling mills were in operation in the area; none were used for scribbling. Six years later, when the first reports appear of direct action being taken against the machines, it was reckoned that 170 scribbling engines were in use. The slubbing, carding and scribbling machines in Bramley Mill were attacked by women who had been made unemployed by the machines.[15] Indeed, between 1780 and 1786, fourteen mills were erected in the West Riding.[16] In the summer of 1786, a petition appeared in the *Leeds Mercury* stating thousands were now destitute because of the new machinery: each scribbling machine could do the work of ten men, and as they worked twenty-four hours a day, the machines had set over 4,000 men out of work, and the same number of apprentices had been laid off. In consequence, the paper reported, the poor rate in Leeds would increase, and appealed that 'men of common sense must know, so many machines in use, take the work from the hands employed scribbling'. The writer continued:

> How are these men, thus thrown out of employ to provide for their families; - and what are they to put their children apprentice to, that the rising generation may have something to keep them at work, in order that they are not vagabonds strolling about in idleness? Some say, begin and learn some other business. - suppose we do; who will maintain our families whilst we undertake the arduous task; and when we have learned it, how shall we know we shall be any better for our pains; for by the time we have served our second apprenticeship, another machine may arise, which may take away that business also.[17]

Thus, the first glimmering of Luddism in West Yorkshire was sparked by mechanisation and the threat this posed to community and tradition. These new scribbling mills prepared wool and fulled the finished cloth, not only for the mills' owners, but also for other master clothiers: from these beginnings would emerge factories. The scribbling mills allowed a clothier to prepare in one day the same amount of fleece and spin into yarn as had previously taken a fortnight.[18] Many of these mills also took under their roofs jennies for spinning the fleece into yarn. Aldred's Mill in Wakefield, for example, comprised 'the Stockhouse, Warehouse, Engine-house, Fire engine, Outhouses, Garden on the east side of Westgate Common commanding the entire and continual Stream of Water of Westgate Common Beck ... the whole purposely constructed and, in all Respects, well calculated for carrying on the Business of Scribbling, Carding & Spinning Wool'.[19] In terms of machinery, the mill possessed 'one double carding engine, five other carding engines, one very large carding engine, all covered with good cards and in good repair; two carding engines uncovered with cards, one-wheel cylinder, three billies, one willy, two jennies and various other articles'.[20] Aldred was processing raw fleece into yarn far quicker than the traditional home-based domestic system could. These new mills concentrated into the hands of a single miller what had previously been individual domestic trades employing hundreds of families. Yet with the year-on-year expansion of the woollen trade, the displaced labour force was able to find work elsewhere, within the domestic system.[21] However, once the economy began to shrink and employment opportunities ended with the commencement of the war with Revolutionary France, tensions within the community rose. Mechanisation meant unemployment: the machines became the target of community vengeance. Between 1786 and 1795, over a hundred mills had been established across the West Riding – almost ten new mills a year for scribbling, carding, and fulling.[22]

The manufacturing world was changing rapidly. It was an easy step to bring all the processes involved in cloth production into a single, vast building: the age of the factory and mechanisation had dawned.

Chapter 2

COMMUNITY AND TRADITION

As our previous chapter has touched upon, the 1780s witnessed the fulling miller, like Ebenezer Alfred in Wakefield, extend his operations into scribbling. In the 1790s, some clothiers, such as Thomas Wood in Flanshaw near Wakefield, did likewise. In 1785, Wood purchased 5 acres of land and buildings in Flanshaw for £410. He was a master handloom weaver, the son of a clothier. He was literate, as evidenced by the many letters between him and his daughter that survive in the John Goodchild collection. By 1790, he had prospered sufficiently as a weaver and clothier to build a large new fulling mill on his land at Flanshaw, powered by a steam engine provided by Fall Ings Foundry of Wakefield. The mill, known as Hebble Mill, commenced operation in October or November 1791. It was performing the functions of processing the raw wool, cleaning it and straightening (scribbling), as well as fulling the finished woven cloth.[1]

Other changes took place in the traditional woollen trade as the eighteenth century ended. Wool-staplers now began spinning their own yarn in purpose-built factories. For example, in 1788, Samuel and Joseph Holdsworth bought land at Westgate End, Wakefield. The family had been wool-breakers since the 1690s, but they now expanded their operation to encompass the processing of raw fleece into yarn. Like many involved in the woollen trade in the town, various branches of the Holdsworth family were associated with the Unitarian chapel at Westgate End. For example, Stephen Holdsworth had been superintendent of building during the construction of the current Westgate Chapel in 1750–3. The Holdsworth family's mill was in operation by 1790, and eight years later, Murray, Fenton and Wood of Leeds installed a steam engine to power the mill complex.[2] By cutting out the independent spinners working from home, and no longer relying on wool-breakers, scribblers or carders, these industrialists were fundamentally changing the nature of the domestic system in taking over the production of yarn.

By concentrating trades into a factory, yarn could be made more quickly and cheaply. No longer did agents like Mr Loxley, who worked for the Milnes family, have to travel across the West Riding ordering yarn from dozens of different families: instead, yarn could be ordered in bulk from one or two suppliers, who were now located in urban centres close to the weavers' premises. The woollen trade was changing rapidly, and there would be winners and losers in the shift from a rural craft-based trade to an urban, mechanised industry.

The domestic system had reinforced traditional lines of patronage and stratification: the fulling miller, wool-stapler, clothier and merchant all had their own sphere of influence. Once the traditional structure of the domestic system began to change, the clothier increasingly found himself pushed out as merchants and fulling millers came to dominate production. Concentration of looms into protofactories began in the 1770s, when they were technically illegal.

The central point of the domestic system was the cloth hall. Halls were established in Wakefield by 1719 (but had disappeared by the 1740s), in Leeds from 1720, Huddersfield (now demolished) from 1765, and Halifax from the 1770s. It was here that the independent clothiers sold their lengths or pieces of cloth to the merchant for finishing, who then sold it onwards to retail in the home market or for export.

Milnes, Heywood & Co.

The merchant's responsibilities within community tradition was to finish the cloth, and to get the goods to market. The largest of the eighteenth-century merchanting houses was that of the Milnes family of Wakefield. The family originated in Chesterfield and moved to Wakefield in the 1690s as cloth finishers, but quickly expanded the business into the merchanting of cloth. Two branches of the family were involved in the same trade. In 1774, brothers Pemberton and John Milnes – trading as Pem & John Milnes and Co. – became trustees and investors in Halifax Piece Hall, opened 1779, and also Leeds White Cloth Hall. Their nephew, James Milnes – trading as James Milnes & Co., whose agent was Titus Rideal – also invested in both places. In 1775, the surviving partner, Pemberton Milnes, entered into partnership with his nephews to form Milnes, Heywood & Co. Into this venture, Pemberton invested £30,000, John Milnes (son of Pemberton's brother John and known in his own lifetime as Jack

Milnes the Democrat) £20,000, and Arthur and Benjamin Heywood £10,000 a man.[3] John Milnes was the public face of the concern and had a private income of at least £10,000 from the business.

By 1780, as noted above, the family controlled half of the white cloth trade and were importing high quality Saxony fleece for the production of high quality cloth to clothe gentlemen and for export, as well as buying coarser fabrics from across Lancashire to be dyed and finished for the domestic trade.[4] The family worked closely with their co-religionists at Westgate Chapel: the Lumb family were the principal dyers, and Joseph Burrell and the Soulby brothers, wool merchants of Leeds and Wakefield, seem to have been the principal suppliers of local fleece.[5] As previously mentioned, John and Harper Soulby had laid out Cheapside as wool-staplers' warehousing from 1806. The Milnes family network extended into continental Europe. The best fleece in Europe at the time came from the electorate of Saxony, where Spanish Merino sheep had been imported to improve northern European fleece. The relocation from Merseburg of Christian Frederick Gotthard to Wakefield gave the family direct access to this trade; he could travel freely through Europe buying fleece, and being fluent in English and German, negotiated trading terms for the Milnes family. Joseph Scott – again a Unitarian – was the principal cropper for the concern, his premises being based less than 50 yards from Westgate Chapel, and the secretary to the trustees of Westgate Chapel, Samuel Shuttleworth, was one of the clothiers the concern dealt with for the production of superfines.

Beyond the congregation at Westgate Chapel, the Milnes family also dealt with independent clothiers who supplied cloth for finishing, including Jonas Kenyon, clothier of Over Cumberworth near Denby Dale. Cloth was also purchased from clothiers in Wakefield, Ossett, Horbury and Dalton, as well as further afield in Lockwood, Lindley, Almondbury, Golcar and Crosland the latter places being centres of cropping, and Luddism, as we shall see. According to the notebooks of Jonathan Akroyd of Lane Head, and later 29 Northgate and Bowling Dykes Mills, Halifax, for the period 1770–89 the Milnes's agent, Mr Loxley, was buying from Akroyd shalloons and other worsteds, the former costing 32*s.* to 42*s.* a length and the latter, 40*s.* to 108*s.* a length. Rather than rely on spinners in the Halifax area, Akroyd was obtaining his yarn from Joseph Taylor of Dodworth, near Barnsley, as well as from Dunsop Bridge, Tosside and Wigglesworth, situated between the Forest of Bowland and Skipton. Indeed, the Akroyd brothers – James and Jonathan – were highly successful in the practice of distributing yarn and other materials to individuals and families for handloom weaving and production of the finished pieces of cloth. It required five or six spinners and several carders to support one weaver. Records show that Jonathan Akroyd and other local manufacturers sent wool to North Yorkshire, Preston and other parts of Lancashire, as well as Austwick-in-Craven, to be spun. As well as buying cloth to take to Wakefield for dyeing and finishing, the Milnes also bought yarn that had been spun ready to weave into cloth: in January 1778, the Milnes purchased a bale of spun yarn for £10, and a bale containing 150lb of yarn was purchased in July 1776, from Akroyd in Halifax.[6] In 1804, management of Milnes, Heywood & Co. passed to Rachel Milnes, who in 1806 entered into partnership with Thomas and William Holdsworth, trading as cloth merchants under the name Milnes, Heywood & Holdsworth & Co. The business was sold in 1832 to Joseph Clay, ending the Milnes family's link with the woollen trade.

In producing their own cloth as well as merchanting clothing from the cloth halls, the Milnes were both supporting the traditional industry and undercutting it. The lack of clearly defined trade activities of merchant and manufacturers meant that as the nineteenth century dawned, the cloth hall system was in slow, yet terminal, decline.

Change and decay

In order to reduce transport costs and increase production of both yarn and finished cloth, the next logical step was to bring all the processes involved in woollen production into a single location – the factory. Only the wealthier clothiers could afford to do so; the wealth in the woollen trade rested with the merchants who owned mansions in both town and country. By 1790, the Milnes family had converted the premises at the rear of their Westgate mansion into a factory of sorts. Yarn was spun and woven into cloth here prior to dispatch to their dye works at Belle Vue, and then returned to be finished in the Westgate factory. The putting-out system had almost been brought in-house.

If the other merchants and manufacturers were to survive, they had to mechanise to compete economically. With merchants producing their own cloth for sale directly into the domestic and export markets, they cut out the cloth halls and traditional marketing economy. Merchants were not, according to convention, to make the goods they sold. The largest of these early factories was erected in Leeds by Benjamin Gott.

Depending on one's viewpoint, Benjamin Gott was either the hero of Leeds's industrial development and growth or the archvillain in backing capital against labour. Born in 1762 in the Calverley district of the city, he came from an affluent background: his father was the consulting engineer for the Aire and Calder Navigation and was later

Crown surveyor for the West Riding. He had sufficient fiscal resources to afford to launch Benjamin, aged 18, into a career with a leading firm of Leeds cloth merchants, Wormald and Fountaine. Initially, he served as an apprentice, and then a partner – at a total cost of £4,000 (over £250,000 in 2021). John Wormald (who died in 1786) had been elected mayor of Leeds Corporation in 1776. He married, as his second wife, Sarah Atkinson, the sister-in-law of his business partner. His son John was partner in Wormald & Gott until his death in 1803. Joseph Fountaine (who died in 1791) was elected mayor in 1777, and was partner with his brother John in one of, if not the largest merchanting houses in Leeds.

Benjamin Gott, who was young, energetic and inventive, became the driving force of the firm, and when the senior partners died, he took over the business. The timing was fortuitous: trade was booming, with an exponential increase in demand for all types of woollen cloth year on year, particularly for export to America. Steam-powered scribbling and fulling mills had been built in the West Riding from the 1780s – one of the first was built in Wakefield by Ebenezer Aldred in 1786, and the Milnes of Wakefield completed a fulling and scribbling mill in 1792, also powered by steam. Having seen the small steps taken by opulent clothiers in mechanising some processes in the production of cloth, and also technological innovations of the cotton mills of Lancashire such as that of Peter Drinkwater, Gott sought to build his own factory. His goal was to bring all the processes in the production of cloth into a single building, powered by steam.

In 1792, Gott bought a field known as Bean Ing in what was then open countryside next to the river Aire. This is where he began building a new mill (originally called Park Mill), where many of the processes of cloth making could be brought together and mechanised.

The outbreak of war with France brought a sudden massive demand for army uniform cloth and blankets, while trade with the Americas and China boomed. By 1800, the mill was employing over a thousand workers but still could not meet demand. In 1788, Thomas Lloyd had set up another vast mill at Armley (now the Industrial Museum), which Gott leased in 1800 and later purchased, in 1805. Lloyd ran his mill to process corn as well as full cloth: any clothier could pay to have their cloth fulled by Lloyd. Under Gott's control, all that ended: the mill worked for one man and one man only, the greater good of Benjamin Gott, who had taken over his rival to dominate the woollen trade in Leeds. Putting everything under one roof at Bean Ing saved time and money because Gott could better control the quality of the cloth. There were also fewer delays and lower transport costs. Despite these savings, most of the wool making process still had to be done by hand. Wherever production could be mechanised, Gott invested in new machines and in different power sources. His machines could be operated by labourers, who were cheaper to employ than skilled workmen. Thus, after the initial outlay in capital to build the machines, his profit margin increased as his wage bill was lower and he was able to finish a length of cloth in twelve hours rather than almost ninety: he could make more cloth for less money and so monopolise the market.

Gott crossed the line in breaking the statutes on the number of looms that could be legitimately held by a clothier. The community fear was that others would follow his lead and push the small clothiers and weavers out of business, whilst some understood that Gott had broken the law and got away with it, and wished to follow his example. Gott also flouted community custom and tradition because he was a merchant engaging in cloth production. Where Gott led, other merchants quickly followed. In Wakefield, the Milnes family rapidly expanded their operations to include fulling, scribbling, spinning, dyeing and weaving. The merchants in quickly exploiting the factory system were now producing their own cloth, often making cloth to order, and circumventing the cloth halls. The smaller clothiers, lacking the capital to invest in more looms or in building new factories, felt increasingly under attack by the rich merchants, whose aim it was to crush the domestic system. Such feelings are understandable as the domestic system was under direct attack from the merchants, who, according to custom, had no rights to make cloth. Clothiers refused to lose their status as men of importance in their community as well as their much-valued status of craft master.

The new centralised and mechanised factories owned by Benjamin Gott and William Cookson of Leeds, and others like Law Atkinson of Huddersfield or John Brooke of Honley, were producing cloth cheaper than any of their competitors and forcing them to mechanise to be able to compete. Gott was 'creaming off' the best customers.[7] In response, groups of clothiers and smaller merchants developed joint stock mills to challenge the likes of Benjamin Gott. The expansion of such ventures that bypassed the traditional domestic system resulted in community rebuke: in 1794, to protect their independence, clothiers across the West Riding raised a petition objecting to merchants becoming manufacturers. Yet violence did not break out.[8]

Community
The challenge to the clothiers' independence and autonomy from the monopolisers like Benjamin Gott cannot be underestimated. These new

mills drew in unskilled labour from neighbouring towns and villages, and witnessed the beginning of the end of the long-established putting-out system of cloth production through independent clothiers. Increasing industrialisation placed pressure on housing stock as well as on food. The workers became more reliant on markets to provide them with food and the threat of famine became real. No longer could the clothier or spinner rely on his kitchen garden. At the same time, the clothiers realised they had no access to common land, and that they were losing business to the larger factories. A perfect storm of discontent was brewing. The clothiers, croppers and merchants were politically aware. They had been major participators in the 1775, 1780 and 1783 Yorkshire Petitions for peace and political reform. The leaders of the community, men like John Milnes of Wakefield or Samuel Hamer Oates of Leeds, were at the forefront of the political reformist agenda. The petition reported in the press was:

> from certain woollen manufacturers, complaining that a monopoly was introducing into the trade by men of large capitals, to the great detriment and probable ruin of the numerous manufacturers of small capitals and praying general relief.[9]

The petition of 1794 was led much in the manner as that of 1783. Largely, the community was split between Whig and Tory, Anglican and Dissenter. The Tory Anglicans dominated Leeds – particularly the Gott and Cookson families – and the Unitarian Milnes, Lumb and Naylor families dominated Wakefield. In Halifax, the Atkinsons, also Unitarians, were vocal community leaders. The Tories, who were mostly the large merchants and manufacturers, were happy with the societal status quo. The Whigs desired political change: they wanted political representation, to get their voices heard to save their community, rights and traditions. The clothiers had hoped to embrace the prospects of machines and become manufacturers. There is no mistaking the fact that the status of the smaller master clothier and his livelihood was becoming debased. The ideological differences between the two groups were unsurmountable. The clothiers backed political reform and their community traditions, and the merchants backed Tory conservative principles and *laissez-faire* economics.

The likes of Cookson, Gott, and other factory owners from the merchant class, had a differing worldview to the clothiers and croppers. The clothiers' view is understandable: this was the worldview until Necker's economic revolution in France in the 1770s and 80s, which realised that finance was not a finite resource. This revolutionised economics, and brought with it a differing worldview: free trade or regulated trade. Conflict over these ideas still impacts on the world today. We see Necker's thinking – and support of free trade – reflected in the worldview of the merchants. If the merchants took a bigger slice of cake, then the clothiers would suffer. This was a narrow worldview. For the merchants, the economy and business could expand exponentially, and was not like a cake; commerce was not finite. This idea, coupled with the *laissez faire* economics of Adam Smith, whereby market forces regulated the economy and that regulation of the economy defining who could do what, the idea of fixed prices, labour laws, guilds and apprenticeships all stood in the way of profit. A regulated economy meant that people and workers knew their place, prices and profit remained largely static, and any change to this was resisted. Making cloth to order, the larger manufacturers like Cookson et al, circumvented the cloth hall. It created a two-tier system: one where the smaller clothiers travelled to the halls to sell their goods to an increasingly smaller domestic home market as the economy shrunk, and the larger merchants' profits increased as they produce their own goods direct for sale to the market. Most cloth produced in the West Riding was white: it was sold at the cloth hall, where it was purchased by the merchant, who finished and dyed the cloth for sale. By processing the yarn, weaving the cloth, dyeing and finishing the cloth, the industrials controlled all stages of production: it was a logical conclusion to bring all the differing trades into a single locale. Yet what were the dyers, weavers, spinners to do when they found that the 'monopolisers' no longer desired their services and goods? A deflating economy from 1792 meant it was increasingly difficult to raise the capital or credit needed to buy land, and as the larger manufacturers came to dominate the market, the newcomer was, by necessity, obliged to devote more time to cloth production as his sole income. Without a portfolio of land investment to provide a secondary income from rents or sale of produce, when the economy shrank, the newcomer to the industry, like the smaller clothiers, found it almost impossible to carry on. The small clothiers failed, or had to give up their status as masters and become dependent artisans in a factory. Land price was linked to credit: to feed the economy, land prices had to increase and be kept high. Without access to cheap land to expand the agricultural smallholding or enlarge the tenter field (where cloth could be stretched to dry evenly in the process of manufacture), small and middling clothiers were being squeezed out of business by the monopolisers, of whom Benjamin Gott stands sentinel.[10]

The new factories forced many master clothiers out of business and they had to seek work for themselves within those same factories. For many, the factory system was to blame: they had brought about bankruptcies, had taken the work from their hands, and were stealing the bread from the mouths of their families. For men like Cookson of Leeds, destroying the clothiers was a good thing, as it meant that the merchants could control the market: factories were the future. In Leeds, by 1800, thirty-five mills were at work.[11] No fewer than eighty-one steam engines were powering machines as the eighteenth century ended.[12]

The small clothiers legitimately feared that their way of life would be quickly destroyed and their social status as masters would be eroded by the new factories, where machines replaced skilled labour in the finishing trade, where journeymen weavers had no place in society. The desire to maintain the static, conservative society and tradition led the community to embrace radical action. Communities under economic stress and fearful of change resort, in some cases, to extremes in order to remove the threat to their community. Benjamin Gott and William Cookson were hellbent on the imposition of the factory system, mechanisation of cloth finishing and the removal of all legislative restrictions to woollen production. The clothiers and croppers, feeling themselves under attack, fought back: they embraced Jacobinism and took direct action to safeguard their community and tradition. Some found support from scripture in their radical views in seeking to overturn the established order. The rich merchants sought to preserve their position and status in society by, naturally enough, embracing 'Church and King' conservative loyalism: the preservation of a stratified society with the king at the top and the working man at the bottom. Social conservatism drove two communities into polar opposites. For the factory owners, buoyed by a growing confidence in *laissez-faire* economics, the capital these men accumulated was radically reshaping custom and tradition and replacing it with a new vision, from the top down. The woollen trade had been governed by consensus and had placed major store in tradition. The change to a position where monetary might replaced community vision was impossible for many. Luddism was not simply about machine breaking; it was a cataclysmic difference in ideology, in which the politics of the French Revolution loomed large.

Chapter 3

ENCLOSURE

Luddism, when it appeared, was not just concerned with the breaking of machinery involved in the woollen trade: machines on farms, as much as walls and gates restricting access to common land, were attacked as symbols of oppression by the elites over the working man.

The changing nature of late Georgian society, which witnessed the transformation of a largely agrarian economy into a rapidly industrialising one, placed extreme stress on food supplies. From the end of the American War, the economy boomed: the West Riding woollen trade experienced an unheralded era of continual expansion and mechanisation. At the same time, the rapid enclosure of land and modernisation of agriculture with the introduction of new technology and working systems, as well as the centuries-old way of land ownership and access to land being changed through enclosure, drove rural labourers into towns to seek work. This created an underclass of the poor. Poor relief was raised from rates levied against wealthier households. Charity was distributed to claimants through local overseers, who examined settlement claims and assessed how much money individuals should receive. As well as apportioning financial handouts to people in their own homes (so-called 'outdoor relief'), many parishes also awarded relief in kind – in clothing and fuel during winter months, for example, or in loaves of bread. Legislation passed in 1722 entitled parishes to provide poor relief in specially built workhouses. By the 1770s, there were about 2,000 such workhouses in the country, with nearly 100,000 people in residence. Ninety separate workhouses operated in London alone, sheltering about 15,000 inmates.

It is undeniable that enclosing land made agriculture more profitable: crop rotation made farmland more productive, land increased in value, and not all labourers lost their land. Yet enclosure, changing working practices and mechanisation meant fewer labourers were needed on farms, and centuries-old ways of life came to an end, literally overnight, with the erecting of fences. The magistrates, justices of the peace and Parliament had the arbitrary power to redistribute land from the people to their own interest. The most productive land naturally went to the great and good, as was their right, the more marginal land being retained as common, or parcelled out to smaller farmers. Enclosure also entailed the conversion of commons, wasteland and open fields to formally enclosed units of land, the conversion of arable land to pasture and the partition of large areas of communally farmed land into small fields to be farmed by individuals. The resulting drop in agricultural labours' employment and wages led to a rise in the urban poor, who were reliant almost totally from 1795 on poor relief, levied at parish level. Over time, these people would be drawn to work in the great textile factories instead of the skilled clothiers and croppers. The government was happy to impose sudden dramatic change on the people, but refused any hint of political revision that would endanger the elite oligarchy's consolidation of power. Whatever the rights and wrongs of enclosure, it is undeniable that it allowed for greater crop yields.

However, unlike woollen manufacturers in the west of England who relied solely on woollen goods for income, many West Riding clothiers developed dual incomes: most master clothiers owned looms as well as smallholdings for growing staple crops of hay, oats, beans, peas and wheat, and depended upon common land for grazing their herds of cows and sheep. Many clothiers, spinners and weavers gained essential income and food from market gardening. The sale of the excess wheat, oats or other goods supplemented the clothiers' income, when shorter winter days and the natural rhythm of season – muddy roads or snow making trade almost impossible, for example – affected the amount of cloth produced as well as slack periods of work. Without small-scale agriculture, many smaller clothiers simply could not afford to remain in business. Akroyd's dealings with the Milnes family exemplifies the seasonality of the trade. In the first quarter of 1777, the Milnes purchased cloth to the value of £166 18s., in the second quarter, £49 10s., in the third quarter, a mere £25 3s., and the fourth quarter, £48 16s.[1] Cloth could not be dried and stretched – tentered – in the winter months, so much of the Milnes' work was restricted to the summer. Winter storms also prevented their ships setting sail to America or Russia. Therefore, the Milnes, like many others, supplemented their income from agriculture.

The agricultural foundations of the clothier's economy allowed them to draw rent from the land if they did not farm it directly, and if they did farm it themselves, the sale of produce provided a financial cushion to mitigate fluctuations in the wool trade. Home-grown produce from the kitchen gardens attached to most clothiers' homes offset the reliance on staple goods bought from market. The lack of common land for cows, sheep and goats through enclosure, along with the increasing demand for land for housing in rapidly growing towns, meant that, for the first time, clothiers faced famine and scarcity. So too did many urban poor. Enclosure and the lack of land meant the rural communities were under stress, and urban centres had an increasing number of workers who relied solely on factory work for their income: in consequence, the urban working class was born. Recognition of this phenomenon is evidenced by the ever-increasing poor rate, a fund designed to pay the poor of a parish 6s. a week – barely enough to live on – levied in a parish to keep the unemployed from total destitution. Riots against paying this tax broke out in 1801 as the middle class were struggling to meet the ever-increasing tax burden.[2]

Enclosure also had another detrimental effect on local community and tradition. Land now became an asset to be bought and sold. Enclosure ensured that the value of land would rise, and it would never fall: vast fortunes were made selling off land that landlords had obtained free of charge thanks to the commissioners. Enclosure was overseen by a body of commissioners who had been chosen by the local magistrates. Often these men were wealthy landowners who stood to make considerable gains through enclosure.

The smaller and middle-ranking clothiers of the West Riding were uniquely vulnerable to land price increases and enclosure. Many clothiers, and dyers, for that matter, needed land for tentering cloth, a couple of acres for their riding and driving horses to take goods to and from the cloth halls, and relied upon a kitchen garden, a couple of cows, goats, chickens, and possibly a few acres under crop for corn, oats or barley. In Armley in the 1790s, it was reckoned that a clothier held 3 acres, and kept a Galloway pony and a cow. In Leeds in 1793, the average amount of land held was 2 to 5 acres, which previously had a rentable value of 10s. an acre for arable use but was now worth 30s. to 50s. an acre due solely to the rise in manufacturing in the area and the new policy of enclosure.[3]

If a clothier sought to expand, he needed land where he could tenter and dry his cloth: increasing land prices around towns and villages made it almost impossible for a clothier to expand without a considerable investment of capital, which many simply did not have. The domestic system allowed for a young entrepreneur to set themselves up in business to manufacturer cloth, and to take their cloth to the public fulling mills for a set charge rather than have the expense of buying and setting up his own fulling stocks or scribbling mill. Hence, the net effect of increasing land prices was squeezing the smaller clothiers out of business as they could not buy land for their tenter frames and smallholdings. This, coupled with the rise in production speed from mechanisation and therefore production scale by the merchant manufacturers, meant it was now almost impossible for a new entrant to the trade to set up in business.

Anti-enclosure riots broke out in Sheffield in 1791 in response to the enclosure of 6,000 acres of common land. The greatest beneficiaries in Sheffield of the enclosure process was the lord of the manor, the Duke of Norfolk, who received 1,345 acres (22 per cent of the total), and the vicar of Sheffield, the Reverend James Wilkinson (81 acres). The Reverend Wilkinson, Vincent Eyre, the town collector and steward for the Duke of Norfolk, lord of the manor, and Joseph Ward, the Master Cutler, reported that 'considerable numbers of disorderly people' drove the commissioners 'from the Commons near this Town' and 'menaced them with the greatest personal danger if they attempt to proceed in this Inclosure and have actually burnt the farming property and broke the windows of several houses and menaced the lives and property of the freeholders friendly to the Inclosures'. In response, he asked for 'military aid to suppress the rioting of many profligate people'.[4] The soldiers, two troops of 4th Dragoons and two from the 18th Light Dragoons, arrived at noon on Monday, 27 July. The *Sheffield Register* reported that:

> The sudden news on Wednesday morning, of a party of soldiers being expected in town, excited the alarm of some, and the curiosity of all. A great concourse of people went out to meet them, and on their entering the town, the streets were lined with the populace ... the unthinking multitude, thus successful in their first outrage, pursued their violence. Broomhall was now the cry – the house of Rev. Mr. Wilkinson our vicar. All his windows were broken, part of his furniture and library damaged and burnt, and eight hay ricks set fire to, four of which were entirely consumed. Before the populace had been too long at Broom Hall, they were followed by the Light Horse who presently dispersed them.[5]

The officers were billeted in the Tontine Inn. Sheffield was 'an accident waiting to happen', in the days before the riot broke out, and one commentator reported: 'The lower classes of the people, both here and in the neighbourhood, are so much enraged, that their common cry is *"Liberty or Death"*.' Local elites told the Home Office:

> The many treasonable Inscriptions daily repeated upon walls and doors in several places in this Town for several weeks past give the Friends of Government and of the Peace of Society fear that many here are ripe for mischief. ... The peaceable inhabitants of this large and populous Town and neighbourhood are under the most serious apprehensions by the very alarming Riots and Disturbances lately at Birmingham and more so from the arrival here of some of those Rioters who have industriously mixed with the disorderly people of this town.

They believed that on the previous night, 'several of these Incendiaries ... used strong endeavours to raise a Riot by ... inviting them to bring about a Redress of Grievances as they had done at Birmingham.'[6]

The riots had their roots in popular reaction against larger programmes of urban development and improvement, as well as the lack of access to common grazing land. The common land was vital if the poor were to tend to their own livestock, and was a centuries-old tradition. The groundswell of anger against the rich elites taking the common land for themselves and ending a traditional way of life was real enough, and for many it was justifiable, and can be traced back to 1788.[7]

Jacobinism

Against the backdrop of growing social tensions, '5 or 6 Mechanicks' began to meet in Sheffield to discuss 'the enormous prices of provisions' as well as 'the mock representation of the people'. The meetings in Sheffield were expressing the views of the Yorkshire Association, but importantly, of the working man, who now exhorted their brethren to defend themselves against exploitation by the assertion of their natural rights as eschewed by Thomas Paine.[8] The Sheffield Constitutional Society was one of a number of radical groups that sprang up in summer 1791. Support from both the middle and working classes had grown to such an extent that by December 1791, the alarmed Magistrate Joseph Hunter described political reform and Jacobinism as an 'infection' amongst the working men of the town.[9] Anger at enclosure, anger at mechanisation, and at the lack of political representation in order for the people to express their views to the Crown coalesced into a radical underground movement that would become the United Englishmen, who modelled their societal idealism on the French Republic.

The French Republic had declared that the 'natural and imprescriptible rights of man' were to be defined as 'liberty, property, security and resistance to oppression'. The republic demanded the destruction of aristocratic privileges by proclaiming an end to feudalism and exemptions from taxation. It also called for freedom and equal rights for all human beings (referred to as 'Men') and access to public office based on talent. The monarchy was restricted and all citizens had the right to take part in the legislative process. Freedom of speech and of the press were declared, and arbitrary arrests outlawed. The declaration also asserted the principles of popular sovereignty, in contrast to the divine right of kings that characterised the French monarchy, and social equality among citizens, eliminating the special rights of the nobility and clergy. This battle of ideology, more than anything, defined the conflict.[10]

It was a war of ideas, quite literally, of Burkean conservatism against the Rights of Man and Thomas Paine, who crystallised the ideals of Jean-Paul Marat. Edmund Burke, the father of the modern Conservative Party ideology, argued when confronted by the French Revolution that political reform was dangerous and irresponsible, that society was naturally ordered between the rich elites and the working class, who were little more than slaves. For Burke, only the wealthiest in society should have a say in how society was run. Marat, living in Newcastle upon Tyne from about 1770 and later lecturing at Warrington Academy, where future Dissenting Ministers were trained, held a counterview that government was to be for the benefit of all people, not just for the rich. He argued that the people had the right to choose their government and if needs be, to overthrow the state to bring about change, to make a fairer and more egalitarian society, which he explained his seminal work *The Chains of Slavery*.

It was a war of religion as much as politics, and economics of capital verses labour. Fundamentally, during the Napoleonic Wars on the home front, the conflict was a battle over what it meant to be British, and ultimately, who had power. The men who had been consigned to the economic scrap heap on the whims of rich oligarchs and an uncaring House of Commons found their voice through Paine, Marat and extreme religious sects. Unified in their righteous indignation and empowered by God, they had one sole object: to take on the leaders of the land, by force, if necessary, to maintain their way of life, customs and traditions. All it required was a single spark to turn simmering anger into flame.

Fearing that their way of life was coming to an end, many Luddites found solace in religion, and often a religion that viewed anger against the elite as a legitimate expression.

Religion
Today, it is hard to imagine the influence that religion once enjoyed. The 1790s witnessed an exponential growth in nonconformist denominations. One that emerged was the New Jerusalem Church,

or Swedenborgians, established in 1787, who opened a church in Hull in 1805.[11] Religious belief was an accepted part of everyday life. Religious affiliation, perhaps more than politics, defined a person's worldview. War, the violent overthrow of social structures, pestilence and famine, are all powerful themes in the Bible, linked to divine vengeance and wrath. The events of the day struck a chord with many, who found parallels in scripture, most notably in the texts of the book of Ezekiel. The words of Tom Paine, the ideals of Jacobinism coupled with religious revival, were exemplified by the Ezekielite and New Jerusalem movements. The Ezekielites were reportedly indoctrinating members by taking illegal oaths based on Ezekiel 21:

> And thou, profane wicked prince of Israel, whose day is come, when iniquity shall have an end, thus saith the Lord God; Remove the diadem, and take off the crown; this shall not be the same: exalt him that is low, and abuse him that is high. I will overturn, overturn, overturn, it: and it shall be no more[12]

The poor, the dispossessed, the starving found solace in these words, and believed it was their divine duty to overturn the state. So concerned were men like the Reverend William Atkinson, vicar of Bradford, and his brother Johnson Atkinson Busfield, the Bradford magistrate, that he wrote to the Home Office, raising concerns and assuaging fears about the nature of the Jerusalemites' radicalism inspired by the Reverend James Bicheno:

> they pretend to be perfectly harmless and inoffensive and profess a total disregard for the things of this World but there is one of their tenants which clearly militates against this. Viz. that they no longer consider themselves as the subject of an earthly potentate.[13]

Busfield added that they were determined not to rest 'till the threats denounced' in Ezekiel 'are fulfilled' and that the members 'do not breathe the lamblike spirit that these wild enthusiasts profess'. In March 1801, he began to wage a new war of words from portable pulpits, backed up with pamphlets in support of disturbances against the state.[14]

Bicheno preached:

> neither the love of our country, nor the power of self-interest, can exclude even our enemies from an interest in our prayers ... It appears to me to be the duty ... of every man, however humble his station, who knows any thing of the worth of our constitution and liberties ... political

institutions promote the distribution of impartial justice, and which are formed for the promotion of general good and happiness, may for ever be said to be on the Lord's side; whilst the corrupters of his worship, the persecutors of conscience, and the people whose institutions are formed for the oppression of mankind, must ever be considered as the ungodly, and as those who hate the Lord.[15]

The Home Office understood that the New Jerusalem Church and Ezekielites were nothing more than Jacobins.[16] One commentator went further, arguing that:

> when sedition and disaffection are attempted under the mask of religion, it is undoubtedly the duty of Government ... to provide effective remedies to this poison ... this abominable and misguided sect have given themselves the appellation of Ezekielites ... the danger of their fanaticism. [17]

Driven by famine, their livelihoods made extinct through mechanisation, one can see why thousands of the working class found comfort in a religion that told them to tear down the king 'and abase him that is high'.[18]

Comment

Two other factors drove Luddism: the monopolisers' demands to end statute legislation on apprenticeships and the numbers of looms. Gigmills and apprenticeships did not directly threaten the clothiers – it was rather the case that Benjamin Gott and Cookson had been allowed to break the law and control more looms than the statutes allowed for. Factories were illegal. The statute of 1551 limited the number of looms allowed in one building, so factories with hundreds of looms broke the law, and also placed the clothier at a huge disadvantage. The rich elites like Atkinson and Gott literally used their privilege to use illegal gig-mills, ignore apprenticeship legislation and erect vast factories knowing full well that the Crown would back them, whilst the small clothier, often with no more than four looms, as the statute dictated, had no option but to work within the existing legal framework. Little wonder that the clothiers and master and journeyman weavers joined the croppers' crusade against the Crown. Weavers worked from home, and as well as weaving cloth, often supplemented their income from produce from a smallholding. Concentrating looms in factories meant that a household's income was tied solely to weaving cloth. It made the master weaver a worker no longer in charge of his own affairs and totally reliant on being employed as he could not tend his garden and smallholding. The factory ended the independence of the clothier and weaver and created a new class of urban working-class labourer who was totally reliant on the mill owner.

Yet, conversely, the West Riding woollen manufacturing community was not dogmatically rigid: the extension of fulling mills to scribbling and other preparatory processing of fleece became accepted. So too was clothiers expanding their operations and building small factories. What mattered was when this change from within the community was threatened: change led by the community itself was acceptable, but hated was the change imposed directly from the top. The small clothiers legitimately feared that their way of life would be quickly destroyed and their social status as masters of their profession would be eroded by the new factories, where machines replaced skilled labour in the finishing trade, where journeymen weavers had less value in society. The desire to maintain the static, conservative society and tradition led the community to embrace radical action. Communities under economic stress and fearful of change resort, in some cases, to extremes to remove the threat to their livelihoods.

Chapter 4

FIRST STIRRINGS OF DISCONTENT

Mechanisation of scribbling, carding and spinning had rendered a whole working community obsolete. But rioting and unrest had not broken out ... yet. While every worker could move within the woollen trade as long as it had the capacity to allow those displaced by machines to enter new areas of operation, all was well. Throughout the middle decades of the eighteenth century, the woollen trade in Yorkshire experienced continual growth, which afforded a high degree of job and community protection. The grudging acknowledgement of mechanisation as being a good thing helped to keep community tensions low as the labour-intensive and very dirty jobs of washing, sorting and carding the fleece by hand had been eliminated.

However, when displaced workers could not find work, and when mechanisation moved into other spheres, notably the finishing of cloth, then real trouble was brewing. Traditionally, cloth had been hand finished by men known as croppers. Mechanised finishing of cloth had been illegal since the 1540s, yet men like Benjamin Gott, in seeking to maximise profits, began a campaign in the early 1790s to adopt machinery to finish cloth: the gig-mill and shearing frame. Joseph Atkinson of Bradley Mill, near Huddersfield, had illegally adopted gig-mills by 1784 and shearing frames by 1800. In 1787, he was convicted of using gig-mills to finish his cloth.[1]

As war descended across Europe, export markets began to be closed off: the first major market lost to British merchants was Russia. The Milnes family of Wakefield had traditionally exported into Russia, apparently to clothe the Russian Army.[2] Their back cargo was Baltic timber and other Russian-made goods. Opposition to the British

Crown closing exports to Russia resulted in merchants petitioning Earl Fitzwilliam – soon to be Lord Lieutenant of the West Riding – the leader of the Whig faction in Yorkshire, to raise their concerns with government. The petition failed to make any headway, and the loss of this lucrative trade heralded the death knell for Milnes, Heywood & Co. and many others.[3] Fitzwilliam, rather than seeking to confront the Crown over the issue, felt that the consequential increase of the British Army and Royal Navy, and thus an increased demand for woollens, would result in the increase in domestic trade offsetting any losses from exports. Yet as one mill owner in Birkenshaw remarked, the trade would 'not last indefinitely' once the needs of the army had been met: war threatened free trade, especially the export market, upon which the West Riding was almost solely reliant.[4] The closure of export markets to Russia and increasing tension across Europe in a 'cold war' before the British Crown went to war against Revolutionary France meant that if the woollen trade was to survive the economic downturn, ways had to be found to reduce costs and to make cloth production economically viable in a fluctuating market: mechanisation was the obvious solution.

Perhaps 60 per cent of the production cost of a length of broadcloth was in the finishing stage, where the nap was raised and a finished surface was 'cropped'. Since the reign of Edward VI, the use of machines in the process had been made illegal in order to preserve the 'croppers' trade'.[5] It was reckoned that a skilled cropper would take eighty-eight hours to finish a length of cloth: a gig-mill could do the same work in twelve hours. The economic argument for mechanisation was overwhelming. It was perhaps inevitable that, in November 1791, Leeds merchants began a campaign to repeal the legislation that prohibited the machine finishing of woollen cloth. The merchants remarked that:

> in the manufacture of Woollens, the scribbling mill, the spinning frame and fly shuttle have reduced manual labour nearly one-third, and each of them at its first introduction carried an alarm to the work people, yet each has contributed to advance wages and to increase the trade, so that if an attempt was now made to deprive us of the use of them, there is no doubt, but every person engaged in the business would exert himself to defend them.
>
> From these premises, we the undersigned merchants, think it a duty we owe to ourselves, to the Town of Leeds, and to the Nation at Large, to declare that we will protect and support the free use of the proposed improvements in cloth dressing by every legal means in our power.[6]

The merchants wanted the expensive croppers replaced by machines. The skilled carders and spinners had been replaced by largely unskilled labour-managing machines.

For the factory owners, this was a win-win situation. They were able to process a fleece to finished cloth in their own premises, free of restrictive legislation and with cheaper labour costs. They saved the expense of croppers' wages, master weavers and journeymen were no longer required, and those who worked in the mills toiled for considerably lower wages. The clothier, cloth merchant and wool-stapler were all now facing economic extinction as the rich elite maximised their profits.

The days of the artisan's skill and time-served apprenticeship to become a master craftsman were coming to an end: in the name of profit, war had been declared between the factory owners and merchants against the clothiers and croppers. Violence ensued ... but not immediately.

In the west of England, the firm of Bamford and Cook set up gig-mills and shearing frames at their factory at Twerton, near Bath, in 1797. A few years earlier, Bamford had erected scribbling and carding machines and generated local hatred by displacing hundreds of workers. William Eales, a wool comber from Plymouth who had worked at Bamford's factory, testified that the machines at Twerton were powered by water and could 'clear out 18 pounds of wool per hour', a size of output that Eales stated could only be equalled by the best workers in thirty hours. Indeed, such was the scribbling machine's productivity that soon, Eales and most of his fellow wool combers were laid off.[7] Fearing that they would share the same fate as the scribblers, croppers then set out to destroy the machines. To make good their promise, about 300 croppers assembled and broke into a grinder's shop that sharpened the shears for Bamford's at Nunney. The crowd, now 900 strong, then march to Bamford's with the intention of hanging 'up Bamford and two of his men, to burn down his works and those of Collicott & Co.'. The intervention of the yeomanry prevented the two factories being burned to the ground.[8] This was just the beginning of the Luddite rising in Trowbridge, as we shall see. Yet it would be two years before violence would break out again.

The threat of mechanisation and changes to working practices put a community on the defensive. The croppers of the West Riding and their counterparts in the West Country believed that they had customary rights at its core. The culture of the clothiers in the West Riding was built on its permanence, and continuing stability: it was a culture built on capitalist economics, but one that also assumed fixed economic functionality, and that, moreover, market forces could only be applied within strict boundaries defined by the customs and traditions of the community. Traditional rights and customs transcended external market forces, yet were increasingly under attack from mechanisation and the centralisation of services. The centuries-old domestic system was giving way to the new factories, and the labour pains of this birth would set the West Riding on fire. The growth in production through mechanisation was taking place at the expense of the small clothier: these men, with only a few looms and few other machines, had been the bedrock on which the domestic system was built. These smaller clothiers felt increasingly under attack and marginalised; they resented the attack on their social and economic status. Many master clothiers were forced out of business by the new factories and had to seek work in the factories. The new factories were to blame: the factories had brought about bankruptcies; they had taken the work from their hands and were stealing the bread from the mouths of their families. For men like Cookson of Leeds, destroying the clothiers was a good thing, as it meant that the merchants could control the market: factories were the future.

Making matters worse, a bad harvest in 1799 witnessed food prices increase massively: wheat for making bread had been 53*s.* a quarter in 1789, by 1795 it was 79*s.*, and by 1800, 120*s.* By May 1800, it was estimated that no more than seven days' worth of corn existed anywhere in Yorkshire. The other staple foodstuff, oats, was selling at 70*s.* a quarter. Unable to afford bread, or make a pottage, the poor were starving once more. They had a stark choice: it was starve and pay the rent, or eat and be homeless.[9] On average, 8 per cent of an artisan's wage was spent on accommodation, the remainder went on food: cheese, mutton, beef and pork cost 4*d.* a pound, bacon 7*d.* a pound, butter 8*d.* a pound, milk 1*d.* a pint, and oat bread 1*d.*, or wheat bread 4*d.* On an average weekly pay of 9*s.*, 90 per cent was spent on food alongside the 8–10 per cent on housing. It left nothing for illness and unemployment, or for price increases of bread and other essentials. Having no work meant destitution. Price rises meant starvation.

It was estimated that in 1790, in Leeds, a woman spinning could earn 2*s.* a week, a labourer 5–9*s.*, artisans 15*s.*, and croppers – the 'kings of the working class' who finished broadcloths – could earn as much as 30*s.* a week. A clothier was reckoned to be of the 'good sort' to earn £50 a year – the price of a two-bedroom cottage to buy. In comparison, in 1786 John Dennison spent the unheard-of sum of £6,100 in constructing Denison Hall, and in 1796, a Mrs Arthington sold a pair of houses in Park Place, Leeds, for £3,000. Most merchants, who comprised the 'middling sort', had an income of £200–600 a year: in 1790, the Leeds

Street Commissioners noted an income of £400 a year would allow a merchant to rent a town house 'with five servants and a princely table'. The merchant princes like Benjamin Gott, Thomas Lloyd and William Cookson had incomes in excess of £10,000 a year, which shows how wealthy these men were: they were the billionaires of their time. The gulf between the rich, the middle class and the poor was staggering, much as it is today. The world of the elite of that era is enshrined in the novels of Jane Austen; the reality of life was 'hellish, short, nasty and brutal'.[10]

As the crisis worsened, it was recorded that 1,200 quarts of soup per day were being distributed to the impoverished. 'The Sum in Hand', the chairman of the Leeds relief committee, Richard Bramley, declared, 'cannot at the present high Price of Provisions last ... for more than the Space of One Week,' adding, 'Humanity therefore calls loudly on the Benevolence of the Charitable,' and trusted subscriptions would continue from 'everyone whom Providence has blessed with the Means of alleviating the Miseries of their Fellow-Creatures'.[11] On 6 May 1800 at Leeds, 'Colliers from some of the Neighbouring Collieries', along with other members of the labouring poor, were led into the market by a collier from Hunslet named Samuel Atack and rioted over the high price of provisions.[12] The participation of colliers in the Leeds food riot re-emphasises the intimacy between trade unionism, protest and living standards. We find in 1812 that Luddites include coal miners.

With unemployment rising and the cost of food increasing, machines were seen as part of the problem: smash the machines and the unemployed would get their jobs back.

The grievances against mechanisation – scribbling machines, gig-mills and the 'dark satanic mills' that had emerged in the 1780s – were still being felt in communities across the West Riding. Croppers, weavers and clothiers had already been displaced by factories and machines in the Pennine belt of the West Riding. The embracing of machines and manufactories by the Atkinsons and the Brooks had cut deep into the community and tradition. In the central belt of the West Riding, Merchants like William Cookson, soon to be Lord Mayor of Leeds in 1802, Benjamin Gott and others were sending their cloths to be finished by Atkinson by the late 1790s. Cookson declared how he sent 1,000 pieces of cloth to Halifax and Huddersfield to be finished by illegal gig-mills. For Cookson, John and Edward Brooke of Hunslet, Pim Nevins and Fisher & Nixon, also of Hunslet, as well as the merchant house of Markland, Cookson & Fawcett, the factory was the future. The half a dozen water-powered gig-mills in Huddersfield were finishing the cloth of Leeds merchants and putting the cropping shops in Leeds and Wakefield out of business. Gott and Cookson sought to erect their own gig-mills to save on transporting their cloth to Halifax. Leeds had the largest cloth market in the country: stopping mechanisation of the finishing process here was vital to keep community and tradition alive.

As could be predicted, violence broke out in April 1799 against the mechanisation of cloth finishing. The woollen trade was a cornerstone of the economic life not only of the West Riding but also the West Country. Fierce competition between the two areas drove mechanisation, as neither region wished to lose out to the other. As a result of this, in the west of England, the use of shearing frames and gig-mills in a mill owned by John Bell led to retaliation by the croppers:

> I send you this to inform you that we – the cloth workers of Trowbridge, Bradford, Chippinham, and Melkshom – are almost (or the greatest part of us) out of work and we are fully convinced that the greatest of the cause is your dressing work by machinery. And we are determined, if you follow this practice any longer, that we will keep some people to watch you about with loaded blunderbuss or pistols, and will certainly blow your brains out. It is no use to destroy the factories but put you damned villains to death.[13]

The letter goes on to warn Bell that he'd burn in Hell for eternity and suggest that the croppers would kill his mother too, as well as Ebenezer Brown, who owed a large factory. Several Wiltshire clothiers seeking to make use of cheaper machine finishing were sending their cloth to Bath. They too were threatened:

> Gentlemen, if you persist in the plan you have adopted, others will certainly follow which will distress many poor families. This is to give you timely notice to discontinue it and if you do not perhaps you may experience a return from a quarter you little suspect. Depend on it a honest man has no need to arm himself against his fellow citizens.[14]

The threat was unmistakable, yet despite the warning, clothiers still continued to send cloth to be finished by machine. In reply, the croppers sent another stark warning: 'Gentlemen clothiers all I hope that you will a warn tak an not no more cloth to Turtn for if you do your own ruen will be for we are determined to go throo with it.'[15]

As famine bit hard in winter 1799, the gig-mills in the mill belonging to Messrs Johnson of Holbeck, Leeds, were smashed and the mill burned to the ground.[16] Local agitation witnessed the gig-mills in Huddersfield stopped.[17] One address nailed up in Huddersfield declared that the first steps for the workers to redress their grievances was that they would 'pull down all machinery and return the manufacturing business to its old ways'.[18] In 1806, merchant and Magistrate William Cookson described the attack on the mills of Messrs Johnson of Holbeck as follows:

> many hundreds were present and some disguised, ... and though a considerable reward was offered from the government and from the magistrates, and the parties were summoned up who were known to be there, and who could not prove an alibi, no argument or entreaty could prevail upon anyone to confess who were active parties in the business.[19]

Why was this? In the traditional woollen industry, master clothiers, croppers or finishers could only take on two apprentices; this primarily controlled both wages and the labour market. This conflicted with the vision for the woollen trade set by the factory owners like Benjamin Gott and William Cookson. Gott, with the use of steam-powered looms, gig-mills and shearing frames, undermined the very fabric of communities. The large manufacturers could produce cloth cheaper and in greater quantity than the 'domestic system' could. In Wakefield, for example, the raw wool market sold fleece to those who would card and spin the fleece into yarn. The yarn was then sold to the weavers. The urban centre was also the distribution point for the finished cloth for sale to merchants. Weaving and spinning in the seventeenth and eighteenth centuries, and into the nineteenth century in the West Riding was a rural-based cottage industry until the advent of the factory system. Moreover, urban entrepreneurs like the Milnes family coordinated the efforts of the rural workers and marketed their finished products. Certain processes – usually the most highly skilled and the most remunerative – remained centred in urban areas. Cloth finishing and dyeing was one such skilled activity, and was centred in Wakefield for a large proportion of the West Riding in the Calder and Aire valleys. The extension of industry into rural areas and the greater integration of urban and rural industry into regional economies had been the principal achievement of sixteenth-century industry. The introduction of mechanisation and building factories that could process raw fleece into finished cloth meant the end of centuries-old ways of life. It meant unemployment. Thus began the struggle by the croppers, the specially trained men who finished cloth, against the mechanisation of their trade.[20]

To guard their livelihood, croppers formed themselves into an illegal trade union, which became known as the Institution. Legislation was passed quickly through the House of Commons, reconfirming the illegality of trade unionism, then known as combinations.

Chapter 5

COMBINATION

Protest meetings and food riots had been a common feature of class conflicts in the eighteenth century, but now, at the dawn of the nineteenth, they represented a different phenomenon. There existed amongst the working class a national movement, formulating its propaganda with a clear political ideology and agitating for resistance against ruling class and state. But how far this was a cohesive, coordinated organisation was (and consequently still is) hard to ascertain. Members were sworn in and given a membership card bearing the motto 'Liberty, Justice and Humanity' and a small eight-page pamphlet outlining the aims of the organisation and its constitution. Each group was to be set up on a cell system, where members were known only to the 'conductor' of the organisation.[1] The accelerating pace of industrialisation and urbanisation at the end of the eighteenth century was a great driver in social change in Britain. As factories that supported new and more mechanised industries grew, so too did the need for a labour force that had the requisite skills and abilities to perform such jobs. That workforce did not exist, but was created through an unprecedented shift of labour from the agrarian jobs of the countryside to the urban jobs of the city: farm labourers became factory workers. Suddenly, new urban areas were flooded with an eclectic mix of social and economic classes, including those from other countries looking for work in these new industries, and that tended to fuel the engines of associations, clubs and societies. The common thread for many of these men was that the social and economic constructs they were so accustomed to had been severely disrupted. The formation of these organisations, whether for political, cultural or other circumstances, served to connect people of similar interests, but not necessarily the same backgrounds. As we touched upon earlier, the desire for equality as well as political representation drove reform as much as the desire to protect community, tradition and jobs. A Parliamentary Secret Committee attributed success to this movement especially amongst the working class because:

> Many ignorant or inconsiderate persons throughout the country were gradually involved in these transactions and the influence of the destructive principles from which they proceeded was still further extended by the establishment of clubs among the lowest classes of the community which were open to all persons having one penny and in which songs were sung, toasts given and language held of the most seditious nature.[2]

The fears of the ruling class were expressed in the committee's summary of the aims of the republicans in both Britain and Ireland as:

> the entire overthrow of the British Constitution, the general confiscation of property and the erection of a Democratic Republic founded on the ruins of all religion and of all political and civil society, and framed after the model of France.[3]

These fears were to resurface at every assertion of strength by the working class, and at every alarming display of organisation such as the Institution, which was influential in trade union disputes, as we shall see across the West Riding. The radical nature of Luddism as a political force was acknowledged by journalist Frank Peel in the 1870s, but the compartmentalisation of Luddism by some writers has downplayed the armed insurrectionary nature of Luddism,[4] whilst others have stated that Luddism had no political or religious nature or motivation, which is clearly wrong.[5] Some writers have gone as far as to suggest that Luddism was industrial protest that had no real aims or intent beyond machine breaking, and has become, sadly, a common misconception of Luddism.[6]

To combat trade unionism, the Combination Act pulled together a long sequence of acts relating to particular trades, sought to end collective action, and by this very means encouraged among workers a sense that they were facing a common threat. It spectacularly backfired. A government spy reported:

> a general spirit of dissatisfaction created in every class of artisan and mechanic by the late bill against Combinations and which I am afraid has caused more to combine than would have thought of such a measure but for the bill itself ... it is a measure the democrats rejoice in most extravagantly will most assuredly strain every nerve to profit by it. I have found within these last 14 days ... proof of a connected and desperate opposition being in preparation.[7]

The same month, another government spy claimed, 'The members of the new society are exceedingly numerous. It originated in Sheffield in the Republican society there- is connected with the principal manufacturing towns of Yorkshire.'[8] A spy reported that the Sheffield and Leeds Jacobins went to great pains to ensure that 'Loyal and patriotic men' were not admitted, and the avowed aim was to petition Parliament to ban gig-mills and monopolies, and to enact Universal Suffrage.[9] The politicisation of the haves and haves-nots is perhaps best exemplified through the role of magistracy. The magistrates with the passing of the Combination Acts of 1799–1800 had a direct role in suppressing illegal combinations with the wholehearted support of a narrow group of Anglican Tory merchants.

As a result of the Combination Act, the Huddersfield cloth dressers society, which was presumably the local form of the Institution, was dissolved and its funds disbursed. It called in over 500 membership tickets. Yet within eighteen months, institutions would rapidly reappear across the West Riding. Without a class ticket, croppers could not find work. Because of the Institution, Benjamin Gott, the merchant and owner of the largest woollen factory in Leeds, was unable to recruit strike-breakers in Trowbridge. Behind this agitation was the desire to protect the domestic system of production as a whole.[10]

In May 1799, the Lancashire Association of Weavers appealed to the public that, 'We … are firmly attached to our King and Country. … We shall neither interfere with church nor state, but strictly confine ourselves to a private grievance.' While expressing support for the recent Seditious Meetings Act, the weavers insisted that it did not restrict citizens from lawfully petitioning government in their own private interests: 'We are determined that those who are appointed by the constitution of our country to redress our grievances, shall have our real state laid before them; and it must be their wisdom that must determine this point.'[11] The Lancashire cotton weavers and spinners were, like the stockingers of Nottingham and clothiers of the West Riding, mainly outworkers, producing cloth on hand looms in their own homes and paid by the piece. Their overall conditions and status as artisans had been eroding for several decades, partly as a result of a huge influx into the trade of unapprenticed workers, many of whom had been forced off the land by the enclosures. As in the West Riding, the factory system, with its vast mills and steam-powered looms, its long hours of dangerous work and its cheaper cloth that undercut the cottage weavers, exacerbated their declining income occasioned by the hated war. The Reverend Thomas Bancroft, parson and magistrate, informed the Home Office that:

we have an Association in this town & Neighbourhood which at present seems to threaten Harm. It is ostensibly formed for the deputation of the [illegible] of the weavers in the cotton trade, but their publications & the arrangement of the plan [illegible] & great. Their aim is as they phrase it, is to <u>move the country</u> & [illegible] to petition parliament for a redress of Grievances. It is distributed into divisional committees & a central committee & pains are taken to confederate the neighbouring towns ... we have ... forbidden their meetings.[12]

Colonel Ralph Fletcher of Bolton believed that the weavers campaigning for the minimum wage were engaged in acts of sedition, despite their protestations of loyalty.[13] As the price of bread rose, the economy shrank. Wages fell, unemployment rose. The woollen trade contracted rapidly. At the same time, the demand for coal fell and thus wages: in the period 15–20 July 1799 at Tong Colliery near Bradford, 1s. 3d. was paid to John Webster for endheading (driving a coalface forward). By 10–15 March 1800, the piece rate had fallen to 1s. 1d. The average earnings for one collier, Samuel Hargrave, in the same period was just over 1s. per day; thus it was inevitable that colliers at Mr Thorpe's colliery near Wentworth struck work. 'Every man at his colliery has deserted it by combination,' wrote the overseer in May 1799, who noted, 'The Reason of the quitting was, that he [Thorpe] wanted to reduce their prices to the same Terms as those given at the adjoining and neighbouring Collieries, which they wod not agree to' and 'formed a confederacy to leave'.[14]

At the same time, the Home Office received alarming reports from across the north of England: the republican society in Sheffield had established like-minded groups in Leeds, Bolton, Manchester, Stockport and Bury.[15] Many of the members were reported to have enlisted in the volunteers to learn the use of arms, and gain access to firearms. The Home Office recorded that in Lancashire, 60,000 were ready to rise, 50,000 in Yorkshire and 30,000 in Derbyshire: their grievance was the repeal of the Combination Acts as they made 'masters Tyrants and servants slaves'.[16]

Later in the month, information was received from a spy that the workmen were preparing to use whatever force was necessary to overturn the Combination Acts, and opined that 'there has been more persons turned Jacobins within the little time elapsed since the Bill was passed than for a year before'.[17] By September, the spy had infiltrated the group in Sheffield, and noted that Timothy Gales – a journeyman printer – was at the epicentre of the movement. Gales disclosed to the spy that a 'business meeting' had been held in Castleton with delegates attending from Sheffield, Manchester and Derby.[18] The spy could not prove such links, but reported that Sheffield maintained a Jacobin and Republican general committee, which was fuelled by a rise in atheism and attendance at lending and subscription libraries, one of which was centred at Upper Chapel on Norfolk Street and provided access to the works of William Godwin and Voltaire.[19] When news of Napoleon's return to France reached Sheffield, the spy wrote in alarmed tones of large crowds parading through the streets wearing French cockades, singing the *Ça ira* and also *La Marsellaise*, noting the slogan was 'Death or Liberty'.[20] Barlow's reports were taken 'with a pinch of salt' by the Home Office, and furthermore, a former United Irishmen, George Orr, reported, 'I do not find any attempts are making in this country at a reorganisation of the United Irishmen or of the disaffected.'[21] Barlow may have exaggerated the situation in Sheffield, but Magistrate Bayley darkly warned in November that a new tide of disaffection was on the increase in the form of agitation against the Combination Acts. The cotton weavers of Manchester demanded that they 'must either have positive laws to protect them from imposition' or else they would be 'reduced to a state of slavery and subject to the capricious dispositions of those who employ them', he reported.[22] Discontent in Lancashire was rising due to the rise in the price of bread, increasing levels of unemployment due to mechanisation, a drop in wages, and grievances with the Combination Acts.[23] Unlike the workers in the woollen trade who resorted to violence, Lancashire cotton weavers and printers took on the Crown through petitioning. It is notable that opposition to the Act in Lancashire originated with the handloom weavers and cotton spinners, calico printers and other more skilled trades. By spring of 1800, the weavers' petition had allegedly collected 23,000 signatures and was presented to Parliament by Colonel Stanley. As was ever the case, the weavers' demands were not met by Parliament, which passed a compromise measure, the Arbitration Act, whereby weavers could negotiate wages with their employers, judged by a magistrate.[24] The woollen trade took a markedly different line to that of the Lancashire cotton weavers and printers. The legislation against combinations drove labour organisations underground and into the arms of the radicals.

In Nottingham, a spy working for Colonel Fletcher reported, 'The poor are for a general rising for a revolution. The Gentlemen are not, but are for obtaining redress by very strong petitions (worded alike) from Every town in the Kingdom.'[25] The obvious solution to the famine and a faltering economy was an immediate cessation of hostilities with France. The Reverend Wood thundered from the pulpit at Mill Hill Chapel: 'War is in all cases displeasing to God and hurtful to man; in the end, destructive alike to the victor and the vanquished; pleasing to none, but harpies who fatten on human blood.'[26] From this came a mass mobilisation of the clothiers and manufacturers for Peace: war was destroying their businesses. Samuel Hamer Oates, a leading Unitarian, claimed, in a letter to Charles James Fox, that the anti-war liberalism in the West Riding was supported almost to a man by the manufactures.[27]

In spite of opposition, more than 42,000 freeholders of Yorkshire signed the petition. It was the largest mass participation political act since the Yorkshire Association petition of 1783. Yet it achieved nothing. The despised war continued; food prices did not drop. The government, it seems, literally took no notice at all of the voice of the people. As the famine continued, the anger from the working class got louder. The peace petition may not have brought peace, but it empowered an entire generation of the working class into collective action. The Foxites, along with elements of the emerging industrialists, the urban middle class, Unitarians and some other nonconformist Dissenters were largely of the same mind about the war: it was unnecessary, morally wrong, economically unsustainable and causing real suffering at home. The war showed starkly the gulf between the haves and the have-nots and the war and peace factions.

The idealism of the peace agitators did overlap with working-class agitation against the Crown and elites, and both urged peace on Christian and economic grounds.[28] Disillusioned by legitimate lines of protest, direct action was, for many, the only way to get their voice heard.[29] The working class and urban poor in the new towns of the industrialising north and midlands had suffered the most from the famine. A room measuring 6 feet by 9 feet cost 4*d*. a week. It had no access to running water, which came instead from a pump on the end of the street; sanitation was a bucket tipped into a drain; and cooking was on the open fire. An entire family would live and be raised in such conditions. A room measuring 10 foot square carried a rental of 9*d*. a week, and often housed a family of five, according to a 1790 report by the Leeds Street Commissioners. Imagine living in a cellar, lit only by a candle, washing in a bucket of stagnant water, cooking over a smoky coal fire, and having to defecate in a bucket kept in the corner of the single room that served as bedroom, kitchen and parlour! Little wonder that the working class found grievances with their social superiors.

Considering the struggling families making the choice between paying the rent or eating, seeing loved ones die from disease, is it easy to see why the working classes flocked to the banner of the radical cause and were bound by a test that promised to 'Remove the diadem and take off the crown ... [and to] exalt him that is low and abuse him that is high'. The link between the famine and radicalism was proved when Lord Eldon was informed that due to the high price of food, many thousands were taking the United Englishmen's Oath in the counties of Cheshire, Derbyshire and Lancashire, particularly in Saddleworth. The informant noted that there would be widespread revolution if the farmers were not forced to bring their produce to market at lower prices instead of hoarding it.[30] In the north of England, the underground movement put out streetlights: hence the sobriquet the 'Black Lamp'.[31]

Resistance to mechanisation was both transregional, as is evident in the links with the west of England in 1799–1803 and with links to Nottingham and Manchester in 1811–13, but was also transoccupational: opposition to machinery and the factory system came not just from croppers, but from clothiers, who represented the largest occupation element of the domestic system. Economic and political repression led naturally enough to resistance, and there is overwhelming evidence of the continuity of the struggle against machinery and the erosion of the domestic system, community and tradition, from 1799 to 1812 and afterwards. This is the milieu in which they lived and worked, and which shaped their ideology. Luddism was part of a broader working-class movement that sought to bring about change: it was a key component of a wider class struggle. Therefore, for the croppers, scribblers and all others engaged in the woollen industry, it was increasingly evident that Parliament was clearly on the side of the manufacturers regarding the machinery question and *laissez-faire* economics that threatened to destroy community and tradition. Class bias at local and national level solidified through the actions of the armed, judicial and the legislative branches of the state.

The British Crown and the merchants shaped what happened next: economic repression imposed by the advance of machinery and its resultant deskilling of the artisan and imposition of factory discipline – if not the loss of livelihood entirely – gave rise to community unrest. When combined with the political repression of the cropper's organisation and the obstruction of any route to legal challenge, the actions of the merchants and the Crown resulted in a wave of violence, which we know as Luddism.

This was a foreboding portent of what was to come. Jacobinism and industrial grievances were happy bedfellows. Ironically, the Crown had created the perfect conditions through repressive legislation and ignoring the pleas of the working class to witness the emergence of Luddism.

Chapter 6

LUDDITES ARISE

As the economy shrank, the woollen industry in the West Riding experienced severe contraction due to the loss of lucrative export of woollen goods to France and Russia, as well as the contraction of domestic markets. The high prices of basic provisions severely curtailed the purchasing power of the mass population. Wholesalers and retailers demanded in consequence longer credits, or were simply unable to pay their suppliers. William Lupton, a Unitarian cloth merchant attending Call Lane Chapel in Leeds, expressed in his journal his fears about the damage that the lack of credit and lengthened credit periods would have as follows: 'were we to prolong payment ... it would surely derange our system ... we must pay on the nail for every article.'[1] From 1977, a shrinking economy after the boom of a few years previous meant that with less credit and hard cash in the economy, many smaller clothiers went to the wall as merchants could not settle their bills, and the death knell of the domestic system sounded. Rather than buying cloth from the cloth hall, it was now economically imperative that merchants shifted to production of cloth, and rather than putting out the work of dyeing and finishing, carried these tasks out in-house, in a factory. Costs had to be reduced across the board if the woollen industry was to survive the recession. Thus, it was inevitable that mechanisation and centralisation of previously subcontracted stages in the production of cloth accelerated, funded by 'merchant princes' who now came to monopolise the woollen trade. In the 1780s, the competition between merchants and merchant-manufacturers in credit and abatement terms had a degree of flexibility: there was room for both adventurous and conservative factions within the woollen trade. With the economic problems caused by the wars with France, with a contraction of markets, only those merchants who were prepared to be aggressive in business would flourish.

The domestic system could not withstand the economic stress placed on it by the wars.

With difficult trading conditions, it was only natural that the new merchant-manufacturers sought to cut costs. Factory owners in Leeds began to mechanise the cloth finishing process. Since the 1780s, Leeds cloth had been taken to illegal gig-mills in Halifax for finishing. Benjamin Gott, Thomas Lloyd and William Cookson sought to finish cloth by machine in Leeds to save both transport costs and to reduce staff costs. Gig-mills could be watched by unskilled labour who earned perhaps 8s. a week, whereas a master cropper demanded 30s. a week for his skilled labour. Getting rid of the croppers and investing in machines was seen as a short-term fiscal outlay for a long-term increase in profits. Jobs and community did not matter; profit and loss did. William Cookson informed Earl Fitzwilliam that the merchants and manufactures in the West Riding realised that the introduction of machinery in the West Country would inevitably lead either to its introduction in Yorkshire or otherwise there would be a loss of trade in the region. As noted earlier, opposition to gig-mills in the West Country had resulted in rioting, and tellingly, Cookson noted that some of the Huddersfield merchants who used gig-mills – some of which had been working for over twenty years, he tells – had been stopped from working through intimidation by the croppers and clothiers. Community anger was building and the croppers threatened to go on strike if the machines were not taken down. The clothiers, afraid of losing the shipping season for the sale of their goods, gave in to the demands of the workers. Cookson was appalled at the outcome, and informed the Earl, 'It was well known that cloth dressed by machinery was superior to that dressed by hand.' For Cookson, mechanisation meant lower production costs and increased production, and thus, increased profits. He concluded that 'whilst the government must consider the needs of the cloth workers' who would be made redundant by mechanisation, he stressed that the merchants were 'duty bound in the current difficult economic circumstances to use the most economical means possible to ensure a good quality of output'.[2]

In response to the cloth workers' success in Huddersfield, a consortium of Leeds merchants, to a man 'Church and King', sought to provoke a confrontation with the croppers in order to use the croppers' recalcitrance to goad the government in coming down hard on trade unionism, and to also remove what they considered redundant and unnecessary legislation that prevented the legal use of gig-mills, as well as to abolish apprenticeships.[3] The stakes were high as Joseph Beckett, a Leeds magistrate, explained to Earl Fitzwilliam:

> Gott has been threatened very seriously – his windows all broken in the night, and though a man of pretty strong nerves he has thought it advisable to have an armed Guard about his house which I am sorry to say events have proved to be no more than a necessary precaution. This ill-temper towards him arises from his having put up a Gig Mill in his Factory, which the Croppers consider as interfering with their particular employ.[4]

Gott was forced to take down his gig-mills, which was seen as a victory for the croppers. Round one in what became a decade-long struggle had gone to the croppers. There things remained for over a year.

Famine and unemployment in June 1802 prompted Magistrate Richard Walker to inform Earl Fitzwilliam that 'the despondency and distress that pervades this district from the rapid decline of the woollen manufacture' could be the harbinger of social unrest.[5] On 15 July 1802, a group of West Riding magistrates, chaired by J.A. Busfield, was passed intelligence gathered by a spy working for Joseph Radcliffe of Milnsbridge House. The disclosed information reported that 'nightly meetings of numerous bodies of disaffected persons are frequently held for the mischievous purposes of sedition and insurrection … may give rise to serious insurrections.'[6]

As Busfield's letter winged its way to the Home Office, their predictions were proved right. On 16 July, a group of men attacked and burned to the ground Littleton Mill, owned by Mr Naish, where machinery was being installed. Simultaneously, 'Staverton Superfine Woollen Manufactory' was attacked as part of a series of disputes about pay. The mill here was owned by John Jones, a local magistrate. Jones had proposed to make his croppers work from 6 a.m. to 6 p.m. and to have two one-hour breaks, rather than the croppers having five breaks during the day. Jones also cut the wages of his croppers whilst expecting them to work for two extra hours. In response, his croppers went on strike. His mill was one amongst many that became the target for the Luddites. He reported to the Home Office on 18 July that, about 2 a.m., the mill at Littleton was attacked and muskets were fired into the adjoining house, adding that 'no one was hurt although the children of the house were obliged to take refuge under their beds having had no time to get out of the house'. Jones informed the Home Office that the Luddites were dispersed when he arrived with a detachment of the Queen's Bays, the 2nd Dragoon Guards. He feared the Luddites had been former volunteers or members of the Armed Associations who had retained their firearms.[7] Two days later, Jones reported that hayricks were burned and his own workers had gone on strike.[8]

On 9 August, worryingly, the magistrates added that 'The Shearmens' Club' issued printed tickets, the same as those issued in Yorkshire, and noted that without one a man could not work. The Wiltshire bench reported to both Earl Fitzwilliam and the Home Office that from what they had learned, 'there are said to be clubs in every town in Yorkshire and in other parts of England'. James Read believed that 'these clubs, although confined to employment issues at present, could become extremely dangerous'.[9]

Based on this news, the West Riding, magistrates believed that they would soon be seeing a new wave of machine breaking akin to that in the West Country.[10] The West Country violence, according to Magistrate John Jones, was such that the West Country was to be garrisoned by the army to keep 'the peace', noting that mills were 'being destroyed weekly all over the country and hay ricks burnt almost nightly'. He added that 'a great number of the perpetrators come from Leeds in Yorkshire'.[11] William Cookson informed Fitzwilliam that:

> the complete power which the cloth workers have attained over their employers by union as they call it, it may upon similar principle- give ascendancy to every class of the lower orders-The combinations amongst the cloth workers is directed steadily to their own immediate concerns- the proscribing the use of any machine which will finish woollen cloth in a superior [illegible] or cheaper manner. The workmen who [illegible] continue in the employ of a merchant using such machinery would be [illegible] of his [illegible] and become an outcast & the merchant who employs such a man under such proscription must have his work performed by such only, but none such are to be found. Death & Destruction to the works of such employers are loudly [illegible] the shocking outrages in the west shew that the cloth works are capable of realizing their threats.[12]

Cookson added that Leeds merchants had to adopt gig-mills because Halifax and Huddersfield were drawing the finishing trade away, and the merchants' 'slack purse' due to the fall in trade, meant that the merchants had no option but to adopt cheaper means of production to remain competitive. He further felt that the machine breaking in Wiltshire was being directed from Leeds and that many hundreds of Black Lamp members were at work amongst the cloth makers.[13] Three days later, Cookson told Fitzwilliam, 'From a respectable source near Trowbridge, I learn that a sum of money was rec'd there from Leeds last week & this week Monday coming a letter to Trowbridge (with bill inclosed) was put into the office,' adding that a gig-mill and shearing machine had been destroyed in Trowbridge.[14]

Days later, Cookson wrote again to Earl Fitzwilliam in dismay at 'the momentous shape which the spirit of combination amongst workmen of almost every class (but particularly amongst the croppers) had now assumed', commenting further that the bench in Leeds were:

> aware that the Clothworkers have for a first object, the absolute putting down all machines in the finishing of cloths ... the second ... Perquisites, privileges, time, mode of labour, rate, who shall be employed, &c., &c. – all are now dependent upon the fiats of our workmen, beyond all appeal; and all branches are struggling for their share of these new powers. It is now a confirmed thing that a bricklayer, mason, carpenter, wheelwright, &c., shall have 3s. per week higher wages in Leeds or in Manchester than at Wakefield, York, Hull, Rochdale.[15]

Magistrate Radcliffe, who was rapidly becoming one of the most hated men in the West Riding, wrote to the Home Office his own appraisal of the events taking place. He had been informed by Mark Haigh, a yeoman farmer, of seditious meetings taking place at the home of David Midgley in Almondbury and of Samuel Buckley for '5 or 6 Sundays past, eight or ten people who are strangers in Almondbury have come ... during the whole of the afternoon service of those days ... books or accounts of seditious society are kept in the house of the said Midgley'. Radcliffe added that a second informer, Edward Hasling or Harling, said that meetings also took place at night in the same houses. Radcliffe had arrested Robert Lodge of Almondbury for being a suspected member of the society. Lodge reported that Sykes was a member of the society and had given him a membership card in exchange for 1d. Radcliffe sought permission to enter the men's houses under a warrant and to take evidence. Radcliffe was utterly convinced of the danger to society from the 'secret meetings' of the Black Lamp. Furthermore, Radcliffe, thanks to the efforts of a spy, Thomas Hirst, had uncovered the leaders of the Almondbury cell. Radcliffe reported to Lord Pelham that Hirst had made contact with members of the Black Lamp in Almondbury and obtained oath cards signed by Thomas Sykes, David Midgley, Josh Kaye and Samuel Buckley, the superintendent of the committee there. He added that women met in groups, and talked in hushed voices. He observed that the women knew something was being planned, but none of them would 'let the cat out of the bag'.[16] Magistrate Cookson noted that 'the Black Lamp', a meeting took place 2 miles from Birstall, and that scouts were placed some distance from the meeting, who communicated with whistles to warn of approaching constables and soldiers. A 'gentleman' was the leader, and 200 or more had gathered to petition for an abolition of taxes, the 'full enjoyment of natural rights' and to raise wages.[17]

In early September, Fitzwilliam had received from the Home Office convincing evidence that demonstrated a clear connection between the organisation of the croppers in Yorkshire and the shearmen of the west of England. The Home Office had employed spies to intercept letters carried between Leeds and Wiltshire.[18]

Every man out

The letters between Leeds and Wiltshire revealed the degree of organisation present between the two groups of croppers: this organisation was known as the 'Institution'. This was an illegal trade union that had an almost virtual monopoly on the cloth workers of both regions. So strong was the Institution that it was commonly believed that less than twenty cloth workers in the West Riding were not members. The Institution represented the first national trade union organisation and was a clear target for the Crown to bring down in an early precedent of the fate of the National Union of Mine Workers in the 1980s.

The Institution was based in Leeds and communicated with similar organisations in Wakefield, Morley and the west of England. In an intercepted letter, George Palmer of Leeds wrote to Mary Tucker of Trowbridge on 27 August 1802, acting on behalf of the Leeds Committee, promising that Leeds was sending money to support the strikers.[19] From Trowbridge came a letter of thanks on 5 September, which was again intercepted.[20] Another letter from Palmer to the Wiltshire committee was intercepted on 27 September, was sealed and sent on to ensure that the Committee did not know their communications were being read.[21] A letter to Palmer was intercepted in October by Home Office agents. James Read reported to Home Office Under Secretary John King that the letter was certainly intended for a shearman named Joseph Warren, who ran off from Trowbridge five or six weeks earlier. Read noted that Warren was the nephew of James May, one of the men in prison for administering oaths, and may have been involved in the arson attack at the mills of Mr Naish at Trowbridge. Read noted Warren was an associate of 'a certain Hiliker', who was in prison charged with arson at Littleton, and is believed to have spoken about providing an alibi for Warren. Read states that all was quiet but forwarded to King a printed paper that was stuck up in the clothing towns of Wiltshire and Melksham seeking to recruit shearmen for the manufactory of Messrs Wormald, Gott and Wormald's near Leeds. Read told King he had spoken to their agent, who confirmed that their lack of workers arose from the refusal of the Leeds men to work for those manufacturers who have taken on apprentices after the age of 14, and admitted that they were not expecting to get many recruits.[22]

So strong were the links between the two places that delegates from Wiltshire gathered in Leeds in December 1802. An intercepted letter noted that members of 'The Institution' paid a weekly or monthly subscription. From this, money was drawn to pay for a solicitor working on behalf of the Institution, identified as a Mr Wilmott, who was engaged in drawing up a petition to Parliament to prevent mechanisation: £50 was paid from the Leeds Committee on 16 December for this purpose and a further £100 was raised on 28 December, again from Leeds. Money was also pledged from the West Country, Manchester and Oldham to cover legal costs.[23] The fund was also used to pay a weekly dividend to sick, old, infirm and unemployed cloth workers. In Leeds, 1*d*. a week per man was collected and in Halifax 3*d*., and 1*s*. 6*d*. in Huddersfield.[24] In acting as a sick club, The Institution complemented or replaced the role of Friendly Societies. Acting in such manner also meant The Institution was not a combination, and thus was a legal organisation, although the Crown did not share this view.

The Leeds Central Committee met four or five times a year, its primary focus of concern was to police recruitment into the woollen trade. It ensured that any employer not agreeing to its terms found that overnight, it had no workers. Employers met the union's demands, or felt the immediate consequences.[25] The union gave a sense of power and purpose in a common cause to its members, reported William Cookson to Earl Fitzwilliam.[26] The Central Committee met at the White Swan public house, Birstall, and meetings were held in Roberttown in the new year of 1803, reported a spy.[27] Leeds was always 'headquarters and until an effectual extinguisher be applied here, I am convinced no efficient measures to prevent combinations among shearmen will be practicable'.[28] So strong was the union that William Cookson reported, 'the law against the gig-mill is now as complete in effect – nay more so – than if enacted by Parliament.'[29] One magistrate noted to Fitzwilliam that:

> some Magistrates have stopped manufacturers erecting shearing mills for fear of the consequences. Masters themselves are thinking of an application to parliament for further restrictions against the combinations of the journeymen, although experience suggests that such laws are ineffective. The manufacturers need to be protected against all violence and threats of terror.[30]

Rather than resort to Parliament, Benjamin Gott took matters into his own hands. In September, Gott sought to take on boys aged over 14 as apprentices in his mill. Traditionally, the maximum age had been 14. Gott engineered the conflict that followed when eighty of his croppers gave him notice that they would quit when they had finished the job in hand, and threatened that should he bring in other boys to do the work or send it out to another factory for finishing, they would go on general strike. The croppers declared they would not work for him, nor let any others come in to work for him. Furthermore, the croppers declared that if Gott sent the work out to other mills, these manufacturers would be 'proscribed'.[31] Gott had brought about the showdown he had wanted all along. He could now challenge the Institution and what he felt to be archaic legislation. In defiance of the law, he took on more boys, aged over 14, to replace the strikers, and would oversee the hated gig-mills and shearing frames. Gott believed that the machines 'make a better job of the work than the croppers'.[32] When challenged by the Institution, Gott refused to dismiss the boys he had taken on and with his ally William Cookson, held a meeting at the White Cloth Hall on 27 September to debate the rise in illegal trade unionism, the use of gig-mills and the state of the cloth trade. Gott was confronting community and tradition head-on, and he refused to lose. Leeds Magistrate John Beckett noted that hundreds of croppers assembled in the yard to oppose the merchant's plans. The croppers consulted four magistrates over the illegality of Gott's actions.[33]

In order to seek a final showdown between himself and the Institution, Gott argued that the legislation concerning apprenticeships had never been maintained. He and his allies paid for a legal review of the statutes concerning apprenticeships and the use of machines to finish cloth, resulting in a judgement dated 30 September 1802:

> Disputes having arisen betwixt the Master Cloth Workers in Leeds and their journeymen concerning the legality or illegality of taking on apprentices above Fourteen years of age ... to constitute a legal binding they must be bound for seven years before the age of twenty-four.[34]

The case heard in Leeds overturned the previous judgement, and allowed apprentices to be taken on up to the age of 17. Boys aged 14 now manned what were still illegal gig-mills, on wages less than half that of an adult cropper, one boy overseeing several machines, taking over the work of several men.[35]

Earl Fitzwilliam felt the strike was a private dispute, and noted Gott had not broken any law but had impinged on regulations and customs of the community. He said that as long as the strike lasted, not one piece of cloth could go for sale, and what would happen, he pondered, to the thousands unable to work. Fitzwilliam confessed he 'felt a strong bias' in favour of mechanisation, but warned that it would provoke violent disturbances, which the civil powers were inadequate to contain. The Earl also admitted that the laws against combinations was in effective, and confessed it was impossible to ban union activity. Indeed, any such outright ban would impinge on general rights, and that the masters had the right 'to use such means as he thinks proper in his own concerns'. However, he did admit that mechanisation 'would render these men useless'.[36] Mechanisation it was to be, as it would break the strike and break the unions.

The strikers were supported financially by the institution and donations from the wider community, just like the miners' strike of the 1980s.[37] The bricklayers of Leeds were amongst the most vocal supporters of the croppers.[38] Support was also given by the journeymen cutlers of Sheffield.[39]

The Croppers' Institution, since its inauguration, had acted as a friendly society and had amassed a considerable pool of funds. Members paid in 6*d*. to 1*s*. per week into a central bank account, which by summer 1802 held tens of thousands of pounds. The workers from Gott's were initially paid 18*s*. out of the common fund. In all, 1,500 men claimed the allowance in the first week, which so depleted the resources of the Institution that the allowance was dropped to 10*s*. By January, the fund had fourteen days' money remaining.[40] Where this money came from, we can only speculate. Presumably, some clothiers and smaller merchants also contributed, and perhaps also did other radical groups.

Unity amongst clothiers and croppers in Leeds, and across the country, meant that when Gott tried to bring in strike-breakers from Wiltshire and Somerset to his factory in Leeds, it came to nought.[41] When Gott tried to induce croppers from Wakefield and Huddersfield to work in Leeds, the Leeds croppers cried, 'None but Leeds Croppers shall have admittance into this town, we know how to prevent strangers coming here.' In reply, the merchants felt that they were slaves to their workers, and would 'not endure slavery any longer'. Yet the magistrates acknowledged that the Institution, acting as it was, represented a 'trifling' infringement of the law.[42] Both sides were guilty of breaking the law: Gott and Cookson erected illegal gig-mills and the croppers sought strength through unity, which was also illegal. Despite the illegality of their actions, the strike was unacceptable to men like William Cookson, the Tory Lord Mayor of Leeds, who sought to destroy the influence of the cropper. He remarked that they 'were no longer an order of men necessary to the manufacturers and if the merchants had the firmness to do without them, their consequence would be lost ... their combinations would fall to the ground'.[43]

The debate in Yorkshire about apprenticeships and mechanisation was witnessed by other parts of the country reliant on the woollen trade. In Trowbridge, a strike over wages broke out, and a gig-mill was burned to the ground.[44] In both the west of England and Yorkshire, the Institution was not shy in coming forward and using its funds to finance strikes; money was sent from Yorkshire to support strikers in Wiltshire.[45]

William Cookson appears to have operated a large spy network to crush all those opposed to mechanisation. Cookson reported that the cloth dressers in Yorkshire realised that the introduction of machinery into the West Country would inevitably lead either to its introduction in Yorkshire or to the loss of trade in the region. He reported to Fitzwilliam that the fixed object of the Yorkshire croppers and Wiltshire shearmen was 'an absolute putting down of all machinery used in the dressing of cloth'.[46] Earl Fitzwilliam conceded in a letter to the Home Secretary that while accepting that the successful introduction of machinery was of great national importance, the interests of the shearmen and other workers who could lose their livelihood must not and should not be forgotten. He suggested that a meeting of the principal clothiers of Yorkshire and Wiltshire could promote useful discussion about ways to address the reasonable complaints of the shearmen. In Wiltshire, the government sought out spies to find out the views of the clothiers without allowing any suspicion that the government was preparing to sacrifice their interests.[47] The Home Secretary, and no doubt the government, had already decided that mechanisation was the future, croppers would become economically redundant, and thousands would be made unemployed across the country.

In December 1802, seven croppers were imprisoned for intimidating workers operating gig-mills at Law Atkinson's premises.[48] In response, workers at Atkinson's went on strike about the use of machines. Atkinson broke the strike by sacking those workers who refused to use machines. Unable to find work elsewhere in the middle of winter, all bar three had no option but to return to work.[49] Atkinson's Mill then suffered a 'mysterious fire', so too did William Horsfall's Ottiwells Mill.[50]

With tensions rising, the fear of more violence and an industry at near standstill, Gotts's strike was ended by compromise, on 23 January 1803: no gig-mills, but apprentices could be aged 14 to 17 years old.[51]

Chapter 7

POLITICAL AGITATION

Days after the strike ended, John Read of Lincoln's Inn confirmed Benjamin Gott's statement that the regulations forbidding the use of gig-mills did not apply to the machines then in use.[1] The strike had been in vain, yet the violence Cookson foresaw did not happen. Legal routes were resorted to in order to redress grievances.

In the aftermath of the strike, in 1803 the croppers in the West Riding petitioned Parliament against the repeal of the old laws regulating gig-mills and to retain legislation concerning apprenticeships. An estimated 50,000 woollen manufacturers and workers in the West Riding signed. Parliament examined and rejected the West Riding cloth workers' Institution's case against the ongoing mechanisation of the woollen industry and backed the claims of Benjamin Gott, Cookson and other Tory merchants in repealing legislation for apprenticeships and banning the shearing frame and gig-mill. The clothiers were also seeking to retain the legislation that limited the number of looms a clothier could possess: the law stated three. Factories that gathered dozens of looms together were technically illegal. Gott and Cookson sought to change the law to suit their own ends. As could be expected, the committee in its report appeared more concerned about the subversive threat from the institutions, the organisations representing the clothiers and cloth dressers, than about the threat to domestic manufacture from machinery. The Tory *Leeds Intelligencer* gleefully reported that Parliament had rejected the petition.[2]

The matter did not end there. Two years later, over 39,000 people signed a petition that sought to limit the adoption of power looms and gig-mills and enforce apprenticeship laws.[3] When news reached Yorkshire that the petition had been rejected, and that Henry Lascelles, MP for Yorkshire, had led the opposition to the bill, his effigy was burnt in Leeds and half a dozen other neighbouring villages and towns. The local hatred of the man was such that an effigy of him was shot at by the clothiers in the volunteer corps in Leeds.[4]

As well as venting anger against Lascelles, community anger was directed at the new factories and their imposition on tradition and community values stretching back hundreds of years:

> If the factory system prevails … it will call all the poor labouring men away from their habitations and their homes into the factories … supposing I was a parent, and had four or five or six children, and one of them was fourteen, another twelve, another ten; if I was working with my family at home I could give them employment, one to wind bobbins, another to work at the loom, another at the Jenny; but if I go to the factory they will not allow me to take these boys, but I will leave them to the wide world to perish.[5]

Benjamin Gott was producing cloth cheaper than any of his competitors – forcing them to mechanise to be able to compete – and was creaming off the best customers. Unlike the domestic system where workers could fall back on their market garden when trade was slack, Gott dismissed workers and engaged them as he needed, and deliberately employed men outside of the Institution. To circumvent the apprenticeship laws, he also employed men to oversee the machines who had not served an apprenticeship. One commentator went as far as to suggest that Gott's factory 'produced all sorts of baneful moral effects … detrimental to the community'.[6] Factories were alien to the vast majority of the clothiers: working to the clock, rather than the season, challenged their place in society as a master of their trade, and many more were horrified by the immorality of factories as women and men worked side by side. The factory threatened the very nature of society. Women and girls had worked from home, spinning and carding while caring for their family's needs. Their daily toil was repetitive and monotonous. The domestic system, despite its drawbacks, allowed the clothier, weaver or cropper to take work elsewhere when work was slack and to supplement their income from their kitchen gardens. Not so in the new world of mechanisation. Yet factories were the inevitable future. In response to the urging of Lascelles, Parliament agreed to the repeal of laws prohibiting the use of gig-mills and shearing frames and ended centuries-old apprenticeships. Despite the petitions, the government backed the force of capitalism and not labour.[7] The wealthy merchants had won their first battle and now sought to take on the Institution.

Fighting trade unionism

To combat the Institution and to end the power of the croppers, the merchants and manufacturers of the West Riding formed a combination of their own. The Institution was seen as the source of all discontent in the woollen trade, because:

> in their ultimate tendencies are more alarming than in a political than a commercial view...they have a systematic and organised plan and one so efficient and so dangerous both from the amount of its force and from the facility and secrecy with which at any time and for any purpose that force may be called into action.[8]

The fear was working-class solidarity and rights consciousness. In October 1804, Magistrate Dawson of Wakefield reported to the Home Office illegal combinations amongst the cordwainers of the West Riding, which:

> by the percept of a search warrant I got [illegible] of the articles & letters I have the honor to enclsore together with two books, one an account of his movements[?] the other merely the names of the members against each of which was check shewing who had paid their subscriptions and who were in [illegible]; George Foster who appears to have been secretary to the society and one Stephenson were no the evidence against them and their of confesion convicted before the Revd W Wood ... committed them to the house of correction for fourteen days of hard labor.[9]

Dawson, much as he had done to combat the United Englishmen from the 1790s to 1803, relied on spies and informers to root out sedition and trade unionism. Joseph Parkington, the steward of the combination, was sentenced at York to three months' imprisonment. Dawson notes that the combination began as a mutual or benefit club, but was 'extended to illegal purposes'. He feared that all such similar clubs were acting illegally, but could take no action for lack of evidence that would ensure convictions at the Quarter Sessions. Any time working-class solidarity appeared, the government sought to crush it.

In January 1805, five shoemakers in York received sentences of three months for illegal combination.[10] From 1802, there is clear continuity in the struggle against machinery and the erosion of the domestic system developing into the Luddite riots, exacerbated by famine and disease. Despite the boom of 1803–5, for some merchants, the woollen trade was still in decline, with poverty and starvation increasing.

To try to break class solidarity, in Leeds, fifty-four firms signed a resolution not to employ any Institution men. Joseph Stancliffe, a clothier of Hopton, in evidence to the 1806 inquiry, thought that the decision not to employ Institution weavers 'has in some measure prevented them'. However, it led to a bitter dispute. Non-Institution men were referred to as 'snakes' and homes were attacked in Beeston, Wortley and Armley.[11] Among the names of the thirty-one firms signing the Huddersfield resolution are many of those like the Atkinsons and William Horsfall, who were the most prominent advocates of finishing machinery.[12] The battle lines were being clearly drawn in this struggle.

Despite another petition by croppers and clothiers, on 20 February 1806 the Crown issued a new memorandum relating to gig-mills and shearing frames. Much as the Crown had stated in 1803, the legislation then on the statute book concerning the use of gig-mills and shearing frames was not applicable. The Crown believed that the machines prohibited during the reign of Edward Tudor were not comparable to the machines then in use.[13] A howl of rage erupted in the West Country and Yorkshire. Worse was to come.

In March 1806, another Parliamentary Committee was formed to debate the woollen trade. Gott's treatment of apprentices once more came to the fore, along with the Institution. The Crown argued that the cloth workers had broken the law in going on strike, and that Gott had fully understood the statutes of Elizabeth I relating to apprentices. The death knell of a centuries-old way of life had been sounded. The Crown sought to break the influence of the croppers and allied workers, and to allow the merchant-manufacturers to introduce mechanisation.[14]

Electioneering

With the death of William Pitt on 21 January 1806, the King reluctantly called a new government termed 'the Ministry of all the Talents'. Pitt's first cousin, Lord William Grenville, was prime minister, but was in office for barely ten months. The government fell on 24 October that same year. What happened next was a battle between the clothiers, croppers and merchants against the hated Lascelles.

The 1806 general election ran from 29 October to 2 December. Walter Ramsden Fawkes, an associate of the radical Sir Francis Burdett, agreed to stand against Lascelles. It is therefore no surprise that the Whig merchants were the power behind the Fawkes campaign: three stalwart Wakefield reformer merchant princes – John Milnes Jnr., Thomas Lumb and Robert Bakewell – organised the Fawkes campaign in the wapentake of Agbrigg and Morley. They so harnessed community anger against Lascelles and other Tories that, of 9,056 promises for Fawkes across Yorkshire, 6,582 were from the West Riding. Lascelles, when faced with overwhelming opposition, withdrew a week before the election took place and complained afterwards of 'the common cause made against me by the clothiers, and the secret and matured arrangement with which I had to contend'. Leeds Tory, William Cookson, reported to William Wilberforce that the Whigs 'in appealing to the manufacturers' had 'a very unfair advantage. ... the exasperated state of the clothiers in every direction of our Riding, as well as of the general class of workmen, who all make common cause'.[15] The voters amongst the woollen trade workers had sent a stark message to Lascelles and the government. The outcome of the election was that the Whig parliament suspended the Acts allowing a change to apprenticeship laws and the use of gig-mills and shearing frames. The Whig government was not to last, and fell in April 1807 due to the recalcitrance of the King over Catholic emancipation. The nation went to the polls once more. Fawkes withdrew when asked to stand again and rather than allow Lascelles to retake the seat, Earl Fitzwilliam sponsored his son, Lord Milton. The election was hugely costly. Fitzwilliam spoke of spending £150,000 and Lascelles relied on his Barbados slave plantations to finance his electioneering to the tune of £140,000. Wilberforce, who prided himself on the support of 'volunteers' against the 'others', rebuked such extravagance in spending a modest £28,000, enabling him to return half the £64,000 raised for him by subscription in Yorkshire and by his friends all over the country.[16]

The general election ran from 4 May until 9 June 1807. On 19 May, Milton's supporters gathered in Briggate to witness the departure of the nineteen-strong election committee for York – amongst which we find Milnes, Lumb and Bakewell. Milton's supporters were adorned with orange placards, which read 'Milton for Ever'. In the midst of the assembled crowd of jubilant Whigs, two boys wearing placards bearing 'Lascelles' endeavoured to pass through, accompanied by the Mayor of Leeds, Richard Bramley, a member of Lascelles' committee, who seems to have instigated the events. As could be so easily predicted – if not planned for – a scuffle broke out to prevent the boys pushing through the Milton supporters. Lascelles' supporters were booed and hissed in the street, which, according to the Tory press, showed the gathered clothiers' 'great inclination to riot'.[17] The Whig press was at pains to stress that 'not a stone was thrown or any one irritating step taken' by Milton's supporters to instigate what happened next.

The magistrates panicked; fearing a riot, the Riot Act was read, despite no acts of violence having broken out. The mayor ordered 'the military to scour the streets with drawn swords', reported the press, 'who struck down every person who did not instantly disperse', adding that 'the military pursued them, into yards and alleys'.[18] Cavalry are not highly trained at controlling crowds of civilians – people raising their fists, horses pushing, people unable to get out of the way because of the press of people behind them. It was inevitable that a soldier panicked. The crowd became a seething mass trying to escape and many were 'thrown down by the horses and other severely cut by the swords of the soldiers'.[19] In the massacre that followed, twenty innocent civilians were seriously wounded.[20] According to the *Leeds Intelligencer*, one soldier was slightly injured in the affray, which for the Tories and magistrates made the cavalry's actions legitimate retribution. In retaliation, the following day the Lord Mayor's house was pelted with stones.[21] What happened next was always going to happen: the Mayor let loose the cavalry once more and 'numbers of soldiers' were seen 'galloping down the footpaths of the most public streets of the town with their sword drawn … to the great terror … of the inhabitants', reported the press.[22] The Tories claimed that 'the strictest love of humanity, warranted the calling out of the military'.[23] Really? The episode here in Leeds is redolent of Peterloo and Orgreave. The following day, Lord Lascelles ordered twenty-one men arrested for using insulting language about him and causing a riot.[24]

Despite Lascelles' best efforts, Milton's success in the West Riding was in part due to the central committee of nineteen gentlemen who supervised the work of local committees and sixty-seven lawyers who were employed as agents. In Agbrigg and Morley, Thomas Lumb once more ran the campaign.[25] Lumb noted that when polling began, he had problems transporting the voters to the polling booth in York, commenting, 'Something must be done for none of them can be prevailed upon to ride in waggons,' as he could not hire sufficient coaches.[26] Prior to the Reform Act, some voters had two votes. A plumper was a voter who possessed both votes, and chose to support just one candidate when there was also another from the same party on the ballot paper. The support for Milton, who canvassed for plumpers from the West Riding cloth merchants, again proved decisive, providing him with 7,625 votes in the Riding, which contributed 60 per cent of the voters. In Agbrigg and Morley, where Thomas Lumb was chairman, Milton polled 2,959 votes to Lascelles' 1,650. Amongst the cloth workers he won 450 votes in Agbrigg and Morley wapentake, 37 clothiers in Batley out of 50 who polled, 73 out of 84 in Dewsbury, and Idle, 46 out of 50 clothiers.[27] Milton's victory was centred on mobilising the vote of the clothiers, who were mostly non-Anglicans, as John Milnes Jnr. commented in June 1807 to Earl Fitzwilliam:

> the dissenting ministers have had their reward from the liberal endeavours of the later administration and their names being recorded in the poll books for Lord Milton is enough for them; those men from principle and gratitude will be upon like occasions hearty in your Lordship's interest and indeed it will be an interest of some importance to preserve as the influence of the dissenting clergy has of late years become diffusedly great, as nearly one half of the clothing country have become dissenters of one denominations or another.[28]

The Tories could not believe the outcome. The Tory Church of England *Leeds Intelligencer* went as far as to denounce Lord Milton as being a Jacobin, and quite correctly, labelled his supporters as 'free thinkers, rabble rousers and Presbyterians'.[29] The Tories screamed:

> Lord Milton ... succeeded by the assistance of the clothiers ... they supported him as the friend of the ancient exploded mercantile system. They loved him ... as the enemy of the present system of commercial improvement ... eleven thousand freeholders of the County of York, Jacobins or prejudiced clothiers ... that prejudice of the clothiers is ill founded we believe ... the clothiers have gained no object for themselves ... whose minds had been industriously and seditiously inflamed against Mr Lascelles.[30]

Anger against Lascelles was of his own making for backing mechanisation, and it was inevitable that this community anger would be harnessed by the Whigs. The woollen trade was now solidly politically identified as Whig, religiously as dissenting. Such dissent in politics and religion would develop throughout the nineteenth century into trade unionism and define the identity of working-class communities across the West Riding until well into the 1980s.

Chapter 8

ECONOMIC WARFARE

Against the backdrop of the elections was the deteriorating economic situation. Unable to invade Britain due to the Royal Navy, Napoleon sought to cripple the country by other means. He turned to economic sanctions. The Continental System (or Continental Blockade) excluded British goods from the continent, and was signed into law on 21 November 1806. With French hegemony over most of Europe following the treaty of Tilsit, only Portugal remained as a barrier to closing all of Europe's ports to British goods. Thus, in 1807, France invaded Portugal to ensure a total trade embargo: for Britain, the lucrative European market was lost for both the import of fleece and the export of finished cloth. James Ellis, a Leeds merchant who bought 'Portugal, Spanish & Saxony wool', reported to the Home Office that all the workmen in his factory in Armley had been laid off, due to scarcity of wool and trade.[1] To make matters worse, the invasion of Hamburg by the French resulted in the strangulation of the German trade. This left America as the sole export market.[2] On 11 November, Parliament signed into law the Orders in Council forbidding trade with France or her allies.

By closing the import of British goods into Europe, and the export of goods to Britain, Napoleon hoped to cripple the British economy, as well as to boost internal markets within the empire. In retaliation, the British government imposed its own blockade. Trade wars and economic protectionism are as costly as a war fought with pitched battles and the outcome is as unpredictable.

The government banked on having the fiscal resources to weather a ten to fifteen-year recession: long-term economic goals trumped short-term disadvantages to the economy and domestic policy at home. The Continental System heralded in a nationwide depression that is often overlooked for its major impact upon the north of England, and on the cloth trade particularly.

Cut off from the wider world and European trade, the woollen trade collapsed by 21 per cent and the worsted trade fell by 29 per cent, dropping back to levels of commerce not seen since the 1780s. The collapse of the sale of worsted and broadcloths sent many businesses to the wall.[3]

The collapse in trade meant that wholesale mechanisation of the woollen trade was seen as the only solution to reduce costs. However, contrary to the wish of some, and largely in part thanks to the Whigs, Parliament voted to retain legislation against gigs and shearing mills. Yet for some, the Continental System offered new opportunities to trade, which largely offset the lack of European trade. The instability in export markets gave further impetus to the larger manufacturers to become merchant-manufacturers and to undertake the risks of trading directly. The merchants could therefore curtail their commitments in bad years or switch to domestic contracts as needed. This working model, however, placed the medium and large manufacturers at a disadvantage as they would have to stop production, lay off workers and then re-hire them at a later date. Such a working model favoured the domestic system level of production, whereby a clothier relied on cloth production and market gardening or another trade for income. However, the manufacturers with large mechanised factories who were unable – or at least unwilling – to close down their mills in a depression were forced to become merchants. To make matters worse, in bad years, they retailed their produce at or below prime cost. This gave a considerable boost to the business of speculative consignments for export. In November 1807, the French Army invaded Portugal, sparking what would become the Peninsular War. In response, the Portuguese court fled to Brazil, where they sought to administer their dislocated country and its response to the French. In the wake of the court, a number of Leeds and Wakefield merchants and manufacturers sent representatives to Brazil to negotiate lucrative trade deals into South America. John and Jeremiah Naylor of Wakefield gained lucrative contracts in Rio de Janeiro in this way. In 1800, 45 per cent of all woollens made in the West Riding were exported to America, increasing to 66 per cent in 1808. In 1806, J. & J. Naylor & Co. of Wakefield was trading broad and narrow cloth, fancy cloth, worsted, haberdashery and other goods with eleven firms in New York and Philadelphia. Naylor's was the second largest concern in Yorkshire trading with these American states, eclipsed only by Cookson's of Leeds. Milnes, Heywood & Co. of Wakefield are listed as merchant manufacturers, who only had three trading contracts with these American states.[4] By 1829, this firm's trade with Brazil was very lucrative indeed. Unsold goods in Lima were valued at £20,000, Rio some £30,000 worth of stock, and at Buenos Aires another £12,000. Naylor's also benefited materially from the war as army clothiers, but peace placed that profit at risk.[5] As always, there were winners and losers. The winners were the aggressive monopolisers. Those not lucky enough to have government contracts, or unable to profit from new markets, had a bleak future: huge swathes of the West Riding cloth trade was 'on its knees', as one correspondent to the *Leeds Mercury* signing himself as 'P' pointed out in early autumn 1807:

> military cloths are the only species of woollens that have for many months past been in regular demand, and the consumption of which has lately been greater than usual, from the circumstances of a very large part of the army having recently been new cloathed, of course it will be a considerable time before such a demand for the military again occurs; and it is to be feared that manufacturers of white cloth (which is dyed into red and scarlet) will in a short time feel their full share of the severe distress, long experienced by the manufacturers of coloured woollens ... the clothiers, wool-staplers and others connected with the woollen trade ... is in a worse situation than it has been at any period subsequent to the American war ... if very prompt measures are not adopted to remove the pressure on trade, a general insolvency must speedily ensure; and this pressure can only be removed by the restoration of peace.[6]

About the economic downturn, an anonymous clothier wrote:

> I am a plain man, little used to writing, but as you have been so good to undertake in the last *Intelligencer* to give us Clothiers some advice, it may happen that you can help us in our need.
>
> You say we should not petition the King for Peace, God Bless Him, but should follow our callings 'Honestly and industriously', I hope we shall follow them; but if we follow them industriously, can you tell us how to sell the cloth our industry produces; for it is of no use to tell us to make cloth fast, unless you can tell us how to shift it when it is made; and the more industrious we are in these times, the worse we are off, for it only throws us into debt for wool and wares; and you know, if you know anything about us, that hundreds of clothiers like myself have gone to the cloth halls every market day for many months passed without selling a single end of cloth; and so scarce has money been, that we've gone home again without asking to see the stapler or salter, and without taking as much money as would be our distressed families dinner.
>
> If you and other men of war have hearts in your bellies, it would soften them to see us meet our inquiring families on these mournful

market days- for it would melt a heart of stone. A wise man has said that 'Hope deferred maketh the heart sick' and our hearts have for a long while sickened under the deferred hope of selling cloth and receiving money for what we have sold long since. You may be able to hear our distress, as it often happens that folks can hear others folks' misfortunes better than their own. But we feel that something must be done to help us, and we know of nothing so likely as PEACE, nor of anyway of getting it so likely as the way that has got it aforetime. That has been by asking our good old king for it; and this with God's help, we are framing to do again.[7]

Peace was once more the panacea to the economic problems facing the north of England.

Peace petitions

With the woollen trade crippled by the war against France, as could be expected, the Whig leadership, which had organised the election victory of Lord Milton as MP for Yorkshire, and whose wealth was based on the woollen trade, were to the fore in a new round of peace petitioning. The leaders of the Whig movement, by and large, in Yorkshire were wealthy Unitarian, who were members of a new merchant-gentry elite that dominated towns such as Hull, Leeds, Nottingham, Derby, Belper, Sheffield and Wakefield. Outside of the West Riding, by 1800, Unitarians wielded considerable economic power in Liverpool, Bristol and Manchester, and were conspicuous for civic leadership and political influence. Unitarians figure large in the making of provincial middle-class culture across the country.

Lancashire

Through the peace petitioning campaign, a mass popular movement was engendered. In both Lancashire and the West Riding, radicals recognised that it would be more effectual for regions to combine their efforts and choose regional leaders to take the campaign to Parliament. Resolutions passed in Lancashire further expressed a provincial identity in stating that the war was affecting the economic position of the 'lower and middling classes of manufacturing districts of Lancashire, Yorkshire and Cheshire'.[8] Joseph Hanson was regarded as the most suitable 'gentleman leader' by the 'artisans across south-east Lancashire wishing to petition for peace and reform'. Hanson attempted to arrange for a meeting in Manchester to draw up a peace petition but was prevented from doing so by the authorities. The first open mass gathering for peace in Lancashire recorded in the newspapers occurred in Rochdale on 7 December 1807.[9] Diarist Rowbottom lamented:

the poor at this time are in a wretched situation such as was seldom known before all sorts of work Both scarce and a very little for working it and all sorts of provisions at an Enormous price makes the state of the poor to be miserable behind [beyond] description and a great deal of poor familys in a state of actual starvation.[10]

A letter in Cowdroy's *Manchester Gazette* in December 1807 from 'a woollen clothier' thanked Hanson 'at the request of a number of respectable distressed tradesmen in the West Riding'.[11] Hanson then published 'A Defence of the Petitions for Peace', a pamphlet that contained strictures against the Manchester elites for their repressive actions against the working classes.[12] This was a case of north verses south, and manufacturer against merchant: an alliance of Whigs, radicals, merchants and artisans against Tory oligarchs. It was now that a William Dawson travelled to Stockport to address a large body of weavers and was subsequently arrested for sedition.[13]

As in the West Riding, in Lancashire, Unitarians were at the forefront of the campaign. Colonel Fletcher reported that a group of Unitarians from Bank Street Chapel in Bolton attended a meeting to discuss the economic situation facing the town's weavers, who, 'more than once attempted to introduce the subject of a petition for Peace, but this the Chairman repressed as it was not the object of the meeting'.[14] It seems likely that the protestors were probably led by Dr Robert Everleigh Taylor. Another meeting was held in February 1808. Colonel Fletcher, in letter to the Home Office, described that at a meeting to discuss the poor rate and other levies, 'a hundred petitioners burst in, refused to let the boroughreeve speak, crying, "Peace, Peace, Peace"'.[15] Through holding open-air rallies for peace, led by the radical Unitarian minister the Reverend John Holland from Bank Street Chapel, Dr Taylor from Cross Street Chapel, Manchester, the petition here attracted and contained an estimated 13,000 signatures.[16] Manchester's petition was stated in Parliament to have 50,000 signatures, and William Cowdroy, through the pages of his newspaper, claimed Stockport had collected 12,000 signatures and Bolton 18,000.[17]

Strong links between Lancashire and Yorkshire are implied by the *Leeds Mercury* supporting the Lancashire cotton weavers, and Hanson appearing in the *Leeds Mercury* calling for peace:

> We your majesty's local subjects, inhabitants of the towns of Manchester and Salford ... most humbly petition your majesty for a speedy and honourable termination, if possible, of the present war, which has of late, been for us, peculiarly unfortunate ... the very extensive suppression of foreign commerce – considerably lessened the price of labour – threatens

to occasions the want of employ for thousands ... and to reduce many enterprising and ingenious manufacturers, and others, from affluence to comparative poverty.[18]

After a mass meeting to draw up a peace petition was held on Oldham Edge on Christmas Day 1807, the Oldham constables issued an address in the Manchester newspapers accusing the participants of Jacobinism. The Royton spokesmen Henry Whitaker and James Kershaw sardonically admitted to the charge of being 'enemies to the Government' because they believed the government had degraded and impoverished the country by pursuing war and not peace, noting, 'It is true that the Royton people have uniformly opposed both this and the last destructive wars! And if that entitles them to the epithet of enemies to the Government, they freely and gladly submit to it.'[19]

As alluded to earlier, the Reverend John Holland, as with other Unitarian ministers across the north of England, began a petition in January 1808 from his chapel on Bank Street, Bolton. So successful was Holland that he amassed 17,000 signatures in favour of peace. Hanson's Manchester peace petition was presented to the Commons on 18 March 1808. Samuel Whitbread commented:

> this petition, signed by 50,000 persons, in addition to the thousands who had petitioned before, laid a great weight of responsibility on ministers. An insinuation had been thrown out, that some gentlemen on his side had had recourse to artifice, in order to encourage these petitions. He knew nothing of any such artifice; and firmly believed, that this petition was wrung from the persons subscribing it by their distresses. The language of the petition was unexceptionable, and even highly respectful. Unless ministers, therefore, shelved a serious disposition to enter into a negotiation, it would be the duty of the house to interfere, and address the throne on the subject.[20]

Leeds

Over the Pennines, the clothiers and croppers understood that ending the war was the best hope for their community rather than petitioning for a minimum wage. Employers could not raise wages while the economy was on a deflating trajectory; peace would reopen closed markets. Bolstered by their success at the polls in electing Lord Milton, the Whig cum liberal leadership of the West Riding threw their weight behind achieving lasting peace. The *Leeds Mercury*, owned by Edward Baines, a Unitarian attending Mill Hill Chapel, championed the call for peace:

What further advantage can arise from a farther continuance of the War? … It is well known that the petitions for Peace from Leeds, Wakefield &c. gave that alarm which obliged the war faction to retire and give place to Mr Addington, for the express purpose of making peace … the war has been continued without any apparently reasonable object. … We were last year told by our negotiator Lord Yarmouth, that we might have had an honourable and advantageous peace, but the French were not willing to give Dalmatia to Russia, nor to let the Court of Naples possess Sicily … in the name of Common Sense had these objects to do with the happiness of the people of England? The situation of the country imperiously demands from every man who had anything left worth preserving to petition for peace … the clamorous supporters and promoters of war … are the true blood-thirsty Jacobins, whose pious War-Whoop has done more injury to their country than all the efforts of the Corresponding Societies could ever have effected.[21]

Calls for peace came from across the dissenting community. The Reverend Edward Parsons, the minister at Salem Independent Chapel, Leeds, preached a sermon entitled 'The True Patriot', in which he said:

Deluded politicians! Guilty patriots! You inflict the horrors of war, and perhaps, upon unoffending countries … why will you aggravate and seal your own condemnation by a pretended zeal for religion … is an alarming presage of national judgements; and therefore, such criminals, with all their gasconading about loyalty and patriotism, are the worst of all enemies to their king and their country.[22]

As could be ascertained from the success of the petition in 1801, the next petition was managed in a very similar way. The well-established liberal leadership made much use of trade organisations to raise an impressive body of public opinion. Opposition to the war was no longer based solely on economic reasons, but also on moral obligations and political reasoning. In Huddersfield, a Peace Meeting was convened at Honley on 7 December 1807, chaired by wealthy Methodist cloth merchant Thomas Haigh, a noted lay preacher for the Methodist New Connexion, aka 'Thom Paine Methodists'. Haigh condemned the war in no uncertain terms: 'the exclusion of our trade from foreign markets, our goods lay on hand, nor can we in many cases obtain remittances for those already sold.'[23] In Leeds:

the appointed general meeting of merchants and manufacturers of Yorkshire, to consider of the propriety of addressing the King on the subject of Peace, was held at the Mixed – cloth – hall in Leeds, when about 10,000 persons gave their attendance. The chair was taken by Mr. John Firth, and the following re-solutions were agreed to: —

That the restoration of peace Is highly desirable, and is an object of great importance to our own interests and the general prosperity of the nation.

That many of the inhabitants of this commercial and manufacturing country are reduced to a state of extreme distress, which is greatly increased by the pressure of heavy taxes and poor rates.

That the long continuance of the war is the principal cause of these complicated evils.

That it is expedient to present a petition to his Majesty, praying him to adopt such measures as he in his wisdom may deem most advisable, to restore to us at an early period the blessings of peace; and that a petition be prepared to this effect. That we are informed by the papers that the late negotiation was broken off for Russian, and not for British interests and that power having since become our enemy the war has now no distinct object, and cannot therefore be necessary, either to preserve our honour, our liberties, or our independence.

That we have no intention of promoting the interests of any party distinct from the nation at large; the sole object of this meeting being to express our wishes for the restoration of peace, and to make our wishes known by petition. That should his Majesty's Ministers, who-ever they may be, sincerely and earnestly endeavour to procure for us the blessings of peace, on fair and reasonable terms, they will receive our thanks, and deserve the gratitude of the country.

That if, contrary to our expectations, his Majesty's Ministers should advise their Sovereign to reject the prayer of our petition for peace, we will from time to time dutifully renew our application, nor desist from entreaties until it shall appear that peace on reasonable terms cannot be obtained.

Mr. Bakewell, of Wakefield, in proposing the motion of thanks to the Trustees, observed, that particular circumstances made a petition for Peace desirable at the present moment. — He then read a draft of the intended Petition, in substance nearly as follows : — The Petitioners assure his Majesty of their attachment to his person, and the principles of Government which placed his Majesty and his august Family on the Throne; and represent to his Majesty the distressed state to which great numbers of our merchants and manufacturers were reduced by the long continuance of the war, deprived them of foreign markets, whereby many workmen are left without employment, and the smaller manufacturers unable to provide for their families, and they express their apprehension of these calamities being increased by a war with America.

They allude to the heavy taxes and addition to the national debt, and the increased annual expenditure of the country, while the power and territories of the enemy have been enlarged, and our Allies have deserted us to seek his friendship and protection.

The Petitioners further express their fears, that should the war continue, many of the former Allies of this country will be drawn into closer connection with France, and make amity with this country very difficult to be resumed. It implores his Majesty, as the father of his people, to adopt such measures as may appear expedient to restore to us the blessings of Peace, and concludes with assuring his Majesty of their loyalty, attachment, and support, should the restoration of Peace be retarded by any demand of the enemy, inconsistent with the honour and security of the realm, &c. Ste.

The petition was then agreed to, and the meeting separated quietly: but a troop of the 16th light dragoons was ordered from York, and arrived in Leeds on the night before the meeting, on the morning of which they were drawn out with ball cartridge, ready to aid the magistracy had it been necessary to call for their services! ! Was this consistent with the boasted privileges of Englishmen, when a meeting was legally convened?[24]

Bakewell, a Unitarian, who had been gaoled in 1793 for sedition and arguing against the seditious meeting and writing Acts, was outspoken in his contempt for the war:

Gentlemen
I Beg to propose a motion which I have little doubt will receive your approbation, the substance of which will be to return your thanks to the trustees of the Coloured and White Cloth Halls, for their ready compliance in calling this meeting.

If ever there was a time when it was proper for the people to come forward and petition for Peace, it is the present. On three former occasions it has been the pride and glory of the County of York to terminate or prevent the calamities of war. The Petitions, Addresses and Remonstrances from Yorkshire put to a close the War with America; – the petitions on a more recent occasion, in the last war, from this place and the neighbouring towns were followed by peace; – the remonstrances from Yorkshire seconded by other parts of the kingdom prevented a war with Russia. We have in these three instances the political benefit of a petition to oppose all objections against it.

Gentlemen, independent of all general arguments, there are particular circumstances existing which make a Petition for Peace particularly proper at this time. We are informed by his Majesty's late declaration, that as the war was continued to promote the interest of Russia, and as Russia is now an enemy, it were absurd to say the war is continued for her interests; the war must therefore, now be without any defined object whatever; and this must be a time of peculiar felicity to put an end to it.

Now gentlemen, though the war be at present without an object, if it be longer continued, even for a month, for three months, six months, or any further period, other circumstances and other objects may arise which may make it very difficult, if not impossible to treat. But gentlemen, there is another consideration of still greater weight which I wish to press on your most series [serious] attention. We are on the eve of War with America, – a war so calamitous in its consequences to the commerce and prosperity of this country, that the very boldest amongst us must tremble to contemplate them. Gentlemen, we all know that the disputes with America arise entirely out of the circumstance of the present war with France; were we at peace with Europe, the cause of these difficulties and disputes being removed, the effect must cease, and we should also be at peace with America. Thus, by making peace at the present time, we should save this country from great impending calamity; and it cannot be said on the other side that any possible advantage can arise from the longer continuance of the war.

Were any further arguments wanted to prove the necessity of Peace, many of you, I much fear, can read them in the distressed circumstances of your families when you return from these public markets; you can perceive them in the general gloom and dejection which pervades the country; we can all feel them in the fearful forebodings and anticipations of what is to come. Will any man say that we have had added another hundred millions to the national debt, we can make a better peace than at present? Will any man say, when (which is a far more serious consideration,) we have sacrificed One Hundred Thousand of our fellow beings, men of like feelings and passions with ourselves, we can treat on better terms than at present? Will any man say, that when we have ruined some hundreds more of our merchants and manufacturers, we shall gain better terms of peace than at present? NO Gentlemen, the positions are too absurd to dwell upon, and yet it is incumbent on the supports [supporters] of war to prove all these things.

Let us Gentlemen, awake from our delusion, to contemplate the folly of continuing a war which is in its consequences so calamitous, and which can produce no possible advantage to this country;- let us cry aloud and spare not;- let us seek peace and pursue it, nor desist from our endeavours till the object of our wishes be obtained.

Gentlemen, We read from high authority that blessed are the peace makers, for their reward shall be great – every man, however humble his situation who contributes by petition or otherwise, to close the calamities of war, is entitled to the appellation of a Peace Maker, and to partake in this glorious reward.[25]

Bakewell and colleagues could take pride, that in their endeavours they were supported by Samuel Whitbread.[26] The petition that Bakewell and liberal Whig leadership baked, read, in part:

several townships and villages have passed resolutions expressive of the necessity of peace, and of the expediency of petitioning, and have also requested the trustees of the cloth halls to convene a meeting of the Cloth Manufacturers for the purpose of presenting a general petition to the King ... the distress you daily observe will impress this necessity upon you with more force than any arguments which be produced.[27]

The petition was slandered by the Tory Anglicans as 'founded in the deep held system of Jacobin treachery'.[28] Three petitions were distributed in Leeds, Bingley and Saddleworth, generating 60,000 signatures, with some 28,268 gained in Leeds.[29] In Rochdale and Oldham, the petition gathered 36,000 signatures, Manchester 50,000, and Bolton 18,000.[30] In Bingley, out of a population of 2,580 people, the petition attracted 2,542 signatures, and from Liverpool, headed by William Roscoe, came a petition of 15,000 signatures.[31] On 1 March, 10,000 assembled at the cloth hall in Huddersfield, the meeting being chaired by Thomas Haigh. Addresses were given by John Platt, a woollen manufacturer from Saddleworth, and Ben Ingham, the leader of Lockwood Baptist Church. Some 20,000 signatures were collected for peace.[32] Iron founders in Yorkshire and Derbyshire submitted a petition on 20 June 1808 that had gathered 29,000 signatures.

This was a formidable public outpouring against the hated war: over 200,000 signed the petitions, yet it achieved nothing. The Crown was deaf to the pleas of the starving and the dispossessed. Despite the failure of the petitions, as far back as 1919, some historians argued – quite correctly, in my view – that the peace petitions rejected by Parliament in 1808 turned the working classes towards unionised action and radicalism.[33] As could be expected, the Crown was deaf to the will and suffering of the people. One Tory declared: 'The Jacobins have conceived that a clamour at this juncture for an impracticable peace.' Unlike their brethren in Huddersfield, the Methodists in Wakefield, led by the Reverend Samuel Bradburn, sought to distance Wesleyan Methodists from the peace petition movement and branded any Methodists taking part as Jacobins and threatened to expel any members who took part.[34] Bradburn had consistently argued in favour of war with France from its outbreak in the 1790s. He was, furthermore, staunchly opposed to any idea of equality and freedom of religion. He urged retention of all legal impositions against Catholics and Unitarians, and from his pulpit denounced the Reverend Dr Priestley, Thomas Paine and the schismatic Alexander Kihlman. Kihlman had left the Methodist conference with thousands of others as he believed in the ideas of democracy and the rights of man. His nascent denomination became known as 'Thom Paine Methodists'. Bradburn believed that the rich owed their position to God, and the poor were born to suffer and would receive their reward in heaven: he believed that man was born evil, corrupted, and in consequence, society was flawed, and man had no right to attempt to redress these failings. Indeed, Bradburn insisted that original sin was the leading principle of Christianity, and men were only equal to one another in their corruption. Others like Hannah Moore, the influential writer and propagandist, and William Wilberforce, all shared this worldview: salvation and prayer was the answer, not the political ideas of Thomas Paine, Olympe de Gouges – the French radical feminist who inspired Mary Wollstonecraft's *Vindication of the Rights of Women* – Major Cartwright, the Reverend Christopher Wyvill – an Anglican priest with strong Unitarian theological leanings and political reformer – as well as the Unitarian clergy, who denied any such notions of original sin, as we discussed earlier. Two differing worldviews were on a collision course. Bradburn's appointment in Wakefield in 1806 was no coincidence: as past president of the conference in 1799 and his track record of 'Church and King' Tory politics, he was a 'safe pair of hands' in the then town to prevent Methodists being seen as Jacobins, and prevent further secession to the 'Thom Paine Methodists', who worshipped with the 'infidel' Unitarians in Wakefield and were building chapels in Leeds and the village of Horbury, near Wakefield. As could be expected with a strong alliance between Church, State and the growing Methodist movement being in favour of war, the petitioning achieved nothing. The war continued, and the woollen trade continued its downward slide.

Chapter 9

FERMENTING REVOLUTION

The economic slump that had started with the Continental System carried on and became worse due to the belligerence of the Crown. America was sucked rapidly into the economic siege that had emerged between Britain and France. William Lupton, the Unitarian merchant prince attending Call Lane Chapel in Leeds (mentioned in Chapter 6), and a major woollen merchant, reported to his brother-in-law that 'we cannot expect any settled good trade until the American business is settled'.[1] Joseph Rogerson, who carried on an extensive business in Bramley, noted that talk of war with America in the new year of 1808 depressed the export market, as the bulk of the Leeds woollens were exported to America.[2] William Roscoe, the Liverpool Unitarian radical, summarised the effects that the economic collapse of the woollen and other trades would have:

> these circumstances, added to the threatening aspect of public affairs, have at length excited the dormant feelings of the people; and a suspicion, not wholly groundless, begins to prevail, that if they sleep much longer they may awake only to their destruction. Subjects of the greatest importance to their interests begin again to be discussed.[3]

Roscoe predicted Luddism four years before it erupted. Tension and anger was building across the land against the Crown, local elites and business owners. The country was simmering with rage; all it would take was a gust of wind to fan the embers to full-blown rebellion.

Anglo-American relations had been at a low ebb since 1808 and gradually became worse. The Non-Intercourse Act of 1809 effectively closed off the North Atlantic to British shipping. In consequence, the Manchester cotton trade, relying heavily on imports from America, ground to a halt. The woollen trade fared no better. Cut off from its primary market, the trade collapsed.[4]

Increasing mechanisation and lower wages were driven by the contraction in the economy as manufacturers sought to earn a profit. The Tories finally rescinded the legislation concerning gig-mills and shearing frames before the summer recess of Parliament. Machines were cheaper, needed no wages and could be overseen by fewer workers, who were largely unskilled. It was not just the West Riding woollen trade that was seeing wholescale mechanisation; Manchester cotton weaving was becoming increasingly mechanised in factories. In Nottinghamshire, traditional stocking frame weavers found they were being squeezed out of the market by increasing use of new machines. Luddism arose at a crisis point: a whole way of life and community was at stake in three regions of the country, and can be seen as an eruption of pent-up community anger against unrestrained capitalism. The first explosion of violence came from Nottinghamshire, when the stocking frame weavers took direct action against mechanisation in spring 1811.

Nottinghamshire outrages

Echoing the events of 1799, unemployment and vast wealth inequality, coupled with community anger, led desperate people with little or nothing to lose to take desperate measures. Ned Ludd marched forward at the head of a new army of 'redressers'.

The grievances consisted firstly in the use of wide stocking frames to produce large amounts of cheap, shoddy stocking material that was cut and sewn rather than completely fashioned, and secondly, in the employment of 'colts' – workers who had not completed the seven-year apprenticeship required by law. Grievances were also made against the increasing number of female stocking weavers, who were paid less and thus put men out of work. The employment of women and boys was due to a major shift in technology with the use of so-called wide frames. The *Nottingham Journal* reported: 'The depredations have been almost exclusively confined to the destruction of a certain description of stocking frame which being of a new construction are supposed by the workmen likely to prove greatly injurious to the body at large.'[5] These changes threatened custom and tradition in an echo of the grievances of the croppers and shearmen of Yorkshire and the West Country. 'Full-wrought' stockings were made in the form of a tube. However, early in the new century a new form of stocking making was developed using a wider frame, which enabled the knitter to produce cloth in one flat piece. This was not a new technology, having been used for at least two decades without causing dispute to make, among other products, pantaloons and lace. As with the mechanisation of cloth finishing, this kind of frame required a great deal less skill and could be used by women and apprentices with little training.[6]

However, when these wide frames were used to produce stockings, they seriously threatened the framework knitters' trade. The use of the wide frame allowed the stockings to be made in one piece with a selvedge at the back, and were sewn together: such 'cut-ups' were immediately denounced as cheap, inferior products. Moreover, framework knitters believed that such products were contrary to the charter granted to the Worshipful Company of Framework Knitters by Charles II, which decreed that only 'fully wrought hose' might legally be produced. Indeed, the charter provided a sanction, ordaining that frame making 'spurious articles' might be destroyed in order to ensure that hose was not deceitfully made.[7] The Nottingham Luddites believed they were acting within the remit of the law.[8] Ned Ludd's first attack in a decade was on 11 March 1811, when the wide knitting frames in a shop in the Nottinghamshire village of Arnold were destroyed, following a peaceful gathering of framework knitters near the Exchange Hall at Nottingham. In the preceding month, framework knitters, also called stockingers, had broken into shops and removed jack wires from wide knitting frames, rendering them useless without inflicting great violence upon the owners or incurring risk to the stockingers themselves.[9] The local press reported that 'a number of individuals from the adjacent villages' marched into the city 'with a view of representing to their employers the hardships they were subject to and of intimidating others into compliance with their demands by which alone they can be enabled to obtain a subsistence'. The magistrates called out troops but the demonstrators left quietly. Later that day, a large crowd assembled at Arnold 'with a premeditated determination to destroy some stocking frames employed there by hosiers of this town'. Fifty frames were broken.[10]

All was quiet for several months until alarming reports were received of a new wave of violence:

> 'Sir, if you do not pull don the Frames or stop pay Goods only for work
> or m.. in full fashon
> my Companey will [vi]sit yr machines for execution...
> Ned Lu[d'[11]

The recipient was Edward Hollingworth, whose house was attacked on the night of 10 November. The Luddites arrived at Hollingworth's house at around 1 a.m. demanding entry to the property, and that Hollingworth surrender the frames inside. He had removed some of his frames to Nottingham. Hollingworth refused to comply and an exchange of fire broke out. After nearly twenty shots had been fired, the Luddites began trying to break in, using hammers. It was at this point that one of the attackers was mortally wounded by gunfire, and they were forced to retreat. The Luddites regrouped, and driven, we assume, by what they felt was the 'murder' of a fellow Luddite, redoubled their attack. In the meantime, Hollingworth and his men retreated upstairs, and the two groups exchanged fire: the Luddites gained entry to the house and exchanged gunfire with Hollingworth up and down the stairwell. By now, the attackers had started to pull down the partition wall that supported the floor of the room that Hollingworth and his men had fled to. Finding themselves in a hopeless situation, they decided to escape through a window at the back of the house. The Luddites destroyed five wide frames and two warp frames, 'along with the doors, window-frames and household furniture'.[12] Letters dated 13 and 14 November 1811 request that the government dispatch military aid because '2000 men, many of them armed, were riotously traversing the County of Nottingham'.[13] Towards the close of November came reports of more rioting in Nottingham. A mob of 300 armed with firearms and clubs broke into workshops containing stocking frames, 'destroying the stocking frames and other property and threatening yet further outrages'.[14]

The *Leeds Mercury* reported in December that year about the outbreak of rioting in Nottingham:

> what an alarming crisis is this country brought when its Military force, instead of being employed against our foreign enemies, is obliged to act, reluctantly indeed, against our own subjects, made blind and desperate by privation and want. Nor is the cause of this riotous disposition confined to Nottinghamshire—it exists in almost all the manufacturing districts of the kingdom, both in Woollens, Cottons and Iron, though Nottinghamshire, alone, is happily the only scene of popular outrage. And is it not well worthwhile to enquire how all this danger and suffering may be brought to an end? And if the men to whose incompetent hands the administration of the government of the country is unfortunately committed, are unable or unwilling to remedy the evil, does it not behove the People, particularly in the manufacturing and commercial counties, now Parliament is about to assemble, to exercise their constitutional right and meet and instruct their Representatives. Nor ought we to allow ourselves to be diverted from this course by fear of the calumnies of weak and corrupt men, who tell us that the riots in Nottinghamshire are owing to French Gold! and who, to conceal the

true cause of the evil, will tell their shallow dupes anything.—No; these riots owe not their rise and progress to the gold of Napoléon, but to the politics of PITT and his adherents; and so long as the system acted upon by that Minister, whose lofty spirit was subdued at the contemplation of the misery his ill-fated councils had produced, are pursued, we may be distressed, but we cannot be surprised either at disaster abroad or commotion at home.[15]

The frame breaking in Nottinghamshire spread amongst the croppers and other workers in the woollen industry of the West Riding and others deeply affected by the economic slump in Lancashire and the midlands had real grievances with the state. To make matters worse, the harvest of 1811 failed. Food prices rose dramatically. On 12 November, John Pilkington reported from Bolton that:

> The advanced prices at which flour, meat and potatoes are now sold in this district, and the fear of a further rise ... have caused a considerable degree of anxiety ... wages are certainly lower than at any former period, and should a further considerable rise take place in grains & potatoes without an [illegible] advance in the price of labour, the consequences are justly to be feared.[16]

Machine breaking grew from a cost of living crises. On 7 December came news of machine breaking in Derbyshire by men with their faces blacked out and armed with 'guns, pistols, swords & also with large hammers, Iron crows for the purpose of destroying' machines.[17] A spy reported on 27 December that in Manchester there was pressure for a strike from the weavers, to gain an increase in wages, noting that 'even the single man Cannot Live on his Earnings Let alone men with famileys'.[18] Edward Baines, through the pages of his newspaper the *Leeds Mercury*, thundered:

> We have more than once adverted to the unhappy disturbances at Nottingham, and as far as our endurance and efforts could extend, endeavoured to convince the deluded people concerned in these outrages, that they had grossly mistaken the cause of their distress which originated, not in the use of machinery, but in the decay of trade, the unhappy effect of war, and the Orders in Council; we advised them to petition not for Peace, for we considered that was hopeless, but for the removal of the Orders in Council. For this conduct we were denounced as traitors, and branded as incendiaries; but it is a conduct we do not repent of: We offer the same advice to those mistaken persons who are now disturbing the peace of this county by similar outrages. The destruction of all the machinery in the kingdom would not contribute an iota towards relieving their distress. The proceedings

they have adopted are most reprehensible and destructive, they tend to destroy the very bonds of society, they introduce into the very heart of the country a species of Civil War, they put those in a state of hostility with each other, who ought to be the best friends, and ultimately tend to introduce either general anarchy or complete military despotism. We would conjure them as they value their country, their wives, their children, their own lives, to pause in this destructive career, and to abandon, before it is too late, a system which can terminate only in misery and ruin.[19]

A counterview prevailed, however, as one writer opined to the Home Office:

I can form no judgement on the question, the ostensible cause of the dissatisfaction between the Hoziers and the Knitters declarations & assertions are so various, but the dissatisfied have now gained such an ascendancy & system, that unless <u>prompt</u> and <u>powerful</u> measures are applied, I think the season of winter, & the want to which they have reduced themselves, by the extensive destruction of the implements necessary to earn their support [illegible] most serious results. More than a thousand persons are now without their usual means of subsistence, & many persons are entirely ruined ... many constables have been sworn in ... in case of alarm ... <u>small military escorts</u> should be stationed ... the confidence of the populace from having born great mischief in the presence of a few dismounted dragoons has occasioned the ruin of many.[20]

Ludd and Yorkshire

Concurrent to the stocking frame knitters' grievances, the croppers had been fighting to maintain their trade since the 1780s and ever-increasing mechanisation sought to extinguish their trade. As with the miners in the 1980s, the government decided that these men did not matter. In 1806, five mills in the West Riding had gig-mills; by 1817, seventy-two mills, and some 3,378 croppers had been laid off and replaced by boys earning 5s. a week in imitation of Gott.[21] More alarmingly, since 1806, the employed workforce in the West Riding woollen trade had dropped from 20,000 to 9,400, of which just 5,000 were in full-time employment; the number of master clothiers had dropped from 3,200 to 1,870; the number of mills in operation had dropped from 127 to 90. Those in full employment had seen wages fall from 17s. per week to 10s.[22] Exacerbating the fall in wages was a cost-of-living crisis that had seen the price of food rise by 200 per cent since 1790, whereas wages had tumbled and the woollen industry slumped 20 per cent from 1790 levels.²³

Making a bad situation worse, in February 1811, Napoleon acceded to America's demands for free and neutral shipping between America and France, and Britain found herself excluded again from North American markets. At the same time, a shrinking economy meant less demand for goods in the domestic market.

The West Riding woollen trade was uniquely vulnerable as it relied upon exporting perhaps 80 per cent of all goods to America. In desperation, the trustees of the Leeds Mixed Cloth Hall requested a loan from Lord Milton as early as April 1811 to keep the hall functioning as it had been crippled by the closure of American ports.²⁴ The scale of the economic disaster that befell the country through exclusion from American ports can be seen in the drop in the value of exports during the course of 1811, falling to £32,900,000, representing a loss of almost £30,000,000, or half of exports being lost.

The loss of the American market crippled the economy of the West Riding. A year later, an estimated £590,000 worth of American exports lay on shelves gathering dust at the Mixed Cloth Hall. At the Leeds Coloured Cloth Hall were 37,000 pieces of cloth worth a further £185,000. At the Piece Hall in Halifax and warehouses in Bradford and Wakefield was a further £200,000 worth of goods languishing unsold. In total, £2.5 million worth of 'goods chiefly intended for the American market' remained unsold.²⁵ Today, this amount of cloth would be worth billions. In Ireland, the linen trade relied almost exclusively on the import of materials from America: more than 14,000 weavers were unemployed in Belfast alone. In Manchester, the new 'boom economy' based on the processing of raw cotton into cloth came to a juddering halt. Irish weavers who had been displaced by the events of 1798 and ongoing sectarian violence against Catholics, as well as due to the stagnation and decline of the linen trade, and had emigrated to Liverpool and Manchester to find work, suddenly found themselves unemployed.²⁶ As one Luddite historian comments:

> With the 1806 parliamentary report being particularly vitriolic in its attitude to the Croppers/Shearmen and the way they were organised, these workers now had no choice but to go underground. With the declaration of war with North America in and the consequent loss of the American market for cloth goods, the West Riding was hit particularly hard. Allied to the broader context and in this climate, the

capitalists increasingly moved to step up the pace of mechanisation in an effort to undercut their rivals and corner what little trade was now left.[27]

War with America was the death knell for many businesses. One diarist notes: '27 January 1812. The Americans declare war to be necessary against England – work scarce, but money scarcer.'[28] William Thompson of Rawden tells us from his business records that in 1811, he employed 650 men and boys making 6,000 pieces of cloth a year on 210 looms. In 1812, he had laid off 200 men, who were making 4,000 pieces on 150 looms and reported that 'he had never known the poor in such a distressed situation' due to a lack of work and rising prices. Another eyewitness, Thomas Dennison, reports, 'I have been a manufacture for 28 years and never saw anything equal to it in my time' concerning the collapse of trade and increase in destitution. In Saddleworth, Francis Platt stated that the poor had to make do with oatmeal boiled in water with potatoes as the single meal for the day.[29] It was not just the West Riding woollen industry that was in decline. Lancashire cotton mills were facing ruin, as were the iron works in Derby, and the manufacturers in Nottingham and Derby. As the economy slumped, prices rose: a tidal wave of discontent was about to break. It is perhaps no surprise that the *Leeds Mercury* reported at the start of 1812 an 'Extensive failure in the City. We are extremely concerned to hear that the old and respectable Banking house of Messrs Boldero, Lushington & Co. stopped payment this morning.'[30] Banking failure meant that merchants lost thousands of pounds of both hard cash and credit. As in the 2008 economic crash, those with the least to lose suffered the most, as the economy went into free fall. The annus horribilis of 1812 was the direct consequence of Napoleon's Continental System and the British government's actions with America.

Along with unemployment came rampant inflation and a cost-of-living crisis as the economy deflated. On 12 November, John Pilkington reported from Bolton that:

> The advanced prices at which flour, meat and potatoes are now sold in this district, and the fear of a further rise ... have caused a considerable degree of anxiety ... wages are certainly lower than at any former period, and should a further considerable rise take place in grains & potatoes without an [illegible] advance in the price of labour, the consequences are justly to be feared.[31]

Machine breaking grew from a cost-of-living crisis. On 7 December came news of machine breaking in Derbyshire by men with their faces blacked out and armed with 'guns, pistols, swords & also with large hammers, Iron crows for the purpose of destroying' machines;[32] a spy reported on 27 December that in Manchester there was pressure for a strike from the weavers, to gain an increase in wages, noting that 'even the single man Cannot Live on his Earnings Let alone men with famileys'.[33]

The *Leeds Mercury* commented on 11 January:

> it is now our painful duty to add, that this failure has involved consequences more distressing to commerce in this part of the country, than any stoppage during the present calamitous war. ... the banking concern of Messrs. Townsend & Rishworth at Wakefield, experienced on Saturday and Monday what is called a severe run and are compelled to add that the banking house of Fenton Scott, Nicholson & Smith of this place known by the name of the Leeds Commercial Bank stopped payment to the surprise and consternation of the whole town and neighbourhood.[34]

The paper added:

> out of a population of about 9,000 families, of which this town consists, there were found 3,500 families stood in need of the contributions of the benevolent, and that of those 3,500 families, the average sum that each individual had to subsist upon, did not exceed 2*s*. 10*d*. a head, and at a time too when flour is from 5*s*. to 6*s*. a stone, and in a place too where the poor are in a better situation than perhaps any other manufacturing town in the county.[35]

The Oldham diarist William Rowbottom presciently recorded in early January 1812:

> in Consequence of the Badness of trade and the Dearness of all sorts of provisions there is but Little apearance of Cristmas. ... the Lower Class of people ... are absolutely Short of the Common necessaries of Life ... if there be an alteration of times it must be for the Better Except there be Comotions or Civil wars wich God Grant may never happen in this Country or Kingdom.[36]

Rowbottom was proved correct: the government remained deaf to the plight of the poor and working class. Violence was the last resort. With unemployment and starvation rising, is it little wonder therefore that a broadsheet was pasted up on walls across Leeds during January:

> To all croppers, weavers &c & Public at large.
> Generous Countrymen,
> You are requested to come forward with Arms and help the Redressers to redress their wrongs and shake off the hateful yoke of a silly old man and his son more silly and their roguish ministers, all noble and tyrants must be brought down. Come let us follow the brave Citizens of Paris.[37]

Chapter 10

YORKSHIRE MACHINE BREAKING

Not long after the handbill was pasted up in Leeds, on 15 January magistrates received reports of a meeting of croppers, who had blackened their faces and were armed with hammers.[1] It was further reported that there was amongst the croppers a 'conspiracy to destroy machinery of certain Mills in this town and neighbourhood [Leeds], employed in the dressing of cloth'. The Luddites fled before they could strike, one of whom was arrested and taken to York for trial.[2] When fire broke out on the 19th at Oatlands Mill, which housed gig-mills, arson was suspected immediately, especially as combustible material had been piled up behind the main doors to the factory. The *Leeds Mercury* noted, 'The depredators have attacked Oatland's mill near Leeds. ... It appears that the recent riots and outrages in Nottingham have arrived in this county.'[3] The mill was owned by the son of the minister – the Reverend William Wood – and two trustees of Mill Hill Chapel Leeds. 'Oates Wood & Smithson' wrote to the Home Office on 22 January, making it clear that they were offering a reward of £100 for information, and that they requested a royal pardon for anyone who took part who wished to incriminate those involved.[4] In Nottingham, fresh attacks were carried out when stocking frames in Ruddington were destroyed on 26 January.[5]

Unlike Nottingham, where attacks continued into February, all was quiet in the West Riding. A month would pass before the Luddites struck again. On 22 February, 'cropping shops' in Huddersfield and the Spen Valley were attacked. The *Wakefield Herald* reported that a group of 100 armed men with blackened faces 'broke into the dressing shop of Mr Hirst of Marsh, near Huddersfield and destroyed a quantity of shears employed in the cropping of cloth by machinery'.[6] In total, seven shearing frames were smashed along with twenty-four pairs of shears. The group headed thence to Crosland Moor via Longroyd Bridge, where the shops of James Balderstone became the next target.[7] The press reported:

> The same, or a similar party then proceeded to the workshops of Mr. James Balderson, of Crosland Moor, in which machinery of the same description was employed, in which they committed similar depredations, completely destroying or rendering useless the whole of the machinery. The manner in which these outrages were perpetrated, was this:- The depredators, or to use the cant terms, Luddites, assembled with as much privacy as possible, at the place marked out for attack, and divided themselves into two parties, the more daring and expert of which entered the premises, provided with proper implements for the work of destruction, which they accomplished with astonishing secrecy and dispatch. The other party remain conveniently stationed at the outside of the building, to keep off all intruders or to give the alarm, if a superior force, was likely to be opposed to them. As soon as the work of destruction was completed, the Leader drew up his men, called over the roll, each man answering to a particular number instead of his name; they then fired off their pistols, (for they were armed,) gave a shout, and marched off in regular military order. They do not appear to have done any mischief besides breaking the machinery; and one of the party having asked the Leader what they should do with one of the Proprietors, he replied, not hurt a hair of his head; but that should they be under the necessity of visiting him again, they could not show him any mercy.
>
> The depredations appeared to the Magistrates to be of so alarming a nature, as to induce them to apply to General Vyse, of Beverley, for military aid, who dispatched an express to this town, with an order for the Troop of Scotch Greys stationed in this town, to proceed immediately to Huddersfield, and which marched at 11 o'clock on Monday night, for that place. And it not being thought expedient to leave this town without military, a squadron of Cavalry was marched from Sheffield, and arrived about nine o'clock on Tuesday morning, and in the afternoon of the same day, a squadron of the 2nd Dragoon Guards, arrived from York, and on Wednesday proceeded to Huddersfield, to relieve the Scotch Greys who returned to this town on Thursday. The Cavalry from Sheffield left this place on Thursday morning. These military movements have naturally created much anxious curiosity, but no disposition has been evinced in this neighbourhood, to disturb the public peace.[8]

Four days later, the cropping shops owned by William Hinchcliffe at Leymoor near Golcar were attacked and all his machinery smashed. Hinchcliffe in his sworn statement tells us that at least fifty Luddites broke into his workshops about 1 a.m. and broke thirty pairs of shears as well as five shearing frames.[9] In response, cavalry were dispatched to Huddersfield from Leeds.[10]

Now thoroughly alarmed, the *Leeds Mercury* tells us that the merchants and manufacturers in Huddersfield formed a committee on 27 February to resist the 'luddites—the cant term used to describe the depredators'.[11] Magistrate Radcliffe told the Home Office on 26 February that 'the rioters assembled in the night suddenly breaking the machines & departed'.[12] Troops already in the district were immediately placed at the ready as 'so much alarm prevails among the proprietors of gig-mills, that a military guard is nightly stationed for their protection'. In consequence, a reward of 500 guineas was offered for evidence leading to the conviction of the perpetrators.[13]

Two days later, the merchants and manufacturers of Birstall made an appeal to the magistrates for assistance:

> To Joseph Radcliffe Esquire one of his Majesty's Justices of the Peace for the West Riding of the County of York—
> Sir
> We, the undersigned, Inhabitants of Heckmondwike and Liversedge in the parish of Birstall, have received information that several acts of violence and outrage have lately been committed in the Neighbourhood of Leeds and Huddersfield, particularly the destruction of Machinery used for the dressing of Cloth, and buildings containing such machinery, by Bodies of persons lawfully assembled in the Night, and acting on a systematic plan;- and we are induced to apprehend that there is a design formed by these misguided or ill-designing people and their adherents, to carry their destructive plans to still greater lengths; as well from the Extent to which the Frame-Breakers in Nottinghamshire (whom they seem to copy as their Model) have carried their mischievous Operations, as, also, from the arrangement, the secrecy, and the dispatch, with which they have conducted themselves near Leeds, and recently in your immediate Neighbourhood. The Tenor of an anonymous letter this day addressed to the older of an Establishment containing the kind of Machinery above mentioned, threatening the Destruction of such Machinery, and the life of the owner in case his resistance should injure any of the assailants; and, moreover, a threat thrown out very lately in Liversedge, intimating that the principal Inhabitants are in danger from the number of pistols in High Town (in Liversedge) which seem to us to manifest the same spirit, and to bear upon the same point.
>   These and similar considerations induce us, the undersigned, to think that every prudent precaution ought to be used, and every measure pursued by the Neighbourhood to prevent the spread of the mischief, and to detect and apprehend offenders against the public Peace &

security, and [obscured] would greatly tend to this salutary purpose if a body of cavalry could be stationed in Heckmondwike Liversedge and Cleckheaton all in the same Parish, as the presence of a few regular soldiers would encourage and strengthen the defence of Property, which the owners with their confidential servants may be enabled to make.

We therefore beg leave to request that you will be pleased to take into your consideration the exposed state of the machinery and property of this Neighbourhood, and, if you should think it advisable, to give directions that a small Body of Cavalry may be stationed, for a while in Liversedge Cleckheaton, and Heckmondwike for the defence of property there, and for the expeditious pursuit and apprehension of any misguided persons who may attempt to violate the Laws by which property is intended to be secured. Such a measure, we presume, might be of use in facilitating the communication with, and the support of the military in Leeds.[14]

A brief lull followed and then new attacks began, again centred on Huddersfield. Frames and shears were smashed at Slaithwaite, Honley and Crosland. Magistrate Radcliffe informed John Beckett of the Home Office that he had interrogated witnesses to events on 6 March about simultaneous Luddite attacks in Linthwaite at the cloth dressing premises of William Calton and John Sykes:

Milnsbridge house
March 7th 1812
Sir
In compliance with your letter of Feby 26th saying you will be obliged to me for any further information respecting these unfortunate occurrences in the neighbourhood of Huddersfield, I inclose the four informations given to me yesterday after noon, too late for the post, these with the three before sent, happened from half a mile to one mile & an half of my house. These I now send are from Sarah the wife of John Sykes of Hoylhouse in Linthwait, Saml Swallow [ditto], Jno Swallow [ditto] & Jno Sykes[ditto];-

On the receipt of yours of 3d Instant, I immediately wrote to Mjr Gn Dixon for 100 Infantry, & I wish my request to you for them, had immediately been complied with by an application to the War office, as it would have saved time & possibly might have prevent'd mischief.
Yours of the 5th is this day received, & shall be communicated to the comittee at Huddersfield without loss of time, & their determination made known to you as soon as I receive it. & am Sir
Your much Obliged
Hbe Servt
J. Radcliffe[15]

John Sykes informed Radcliffe about the attack at Calton's premises that:

> between one and two o'clock in this morning. A number of people came to the door ... and knocked violently at it, and demanded admittance otherwise they would break the door open – to prevent which the examinant opened the door and 30 or more people with their faces blacked or disguised came in and asked if there were any ammunition, guns or pistols in the house and where the master was, on being told he was not at home they secured or guarded every person of the family and then a number of them ... began to break the tools and did break 10 pairs of shears, one brushing machine ... one of them who seemed to have the command said that if they came again and found any machinery set up they would blow up the premises.[16]

The same day, Radcliffe took the testimony of Samuel Swallow, whose cloth dressing shop was attacked that day. He reported that:

> a number of people rushed in and after procuring lights began to demolish his tools and broke four pairs of shears, 2 shearing frames and one brushing machine ... one man with his face blacked guarded the examinant in bed with a pistol in one hand and stood at the foot of the bed ... when they had broke his things, they bid good morning, told him to lock his door, and then went away.[17]

At the nearby premises of John Swallow, he reported seven pairs of shears were broken and two shearing frames destroyed.[18] This was clearly a planned raid to end machine finishing of cloth in the village, as well as to remove arms that could be turned against the Luddites, and also no doubt to arm the Luddites themselves. Arms raids and machine breaking went hand in hand.

The Luddites clearly had the upper hand after these series of raids, and on 9 March, General Ludd addressed the croppers:

> To All Croppers, Weavers &c& Public at Large.
> Generous Countrymen. You are requested to come forward with Arms and help the redressers to dress their wrongs and shake off the hateful yoke of a silly old man, and his son more silly and their rogueish ministers, all Nobles and Tyrants must be brought down. Come let us follow the noble example of the brave citizens of Paris who in sight of 30,000 Tyrant Recoats brought a Tyrant to the ground. By doing so you will be best aiming at your own interest. Above 40,000 Heros are ready to break out to crush the old government & establish a new one.[19]

The writer is exhorting revolution, to bring down the monarchy and government and establish a new form of governance. The Reference to the events of the French Revolution are obvious and make us immediately think of the United Englishmen's radical activism, known locally as the Black Lamp, 1795–1803, in particular, their desire to bring about radical sweeping social changes and the establishment of a republic. In Manchester, Ralph Fletcher reported that his spies had told him that revolution was being planned.[20] A form of visual communication system was being used by persons unknown across the Stockport area and possibly further afield:

> for many nights past, Signal Rockets have been thrown from various points, which last night were discontinued, & Signals of a different description were substituted. The Signal a blue light suspended from the top of a Pole, which seemed to be worked with the accuracy of a telegraph, forming Circles, & different figures, which signals were repeated at convenient distances.
>
> The Points from whence these Lights last night proceeded, are well ascertained, & will be reconnoitred to night by the active people assisted by the military. The blue lights were seen between Eleven & One in the Morning.[21]

Another attack occurred on 12 March, this time in South Crosland. George Roberts, a cloth dresser, reported:

> between the hours of twelve and one o'clock yesterday morning, he was awakened by a great noise of many people talking and violently knocking at his door and demanding admittance ... [he] opened the door to prevent it being broken and a great number of people rushed in with their faces blacked or covered with black cloth with holes cut in resembling eyes and mouth ... a man with his face covered with black cloth seized [him] and presented a pistol to his head and said if he moved he would blow his brains out, and by force made him sit down upon a piece of cloth which was laid on the house floor.

He reported that two shearing frames were destroyed, with the threat of more violence if Robert's father did not take down his shearing frames in Marsden within a week. As the Luddites left, they fired pistol shots into the air, signalling, we assume, to other groups operating that night that a successful attack had been carried out.[22] On the same night, the premises of John Garner in Honley were attacked when '3 shearing frames, 7 pairs of shears, tumbling shafts and drums for the working of the said frames broken all to pieces, and also 3 cloth covers for the covering of the shearing boards cut and damaged'. As with the attack at South Crosland, the machines were broken by 'a great maul', which we assume to be large hammer. Once the luddites had left the premises, pistol shots marked the end of the attack. No doubt, this was a prearranged signal to other groups out that night smashing machines.[23] In Lockwood, the cloth dressing shop of Clement Dyson fell victim to the same group of Luddites in what was clearly another well-coordinated series of attacks on the night of 12 March. Hannah Dyson reported that her husband was away at the York Assizes in his duty as a magistrate, and that about 2 a.m. she heard three gunshots followed by the doors to the dressing shop being 'forcibly broke down', followed by the Luddites making entry to the dressing shop and proceeding to destroy '2 shearing frames, 1 brushing machine, 7 pairs of shears', adding that they also 'broke the windows of the house and shop which was nine in number'.[24] One of Dyson's apprentices, David Crowther, left us his experience of the attack, noting that he had endeavoured to defend the workshops but was overwhelmed by a force 'upwards of 40 perons' who 'broke open the front doors of his said master's house and called out "House House bring out your shears."'[25]

Up until Sunday, 15 March, Luddite attacks in the Huddersfield area had been limited to the workshops of small master cloth dressers who had installed relatively few shearing frames in their premises. But, at 8.30 p.m. that night, an audacious attack was launched against a well-known merchant manufacturer, Francis Vickerman, who had a large business concern on Taylor Hill, Almondbury, near Huddersfield. Vickerman was on the 'Committee for Suppressing the Outrages' that had recently formed in Huddersfield. For his participation in this committee and for his use of shearing frames he had received a threatening letter prior to the attack to take down the frames or face retribution. The letter was thrown through a window fastened to a brick and read : 'We give you Notice when the Shers is all Broken the Spinners shall be the next if they be not taken down vick man tayler hill he has had is Garde but we will pull all down som Night and kill him that Nave and Roag.' Because Vickerman carried a high degree of influence in the area, he arranged for his premises to be guarded at night by some of the dragoons stationed in Huddersfield. Undeterred, the Luddites endeavoured to break into Vickerman's premises and burn it to the ground.[26] The raid, given the presence of the armed guard, was an especially daring and violent affair.

The *Leeds Mercury* tells us:

> The accounts from the neighbourhood of Huddersfield, are this week very; alarming:- About 8 o'clock on Sunday evening, a number of

armed men with their faces disfigured, assembled upon the premises of Mr. Francis Vickerman, of Taylor-hill and announced their arrival by the discharge of a gun, two of the party rushed into the house and inquired for Mr. Vickerman, and as soon as he presented himself, one of the men said, 'Ned Ludd of Nottingham has ordered me to break this clock,' and without further ceremony, forced the muzzle of his blunderbuss into the clock face. Alarmed by the outrageous conduct and language of the depredators, Mr. Vickerman withdrew into a room above stairs, and a party of the snappers, as they are called, was placed as guard over the family, while a number of others proceeded to the work of destruction in the work-shops, and broke, from 20 to, 30 pairs of shears. Having effected their purpose, a volley from the fire arms was discharged into the parlour window, and a cupboard in the room, near which Mr. Vickerman was accustomed to sit, was perforated in several places by the balls, which on examination, were found to Consist of the leaden seals or stamps usually placed at the ends of woollen pieces, made into a kind of slugs. Providentially, Mrs. Vickerman was placed with her frightened children in such a situation in the room as to escape unhurt, and the men from within the house calling to them without, for God's sake to desist, the firing ceased. As soon as the shears were broken, the cry of 'Out,' 'Out,' proceeded from several voices; they then retired into a field, had their numbers to which they answered, called over, and they dispersed about half an hour before the arrival of the Military Guard, which it was known would be placed at nine o'clock. On entering the work-shops after the rioters had retired, it was found that not content with breaking the shears, they had wantonly laid a sheet of wool and two pieces of fine cloth upon the stove, which were nearly consumed, and in a few minutes, the premises, it is apprehended, would have been in a flame.[27]

Magistrate Radcliffe's heavy-handed tactics in 1799–1802 during the famine and Black Lamp rebellion had made him one of the most hated men in the Riding. His actions against the Luddites increased community anger towards him. The following letter seems to have been the first Luddite threat received by Radcliffe; no threatening letters bearing an earlier date appear in his collection. It is one of the most legible of the Luddite texts and contains a rare Luddite footnote:

For Mr Ratcliffe Esq Millsbridge
Genl Ludd's Solicitor March 20 1812
Jos Ratcliffe Sir
Take notice that a Declaration was this Day filed against you in Ludds Court at Nottingham, and unless you remain neutral judgment will immediately be signd against you for Default, I shall thence summon a Jury for an Inquiry of Damages take out Execution against both your

> Body and House, and then you may Expect General Ludd, and his well organised Army to Levy it with all Destruction possible
> And I am Sir your-
> Nottingham
> March-20th 1812
> Soliciter to General Ludd
>
> * PS you have Sir rather taken an active part against the General but you are quiet and may remain so if you chuse (and your Brother Justices also) for him, but if you Either convict a [one], or coutinance the other Side as you have Done (or any of you), you may Expect your House in Flames and, your-self in Ashes in a few Days from your next move, for our Court is not Governd by Terms But Equity.[28]

A second letter on the reverse of the above read:

> In shewing the General the other Side for Inspection He orders me to inform you the Cloth Dressers in the Huddersfield District as spent Seven Thousand Pounds in petition Government to put Laws in force to stop the Shearing Frames and Gig Mills to no purpose so they are trying this method now, and he is informd how you are affraid it will be carried on to another purpose but you need not be apprehensive of that, for as soon as ye Obnoxious machienery is Stopd or Distroyd the Genearal and his Brave Army will be Disbandd, and Return to their Employment, like other Liege Subjects.[29]

Does this letter confirm a link to Nottingham or was it bravado? On 23 March, a spy reported to his handler that delegates from London, Glasgow and Ireland were meeting to 'plan the business' in Stockport. The use of spies was a marked feature of late eighteenth-century information gathering. Purveyors of 'information' were generally working class, and 'tricked' their way into the confidence of those under investigation. They were paid for their information. It has been suggested by E.P. Thompson and others that the fiscal incentive to provide information made the reports untrustworthy, yet historians Marianne Elliott, Roger Wells and Anne Hone have concluded the reports are generally accurate. The Crown, via its spymasters, sought to create overlapping sources that would either corroborate or contradict each other: from this, the Crown would 'fumigate' the reports to sift fact from fiction as far as possible. It was in the Crown's best interest if they were to prosecute radicals, and secure convictions, to use reliable information. False information would have been exposed quickly once arrests had been made. The Crown did use agents provocateurs to secure convictions and also offered to arrested radicals the chance to turn king's evidence and escape conviction by becoming a spy. In Lancashire, parson, magistrate and colonel of volunteers Ralph Fletcher managed a spy known as 'Citizen Bent'. It was Bent who had uncovered elements of the Despard Plot in 1803. It was Bent who uncovered further details of the Luddite disturbances.

On the night of 23/4 March, destruction returned to the Leeds area when some forty men, again well armed, forced their way into the shearing mill of William Thompson at Rawden, seized the watchman, and then smashed all the shearing frames. For good measure, they also smashed the windows. From first to last, the attack lasted only twenty minutes. In Leeds itself, the workshop of Dickinson, Carr and Shand was entered and 'eighteen pieces of fine cloth, dressed by machinery, torn and cut into shreds'.[30] Men with blackened faces broke into Mr Smith's workshop near Holmfirth and smashed frames. The Luddites then marched about a mile to Horn Coat, where Joseph Brook had his workshop, and destroyed his frames. Finally, the Luddites moved off to Honley, to James Brook's workshop, which contained a recently purchased shearing frame. Having seen the events unfolding in the Huddersfield area, he had the foresight to dismantle the machine. Despite this, the Luddites smashed the machine, but left all his other shears undamaged.[31]

A day later, in a coordinated attack, the shearing frames at William Thompson & Brothers at Rawdon were smashed, and likewise at Messrs Dickinson, Carr & Shann.[32] The press reported: 'They entered the premises through the roof, and whilst no machinery was broken, all of the finished cloth in the shop – around 18 pieces – was cut up or torn to shreds. The damage was later estimated to be between £400 and £500.'[33]

At the start of April, Ludd wrote again to Radcliffe:

Mr Joseph Ratcliff Esquier
Milns bridg
Near Hudersfield
Leeds 8 April Sir,
I ham verrey Happey to Hear of your acktivety in taking of those people Caulled luds for they Have been verrey troubbles Some of late you are verrey acktive just ass as theare are maney more sutch like Skundrils at present mak-ing mutch to do about nothing but striving to take poor people labor from them i think the medson to be given to sutch villons as you is a ledon ball with powder that will not dist jest soner and beter I ham for lud and the poor.[34]

The letter is nearly impossible to read; it is full of grammatical and spelling errors, so much so that previous commentators, relying upon a cataloguer's description, have assumed that this letter was sent by 'the poor', congratulating Magistrate Radcliffe on his efforts to suppress the Luddites. However, I strongly feel that reading the letter as congratulatory would be a mistake, and in fact the letter is couched in ironic and sarcastic terms. If one corrects the grammar and spelling, the letter reads:

> Sir
> I am very happy to hear of your activity in tackling those people called Luds, for they have been very troublesome of late. You are a very active justice[35] and there are many more such scoundrels at present making much a do about nothing, striving to take poor people's labour from them. I think the medicine to be given to such villains as you is the lead ball with powder the sooner the better.
> I am for Lud and the poor.

The letter was nothing short of a death threat, and shows the Luddites' intention of assassinating those the community were felt aggrieved by, especially where machines and not men were being employed to finish cloth. Two of those men hated by the community were Thomas and Law Atkinson of Bradley Mill. Their premises had been the scene of a strike in 1799 and then an arson attack a few years later. The Atkinsons were now back in the firing line for their use of gig-mills and shearing frames.

> Mr Radcliffe Esq Mills Bridge
> near Huddersfield
> Mr Radcliffe Dear Sir This comes from a friend
> I found my Self to be and got into the Seckrets of the Ludites and knowing the dredfull plots that is going forwards I Send this to you there is dredfull Praprations goen forwards for Great Destruction
>   It is reported you back Thos Atkinson it was ordered a wile a go for your place and Bradley Mill to be burnt one Night But I pled it of with great to do.
>   When that Time comes foot nor Horses will be of any use there will be a Great Destruction You must not compell Watching & Warding You must side with the Luds if you Live
>   I should a spook personley to you But durst Not
>   If this was known it is deth to me From Mr Love Good.[36]

By the end of March, most of the isolated workshops of master cloth dressers had been destroyed, or the owners had taken down their machines. Protecting these small and scattered workshops had proved impossible and the Luddites had been able to assemble, break in, and destroy the machines long before the authorities could react. One of the last series of attacks on 'easy targets' took place on 5 April, as Captain Raynes reports:

> On the 5th, a number of armed men, (about twelve o'clock,) with their faces covered, entered the work-shop of Mr. Smith, of Irongate-Head, in the neighbourhood of Huddersfield, and broke all his dressing-frames and shears; they then proceeded to Horn-Coat, broke the frames and shears of Mr. Joseph Brook, and demolished the household furniture and all the windows; they afterwards entered the work-shop of Mr. James Brook, of Reims, near Honley, about three miles further, and broke one frame, which was all he had.
>
> A mill at Southoram, where woollencloth was dressed by machinery, belong, ing to Messrs. Waterhouse, was attacked by about one hundred men, who, after securing the workmen, destroyed two Gigmills, with their furniture, and shattered the windows of Mr. Broadbent, the superintendant.
>
> In the neighbourhood of Huddersfield, no fewer than twenty frames or machines were broken, employed exclusively in the operation of cropping cloth.[37]

For the next week, Luddism abated, yet this was just a pause for the Luddites to gather strength and organise their forces on an even larger level.

Chapter 11

YORKSHIRE CLIMAX

By the first week of April, with the smaller cropping shops and premises either being attacked and the machines destroyed or the owners having taken down their gig-mills, the attention of the Luddites fell on the larger mills. To attack a large complex needed hundreds of men, organised with military precision. This was a marked shift in Luddite tactics: they felt emboldened by their success, and clearly had the upper hand.

The first of these strategic targets to be attacked was the large mill at Horbury, near Wakefield, owned by Joseph Foster. No Luddite attacks had taken place in the Wakefield area, so the timing was perfect for an unexpected attack. The Wakefield press reported that the Luddites:

> Completely destroyed all the shears and frames, the former were not snipped but absolutely broken to pieces ; they then demolished all the windows, and as is actuated by a most diabolical fire, they broke into the parts of the premises, against which these depredators do not pretend to have any ground of complaint, the scribbling mill and weaving shops, and materially injured the machinery and wantonly damaged a quantity of warp ready for the loom, destroyed not merely the glass of the windows, but the frames which were of cast iron, the windows of the dye houses, the counting house, and even the dwell houses contiguous to the workshop shared the same fate.
>
> Some of the depredators had their faces covered with black cloth, others were not all disguised, the number of the lowest calculation exceeded 300: many them were provided with firearms and still greater number with hatchets, and the rest with clubs.[1]

The press continued that:

> At the commencement of these dreadful outrages, a detachment from the main body invested the dwelling house occupied by Mr Foster's sons; they literally shivered the door in pieces, and broke both windows and frame, and proceeded to the lodging room of the young men and demanded the keys of the building under pain of instant death. They dragged the two of them out of bed, and tied them together, making them lie naked on the floor; the other they compelled to accompany with the keys, but this last outrage was completely unnecessary, as many practicable breaches had been made in the building, and a considerable progress made in the work of destruction. The dwelling house occupied by the book keeper was also broken into, and his family threated with the most brutal violence.[2]

Captain Francis Raynes of the Stirling Militia tells us the Luddites set fire to the bookkeeper's house and noted, 'the flames were happily extinguished'.[3] The following day, the windows of the home of Constable S. Rice were broken by gunshots. Rice had attended the scene at the mill and was now a target for retribution.[4]

The press reported that the group had come from different locations, such as Huddersfield, Dewsbury, Heckmondwike, Gildersome, Morley and Wakefield, and had assembled on a prearranged timetable or 'plan of attack'. This was no simple armed mob: the Luddites were organised into sections and numbered off in military manner with officers and NCOs appointed, and moved off in companies, with ten mounted Luddites, with drawn swords, and ten at the rear, again carrying drawn swords.[5] It is hard not to recognise the presence of disaffected Local Militiamen and former Volunteer Corps members being involved with the degree of organisation shown.

Local resident, farmer Matthew Tomlinson, who lived at Lupset farm, about 2 miles from the mill, records:

> On Thursday night, about midnight the nocturnal rioters assembled at Mr Foster's Mill and broke that part of the Machinery which works the shears; their numbers accounted to two hundred with their faces disguised; they also broke many of the doors and windows, and set fire to some of the out housing which was soon put under control. The whole was wone [sic] done in about half an hour – these must be troublesome times.[6]

Following the attack, many of the Luddites had headed across the Huddersfield Road on Grange Moor, where they were observed at 3.00 a.m. Some others went through Horbury on the Wakefield Road –

passing another house belonging to Joseph Foster. Here they fired a volley of shots into the air. Others gathered on Westgate Common, outside Wakefield, seeking to smash Clarkson's Mill, but were driven off by the Royal Wakefield Volunteers and the Wakefield Local Militia.[7] Colonel Campbell reported to Grey:

> I am sorry to say that the Mills at Horbury S.W of Wakefield were on Thursday night attacked by an armed body of 300 men. Very considerable property and machinery was destroyed & many persons very ill treated.
>
> This is the place to which I referred in a former report made to you as having been menaced.
>
> I have learnt from a respectable quarter that these disturbers of the Peace were met on the road between Wakefield & Horbury in the night of Thursday, marching in regular sections armed, preceded by a mounted party of ten men with their swords drawn & an equal number mounted forming a rear guard. It is believed that by a preconcerted plan they had assembled from Huddersfield, Dewsbury, Heckmondwike, Gildersome, Morley, Wakefield &c &c.
>
> From the great intercourse between this Town & Huddersfield information is conveyed which altho' not at all times correct, frequently proves too true.
>
> I hope I shall be acquitted of presumption if I suggest to give the necessity of the office in command of the troops in Huddersfield being very much on his guard, for the destruction of the Bradley Mills in that neighbourhood it is believed is determined upon at all risks.[8]

In evidence later presented by the Reverend William Robert Hay of Pontefract and chairman of the Quarter Sessions, the attack at Foster's Mill was conducted by the United Englishmen, the same body of working-class Jacobins that had threatened rebellion a decade earlier.[9] About the Luddite success at Foster's Mill, Mancunian endorsers wrote to Yorkshire Luddites in support:

> Houghton April 19th 1812
> Dear Brothers & Sisters
> We take the oportunity of answering your letter which you sent by your friend & we are glad to hear that you are all well which these lines have us all at present. Bless God for it. We are glad to hear that you have gained the Victory which your friend related to us which He did the last night & today which we was very glad to listen to him & received him as a friend from you which we believe He is. & we have enjoyed ourselves over a pot or two of Beer. & he read Mr Luds Song. We shall relate no particulars for we sopose you have in of 31 papers & we can give you no satisfactory account And we will leave you to judge about it—

> Yr father & mother gives thier Cind love to you all & we shall all be very glad to see you at the time you have proposed which is all at present from your loving Brothers
> John and Martin Middleton[10]

The letter strongly supports the interaction between Yorkshire and Lancashire radicals. Certainly, Colonel Hanson was named in one Luddite letter as the leader of the revolution that was to come.

Rawfolds Mill

On 11 April, more than 100 Luddites gathered at the Dumb Steeple, still a landmark near Mirfield, and marched on Rawfolds Mill. William Cartwright was one of the most prominent manufacturers in the West Riding and someone who had made clear his intention to press mechanisation to the utmost. He was well aware that his mill was a prize target and he had prepared thoroughly. He had turned the mill into a formidable fortress, erecting a breastwork of flagstones at the windows to allow a protected field of fire for the defenders. Every night, five men from the Cumberland Militia were stationed there.[11] Late on 12 April, a large contingent of Luddites assailed the mill, trying to force the main doors with sledgehammers:

> Mr. Cartwright, for some time before the attack upon his mill, slept in it, with five of his confidential men, and five soldiers. Having received information that it was the intention of the Luddites to attack him, he made such arrangements for his defence as he thought necessary. The windows of the ground floor were secured by strong iron bars, that had been fixed there when the mill was built: there was only one door in front, which was made double, and secured with bars, bolts, &c. The floor above, where they all slept, was flagged; and in the lower part of each window, (about five or more in front,) was fixed a flag-stone, the same width as the window, and about thirty-two inches high, which formed a breast-work. Some of the stones of the floor were elevated sufficiently to admit the muzzle of a musket, which completely commanded the windows below; and the same was done in various parts of the floor, to act as loop-holes, in case an entrance should be effected. The same precaution was taken with the stair-case. The dam protected the back of the building. The assailants amounted to nearly an hundred. They were formed into three companies: first, the musket-men; second, the pistol; and third, the hammer-men; each man answering to his number. They commenced the attack in the middle of the night; and before Mr. Cartwright and his companions had time to put on their cloaths, they were assailed with musketry, and a violent hammering at the door and windows. As speedily as possible, they returned the fire, chiefly

through the loopholes commanding the windows. Shots were fired, inside and out, through the door.

    After about twenty minutes, without having made much impression on the mill, or any one being hurt in the inside, the fire began to slacken, and groans of wounded men were distinctly heard. When the firing entirely ceased, and Mr. Cartwright thought he might venture to look out, he went to the assistance of the wounded men. Several had received shots; but two only were left. : They were so dreadfully shattered about the legs, that immediate amputation was necessary, under which they both died. A wall in front of the mill sheltered them from the shot, otherwise these infatuated people must have suffered much more considerably.

    Mr. Cartwright was frequently threatened with a second visit; but had they been rash enough to attempt it, entire destruction awaited them, from the complete state of defence in which the mill was placed. The wall in front was taken down, and a swivel placed in the second floor of the mill, which would discharge sixty musket balls. This was fixed upon a very ingeniously constructed carriage, and could easily be removed from one window to the other. A chevaux de frise was thrown across the stair-case, which made a very formidable barrier; and lights of a particular invention were fixed outside the mill, by which the features of any person could be distinctly seen at a very considerable distance. These preparations were essentially necessary, from the unextinguishable spirit which raged amongst these deluded people.

    Personal revenge was now added to the evil passions and mistaken ideas by which they were before actuated; and Mr. Cartwright was assailed by threats of the most sanguinary vengeance from all quarters. He was given to understand that the success of a second attack would be insured, by his wife and children being placed in front of the mill; and it would then be seen what sort of a defence he would make.[12]

Diarist Tomlinson adds:

On Saturday night 11th the shearmen attacked the mill of Mr Cartwright at Cleck-Heaton and met with a warm a reception, he having seven armed men besides himself with the Mill; both parties fired until their ammunition were expired, Mr Cartwrights men having only one round of ball cartridge left when the shearmen retired with the loss of 2 men killed and many wounded.[13]

Cartwright himself noted that briefly it looked as if the assailants would succeed but, just as the defenders were fixing bayonets for a last stand, the attackers drew off. Tomlinson is mistaken; the Luddites left two seriously wounded men in their wake, John Booth and Samuel Hartley, but he was correct that others had been hit. Bloodstains were trailed for up to 3 miles from the mill.[14] The terrified bourgeois of Huddersfield:

> have been greatly disturbed by the nocturnal depredations of Shearman and other lawless Characters, associated under the pretence of destroying certain shearing frames worked by machinery – but which your memorialists believe to be only a cover the much deeper designs.
> That such depredations, having succeeded in destroying nearly all the Shearing frames which are not connected with establishments on a large Scale, proceeded on the 12th inst. to commence a regular attack upon a large mill at Rawfolds in this neighbourhood, occupied by Mr William Cartwright & used entirely free shearing with the obnoxious frames; but, after having kept up a brisk and well directed fire for a considerable time, & attempted to force the doors & windows by large sledge hammers, without effect, they were repulsed; and left two of their party desperately wounded upon the spot, who are since dead. … Mr. Cartwright strongly suspects he was fired at within a quarter of a Mile of Huddersfield in broad Day, on his way home from the market, but happily without effect.[15]

Hartley died on 13 April and was buried two days later. The funeral quickly turned to tumult due to the Wesleyan Methodist minister the Reverend Jabez Bunting's intransigence. Bunting was from then on the subject of much hostility to those who sympathised with the Luddites. He apparently had death threats made against him and had to be accompanied on his country appointments for some time by a constable to prevent assassination attempts.[16] Hartley was a corporal in the Halifax Local Militia, in which Cartwright served. Hartley was not alone in being a member of the Local Militia and a Luddite: John Baines the elder and his son John Baines the younger were both arrested for soliciting illegal oaths to a police spy, John MacDonald, and were sentenced to seven years' transportation.[17] A letter was intercepted from Manchester by the postmaster in Huddersfield, and was sent to Joseph Radcliffe:

> Frien I called at Tideswell as you ordered me for to call on your brother but he was not there which I was determined to find him which I have found your father & mother & all together but it was with much Ado I went to Litton & slep all night & was recieved as a friend with Bingham & Bramwell there as an engagement been betwixt the Luds & the Army which the Luds was defeated which was oing to Halifax Luds not coming up as they was apointed There was 16 men stormed the plaise which they had two Cilled there wounded man was carried of and none of them as been taken since which the two men was buried

on Thursday last at Hudersfield which the Corps was put in a Dark room with six mold candles which the friends of the Luds followed them every man in morning with a with aprom edged with Black which the minister refused to Burie them but the Luds insisted on them being Buried in the Church which are to have a grand stone he lived fore and twenty hours after he was taken he was the son of a Church parons which many visited him but He refused to invulge anything I have but sent you all the particulars I have and I hope you will write to me by return of post & send me all the particulars and hif there is any person that ar obliged to come away I have procured a seat of work for them you will please to ax Wiliam pasomell were I may find the wife making in Manchester please to direct for Edward Good over Mill Saddleworth nine Manchester Yorkshire

Which you will not put any name on the letter at all

And put a Cross on the bottom of the letter as I shall see your brothers on Whitson Sunday so no more from yr well wishing friend

G D[18]

As with all Luddite letters and correspondence, the spelling and grammar is problematical, but again confirms broader insurrectionary links across the north of England. Rawfolds was the subject of a letter from General Ludd written in May:

Mr Edward Ludd Market Place Huddersfield To General Ludd Nottingham

I am also desired to say that We lament with extrem regret the fate of the two brave boys who galantly spilt theire blood in a ladeble case at Rawfolds—

They further learn with pleser that a noble attempt was mad about a mil from Huddersfield tho without suckses to destroy the Hytown machenry man

The Generl futher autherises me to say that he trusts to the attachment of his subjects for the avenging of the death of the two brav youths who fell at the sege of Rawfolds—He also wishes me to state that tho his troops hear are not at present making any ostensable movments here that it is not for want of force as the orgenisation is just as strong as in Yorkshire but that they are at present only devising the best means for a grand attack.[19]

A large crowd gathered at Halifax for the funeral of Hartley. To preempt similar popular expressions of grief at Huddersfield, Booth's body was buried there very early the following morning.[20] William Cartwright was 'a wanted man' for the death of Booth and Hartley by the Luddites.

On 14 April, Ned Ludd wrote to a mill owner near Halifax:

> we think it our duty to inform you that we was intent [illegible] your factory on account of those dressing machines that was and still are working it. But we consider ... in justice the humanity ... to give you notice that if you does not cause those dressing machines to be removed within the bounds of seven days from the above date, your factory and all it contains will and shall severely be set on fire: remember we have given you warning and if your factory is burnt it is your own falt ... we are fully determined to destroy both dressing machines and steam looms ... we will conquer both or die in the conflict.[21]

Four days later, an attempt was made to shoot Cartwright as he rode home from Huddersfield.

> On Saturday last, an attempt was made to assassinate Mr. Cartwright, the intrepid defender of Rawfolds Mill, by two villains who fired at him from behind an hedge, as he was returning from Huddersfield. The shots were discharged at nearly the same moment from opposite sides of the road, but happily without effect.
>
> This diabolical attempt upon the life of this gentleman, took place in open day, between the hours of four and five in the afternoon, about a mile on this side of Huddersfield. We have no words which can sufficiently describe our abhorrence of this dark and wicked attempt to murder. Surely, even the deluded followers of Gen. Ludd, cannot approve of private deliberate murder; are his troops already degenerated into a band of assassins? But wickedness is progressive, it is a downward road, the first step prepares the mind for a second, that for a third, until deeds of blood become familiar. And the man who begun his career, probably with the intention only of destroying machinery which he supposed inimical to his interest, ends it by deliberate assassination, There is something in this crime so cowardly, so foreign to the feelings of Englishmen, and so much at variance with the courage and humanity of our national character, that we are convinced, that not one man would have been found to have entered into the association, if it had previously intimated to him, that he was to exchange the character of an Englishman, for that of a cruel and cowardly Italian desperado.
>
> We would exhort and conjure those who are yet innocent of the blood of their fellow-creatures, to abjure a confederation which leads to such dreadful consequences, which sinks them below the level of civilized men, and points to the destruction of Society itself. It is at present possible to retreat; when we have next to address them, it may be too late.[22]

Nine days later, a second manufacturer was targeted: William Horsfall, owner of Ottiwell Mill at Marsden. He was well known in the West Riding for wanting to 'do away with' croppers, trade unions and the domestic system of cloth production and was a prominent figure in the special committee formed to combat the Luddites. As we noted earlier, he had been targeted by Luddites some years before for erecting gig-mills. To protect his mill, Horsfall had fortified it with a stone wall with artillery. Horsfall had boasted that 'he would ride up to his saddle girths in Luddite blood'.[23] While riding home from Huddersfield Cloth Hall:

> On Tuesday afternoon … was shot by four assassins who were concealed in a small wood by the road side; three slugs entered the lower part of his body, he fell from his horse and was dragged a small distance by his leg, but was soon extricated, several persons being near; the assassins were seen run off and have not yet been apprehended. Mr Horsfall lived in great agony until Wednesday evening and expired as the surgeon was extracting the last slug.[24]

Our writer adds, 'This gentleman has shears at work which are wrought by steam, has been very active in apprehending some of those men who were wounded at Cleck-Heaton, and has been very unguarded in many of his expressions.'[25]

The same day that Horsfall was shot, Magistrate Radcliffe interrogated George Whitehead, a Huddersfield deputy constable. He reported that 'on Wednesday evening last the 15th instant, near twelve o'clock he … was going up stairs to bed having a candle in his hand, and that when he had got part way up the stairs, a gun or some other kind of fire arms was fired off at him' as he passed a window at the front of his house which illuminated his staircase. The shot broke 'three squares of glass in the window'. The two shots missed him, but the threat was obvious.[26] Ten days later, Isaac Raynor was the intended victim of a shooting.[27]

Neither the failure of the assault at Rawfolds nor the assassination of Horsfall, contrary to popular myth, did anything to diminish popular support for Luddism. The day after the murder, a master cloth dresser who had already had his shearing frame smashed was roused from sleep by men with blackened faces who told him, 'General Ludd has sent us for your gun and pistol and we must have them immediately. … If you shoot any of us, your wife and children will be corpses in Ten minutes.'[28] Clement Dyson handed over his firearms. A new phase in Luddism appeared: arms raids. The *Leeds Intelligencer* opined:

there is certainly some hidden mystery in this business, not yet ready for development. Their partial insurrections form but a curtain to cover the horrible scenery preparing behind it. ... It is a mere drilling of the people for a field day upon a larger scale. There is a dark, subtle and inevitable agency at work, seducing the ignorant and the inexperienced and encouraging the profligate and the abandoned.[29]

The *Leeds Mercury* noted, 'We believe there is a very general disposition amongst the lower classes to view the actions of the persons engaged in this association with complacency not to say with approbation, this is the strength and life's blood of the organisation.'[30] With Luddism undiminished and the magistrates unable to make arrests, frustration of the authorities increased. 'All these outrages, and much worse, are perpetrated without the detection of even a single individual: and thus escaping, the offenders seem, as must naturally be expected, to increase in strength and daring,' opined the Tory *Leeds Intelligencer* newspaper.[31]

On 23 April, Constable Thomas Atkinson arrested James Haigh at Methley for his involvement in the Rawfolds attack. Haigh had been amongst the wounded Luddites who had escaped, and had been treated by Dr Richard Tatterson at Lepton, who had dressed the gunshot wound to Haigh's shoulder. Haigh was arrested at his sister's house in Methley.[32]

Chapter 12

COTTONOPOLIS

From the late 1790s, Manchester had become synonymous with spinning slave-produced cotton from America. By 1810, the Manchester skyline, and that of surrounding towns, was dominated by mill chimneys. Such was the significance of cotton to Lancashire and Manchester, that the then town became known as Cottonopolis. What been a home-based craft was increasingly dominated by steam-powered mills, one such being owned by Peter Drinkwater. Factories were as alien in Lancashire as they were in Yorkshire, thus it is no surprise that Luddism crossed the Pennines in March. As in Yorkshire, the Lancashire Luddites were fighting the introduction of power looms to the cotton industry, which were undercutting the cloth produced by handloom weavers, who largely worked in their own cottages. As in other parts of the north and midlands, the weavers were suffering severely from a depression in trade – the Orders in Council had hit Lancashire particularly hard – and a series of bad harvests, which had drastically increased food prices. In February, Stockport manufacturers began to receive threatening letters and at least one attempt was made to set fire to Peter Marsland's weaving factory. Despite the exertions of many people who had gathered to try to put it out, the fire grew out of control and by 6 p.m., the whole building had been consumed. Goods worth £100,000 were in the warehouse, but the efforts of those who had removed as many items as possible meant that the damage was limited to £30,000.[1] On 20 March, in the middle of the night, men attacked the power loom factory owned by William Radcliffe. About 3 a.m., a crowd of about 500 people had gathered outside it. Windows were smashed and five torches were thrown in in an attempt to burn down the premises. The crowd then dispersed. The fire was extinguished before it could take hold.[2] Yet five days later – 25 March 1812 – the

Manchester boroughreeve Richard Wood, in a letter undersigned by two constables, reported:

> we have observed with great regret in the London newspapers reports of serious disturbances among the Weavers & Mechanics in this town and neighbourhood, which we are happy to be enabled to contradict. There is no foundation for such reports, on the contrary, it is with pleasure we bear testimony to the exemplary patience with which the working Classes have borne the pressure of the present times.[3]

Disorders broke out in Manchester on 8 April, and were occasioned not by machinery but by politics. Manchester Tories called a meeting at the Exchange to congratulate the Prince Regent on retaining the existing government on his assumption of the Regency. Reformers and radicals, disappointed at the Prince's failure to dismiss the Tories in favour of the Whigs, became determined to stage a counter-demonstration. Handbills were put up across the city calling for inhabitants to attend the meeting to protest: 'Now or never! All those who do not wish for an increase in taxes and poor rates, for a greater scarcity of provisions and no work are called upon to speak for themselves.' The protestors claimed that the Tories did not represent the genuine opinion of the people. Fearing violence, the Tories called off their meeting, but a large radical crowd assembled in the marketplace before marching to the Exchange.[4] Agitation outside the building apparently lasted until one o'clock, when the windows were smashed and the most violent entered the building and destroyed its furniture.[5] Oldham diarist Rowbottom recorded that:

> about one o clock the populace Begun to be turbulent and Begun to Demolish the valuable furniture and the windows Lamps and Chanliers fared the same fate ... the Riot Act was Read and the Cumberland Militia and a party of the Scotch Greys put the mob to the Rout happily no Lives where Lost.[6]

Following the riot, opposition towards Pittism and national events became more militant. Pittism was the political ideology of William Pitt, of, in essence, one-nation Toryism. His worldview was of 'strong and stable' with no hope of political reform, no end to the legal impediments against non-Anglicans. Pitt and his supporters were pro-war and sought to eliminate the ideas of the French Revolution and the Rights of Man, both at home and abroad. Food riots broke out in Bolton, Bury and many other towns and their neighbourhoods.

On 13 April, Stockport spinners, together with colliers and carters from Bollington and Rainow, marched to Macclesfield, where, with local workers, they seized food in extensive disorders.[7] The following day, the steam-powered weaving factory owned by Goodair and Co. was targeted. Goodair's wife recounted that about 9 a.m., a large crowd had gathered outside the factory and began throwing stones at the windows, and then marched into Stockport and smashed the factory windows of other mills containing power looms, including those of Hindley and Bradshaw, Radcliffe, and Bentley and Co. The Luddites also smashed the manufacturers' house windows and, in the case of Marsland, destroyed all his furniture. Then, over 3,000 strong, they returned to Edgeley, where they forced their way into Goodair's mill and 'destroyed the looms and cut all the work which was in progress'. Only the intervention of troops prevented the mills owned by Messrs Sykes from becoming their next victim.[8] In the following days, workers toured the district, led by two men dressed as women and calling themselves 'General Ludd's wives', attacking factory owners' property and demanding food and money from houses they passed.[9] On 14 April 1812, near the beginning of a week of riots in Stockport and its environs, John Goodair's power loom mill at Edgeley was destroyed in a Luddite attack. A Stockport mill owner, Thomas Garside, was caught in the attack, but his life was spared by the timely commands of one of the Luddite leaders.[10]

Food riots broke out in Manchester on the 15th and lasted for five days,[11] seemingly culminating in an attack on the factory of Daniel Burton and Sons at Middleton, 'where machinery is used in great perfection'.[12]

Three days later, rioters eventually succeeded in destroying the large mill at Westhoughton, near Bolton, owned by the firm of Wray and Duncuft, which housed some 170 steam looms.[13] Overt attacks on factories now gave way to arms thefts, insurrectionary plotting, and clandestine drilling in imitation of what was occurring over the Pennines.

Lancashire radicalism was of markedly different form to that in the West Riding. The differing approaches to the economic stagnation caused by the war is in stark contrast, and we have to wonder why. The first phase in February was very limited, and the April rioting was occasioned by politics. One eyewitness, Ralph Fletcher's spy Citizen Bent, reported that following the rioting in Manchester, a 'different cast of political characters' had become involved in the leadership of the disaffected.[14] This seems to suggest that the leadership for the Mancunian Luddites came from elsewhere, possibly Yorkshire.

Historian John Bohstedt argues that textile workers of Lancashire were 'new groups of workers in 1790' and thus, lacked the 'long traditions' of the woollen trade, and therefore, 'had to organise themselves on the basis of regional and industrial, rather than local and communal, solidarity', which is one probable explanation.[15]

Orders in Council

Luddism was a symptom of the war of ideology with France and belligerence with America. The end of access to American markets meant not only a reduction in Yorkshire woollens for export, but also for ceramics from Staffordshire. Thousands worked, for example, as sailors in the shipping industry, importing slave-produced goods like sugar, tobacco, coffee, chocolate, rum, tobacco, mahogany; as workers in ports and warehouses unloading the cargo; as labourers in the various industries refining the products, or in the transportation and retailing of the final products. The closure of ports meant that ships did not sail, and thousands of workers in the allied support trades lost their jobs. Liverpool, led by William Roscoe, began to campaign against the Orders in Council, followed by Staffordshire, led by Josiah Wedgwood, the Unitarian master potter of international fame, to end the Economic war with America.[16] Amidst the crisis, Earl Fitzwilliam realising that if commerce improved, one of the grievances of the Luddites would be removed at a single stroke. The closure of American ports to British commerce had been a hammer blow to the West Riding textile trade, and other areas like Manchester and the midlands. Earl Fitzwilliam wholeheartedly put his weight behind a petition for peace to allow access to foreign markets and end to mechanisation. It was signed by 15,000 clothiers and presented by Lord Milton to Parliament.[17] Hansard records:

> He [Fitzwilliam] said he should have several petitions to present from manufacturers and other commercial persons, complaining of the injurious and destructive consequences resulting to their interests from the Orders in Council: and that, when these petitions should be before the House, he should feel it incumbent on him, to come forward with a motion for the repeal of so injurious a system.

Mill Hill Chapel, led by the Reverend Thomas Jervis and Josiah and George Oates, took a leading part in canvassing the clothing districts, and again circumvented the Tory merchants like Gott and Cookson in Leeds who supported war and the Orders in Council;[18] time and time again, the Unitarians, aligned with the clothiers and croppers, outmanoeuvred the Anglican-dominated Leeds Corporation. Other petitions were raised around Leeds and Wakefield. The two Leeds petitions were each some 40 yards long.[19] The *Leeds Mercury* reported:

> on Tuesday evening the 24th March, three massive petitions left Leeds for London. Each of them was signed by 16,000 to 17,000 people and they were addressed to the Prince Regent and the Houses of Commons and Lords. The petitions called for the rescinding of the Orders in Council.[20]

William Dawson, in a four-page letter about maintaining peace to Earl Fitzwilliam written at the start of May, stated that 'the want of trade and high price of provisions is the cause of the prevailing discontent', but warned that 'so strong is the voice of the people … that unless some very decisive measures are speedily adopted, these parts must soon resort to martial law.'[21] Dawson was perfectly correct: lack of work, poverty and high food prices were driving the working classes to desperation. If disaster was to be averted, then the government had to do something quickly to bolster trade. Political pressure was needed to rescind the Orders of Council, yet the government refused to act. Prime Minister Spencer Perceval stood his ground.

Chapter 13

FOOD RIOTS

Machine breaking was generally over by the end of April 1812. It was a short-lived and violent episode that has come to dominate any discussion of the period. The changing character of Luddite activity reflected the wavering context in all three regions where Luddism emerged: Lancashire, Nottinghamshire and Yorkshire. A key element in each was the presence of unprecedented numbers of soldiers. From April onwards, troops flooded into the disturbed districts to reinforce the already large garrisons. A major aspect of the Luddite movement that is generally forgotten is the arms raids and food protests that took place across the West Riding. Groups of men would arrive at isolated farms and demand the occupier hand over any weapons kept on the premises. Not since 1802 and the Black Lamp had republicans, Jacobins and working-class radicals felt strong enough to embark on the same course of action. Famine along with unemployment and a typhoid epidemic drove the events forward.

Thousands of tonnes of grain had been imported every year to Britain from Russia and America: the Treaty of Tilsit ended this trade, making Britain more reliant than ever on American imports. The Orders in Council ended this importation. To make matters worse, British farmers suffered a devastating series of particularly wet summers from 1810 onwards, leading to a wartime peak in wheat prices in 1812. The price of wheat in June 1802 was 57 shillings a quarter, peaking in August 1805 at 98*s*. and dropping back to 66*s*. by 1807. Prices peaked again in December 1808 at 92*s*., rising to 95*s*. in March 1809, and reached 102*s*. at the end of the year, touching 113*s*. 5*d*. in June 1810. The average price of wheat per quarter reached 126 shillings in May 1812 – double the annual average of the 1790s. This meant that the price of food for people and livestock outstripped the wages of farmers and the working poor. Wheat prices topped out at 155s. a quarter in August 1812, and would not drop until 1814.[1] Making matters worse, typhoid ran at epidemic proportions again through the low-grade, overcrowded housing in Leeds and Sheffield, and was one of the worst episodes of epidemic typhoid in European history. The epidemic was exacerbated by famine.

A seasonally cold and wet spring meant that livestock died of starvation and planted crops were washed out and failed to grow. On 22 March, diarist Matthew Tomlinson of Lupset near Wakefield tells us, 'On Friday fell a deep a snow, yesterday and today it rains so that the [illegible] are full of wet and the rivers overflows their banks.' He adds that he was forced to bring his flocks of ewes and lambs undercover to shelter them from the severe cold, 'but the strong sensation of hunger impresses them to roam over the [illegible] lands and miss the scanty [illegible] for Food.'[2] As March turned to April, Tomlinson tells that his livestock 'still do badly, very badly'. Thousands of lambs, piglets and calves died from the cold and starvation. The loss of livestock meant the price for whatever meat was available rose markedly. A new war began, this time not against machines but for food. Food riots broke out in Manchester, Oldham, Ashton, Rochdale, Stockport and Macclesfield. Tomlinson in Lupset was not immune to the suffering across the north of England:

> national calamities touch on all orders of society and make the lower orders almost desperate for want of employment and bread; they are assembling in different parts of Yorkshire and break the machines and commit other acts of violence and outrage.[3]

In his diary of 12 April, Tomlinson records, 'the season still remains unfavourable.'[4] The day Tomlinson wrote his diary; Sheffield had been the scene of a food riot. On 15 April, it was reported to Earl Fitzwilliam that food 'rioters were dispersed by Huzzars' and the Rotherham Militia had been mobilised. Crowds had gathered for a second time on the 14th, and had been dispersed by the magistrates without recourse to using military force. On the morning of the 15th, 'crowds collected in different parts of the town and began to break open warehouses of potatoes and flour.'[5] The *Leeds Mercury* reported:

> The stock of these they seized and scattered about the streets, or carried away in great quantities wherever they found it, in carts, in cellars or storehouses. Two or three sacks of corn were also emptied upon the pavement and wasted or purloined. Some butter was taken from the market women, and a barrel of red herrings broken, and the fish thrown amongst the spectators.[6]

The mob attacked and broke into the Militia, where 400 stands of arms were stored as well as regimental uniforms. The arms were snatched up along with the clothing, but a timely intervention by the 15th Light Dragoons, who had been called out from Sheffield Barracks, prevented the weapons being dispersed to the crowd. The Strafforth and Tickhill companies of Local Militia were called out by Colonel Walker, officer commanding the Sheffield Local Militia, which was unable to be called up, being on compulsory training in Doncaster. Because of this, Walker also called out the Rotherham and Horton Troops of Yeomanry, in addition to the two Sheffield troops. With the troops mobilised, Magistrate Hugh Parker hoped that tranquillity would be restored to the town, unlike, he lamented, at Morley and Huddersfield.[7] We wonder if the arms raid was to be timed when the Local Militia was known to be absent from the town, and thus the chance of the attack being foiled was judged by the leaders of the group as less likely because of this. Certainly, had it not been for the garrison, the 400 muskets would have been taken and no doubt used by the Luddites against Crown forces. Following the arms raid at the depot, nine people were arrested and later committed to York Castle for trial at the next Assizes.[8] Thomas Fenton, Lieutenant Colonel Commandant of the Sheffield Local Militia, reported that six men were already held in York gaol, and three more were likely to be sent. Fenton noted that the Luddites were helped because several members of the Sheffield Local Militia were amongst the rioters.[9] Magistrate J.A. Stuart Wortley informed Earl Fitzwilliam that the Strafforth and Tickhill Local Militia would be placed on active duty for fourteen days in order to keep the peace, and were to be billeted in Rotherham.[10] The *Leeds Mercury* reported on the trial of Thomas Wilson, one of the men arrested in the arms raid, and was charged:

> with assaulting Archibald Stuart Wortley, Esq. and Hugh Parker, Esq. and discharge of their duty as Magistrates.
>
> Archibald Stuart Wortley, Esq. M.P. stated that he was an acting magistrate for the West-Riding of this county, as was also Hugh Parker Esq. Witness resides about eight miles from Sheffield; was there on the 14th of April; got there about one o'clock. There were a great number of people collected in the market place. The Witness and Constables went to induce them to disperse; the mob at first surrounded, and shewed a disposition to press upon him; the young boys were nearest him, and appeared to be pushed forwards by the people behind. With the assistance of the constables he got them to retreat to some distance; Witness then addressed the mob, to persuade them to disperse, but without effect. In a little time the great body of the mob appeared to have

removed to another place; not knowing where the mob were gone, they thought it right to go round the market-place; found the mob at the head of the market-place, and finding the riot continue, Mr. Parker read the riot act. Being informed that the rioters had proceeded to acts of violence in another part of the town, (in Church-lane) they proceeded thither: when they arrived there they found the mob had begun to break the windows of a dwelling-house; they there read the riot act again. Both before and after the reading of the riot act, they (the Magistrates) were assailed by potatoes and other missiles which the mob could lay hold of. Did not then attempt to apprehend any of the rioters. Very shortly after there was a kind of cheer given by the mob, when immediately retreated. The Magistrates followed them to a potatoe-shop, which they were informed had been broken open; but the mob had then removed to another part. The Magistrates then returned to the market-place, and finding all their efforts to suppress the tumult ineffectual, they thought it high time to call in the aid of the military; but before the arrival of the military, the mob had moved off to the military depot. Thos. Smith, the constable, seized a woman who had her apron full of potatoes; Witness directed her to be carried into the Town-Hall-Prison; two constables went with her, attended by the magistrates; the populace cried out 'rescue,' and immediately a man rushed out of the crowd, and laid hold of the constable; Witness seeing this, darted forward and seized him by the collar, a great body of the mob followed, and endeavoured to separate him from the mob, there was then a considerable scuffle, and in the end the mob released the man. There was then a sort of huzza set up by the rioters. Witness mounted his horse and proceeded to meet the military, and went with them to disperse the mob. Witness remained at Sheffield four days.[11]

Wilson was found guilty, but thanks to good character witness statements, was granted clemency.

Two days after the Sheffield incident came news of information gathering by the Luddites. George Turner, a 10-year-old lad, was riding from Ackworth to Hemsworth when he was approached by an older male of about 30, according to the report, riding a chestnut horse, who asked if Francis Lindley Wood and Messrs Bingley and Watson of Ossett had shearing machines, and stated that they would be pulled down on order of the Pontefract Committee.[12] The Reverend Dr Martin Naylor, editor of the *Wakefield Herald*, opined that 'we acknowledge the hand of distress presses heavily indeed upon thousands of our industrious neighbours ... we sincerely sympathise with their sufferings, nor are we entirely exempt from all share in their misfortune.' The good reverend condemned both the Luddites and the economic and political system that caused the violence, censoring 'the self created market regulator', and urged the Luddites to turn from violence and return to constitutional form of protest:

> to convey these complaints in firm but respectful language to the foot of the throne and the table of the legislative bodies. Let us not despair that those who direct the councils of the nation, are possessed of a benevolence enough to turn an attentive ear to these representations and wisdom sufficient to apply a suitable and effectual remedy.[13]

Naylor was wrong. Westminster brought its own prejudice and tradition to bear over the Luddites and the representations made to it over the proceeding decades, be it for peace with France or to prevent wholesale mechanisation of the woollen trade. The Crown found it impossible to reconcile Luddism with its own policies, economic dislocation and distress. It supported dramatic changes to centuries-old ways of community and tradition. Indeed, the Crown gave fresh impetus to a total transformation to the lives of the working-class by the rich elites. By sponsoring mechanisation, the factory system and inter alia urbanisation, the working class were exposed – often for the first time – to sudden trade fluctuations and dislocation from paid employment. Thus was removed much of the skeletal framework that had offered the working class some form of rudimentary support by making combinations and incipient friendly societies illegal. Therefore, the Luddites' protest cannot be defined merely as a protest against machines. The Crown in Westminster refused to accept that it had brought about the environment that had created Luddism, and inter alia the United Englishmen of a decade or so earlier: rather than addressing the legitimate grievances of the working-class and also middle-class reformers like Major Cartwright, ministers busied themselves by savage and exemplary action to prevent political change.

On 18 April, Radcliffe interrogated George Whitehead, a Huddersfield deputy constable. He reported that 'on Wednesday evening last the 15th instant, near twelve o'clock he … was going up stairs to bed having a candle in his hand, and that when he had got part way up the stairs, a gun or some other kind of fire arms was fired off at him' as he passed a window at the front of his house that illuminated his staircase. The shot broke 'three squares of glass in the window'. The two shots missed him, but the threat was obvious.[14] Ten days later, Isaac Raynor was the intended victim of a shooting.[15]

The same day, Barnsley was the scene of food riots.

George Walker toured Yorkshire in 1814, drawing scenes from everyday life. Here we see croppers at work with their shears.

Spinning fleece into yarn was a traditional craft carried out at home by women, as we see here.

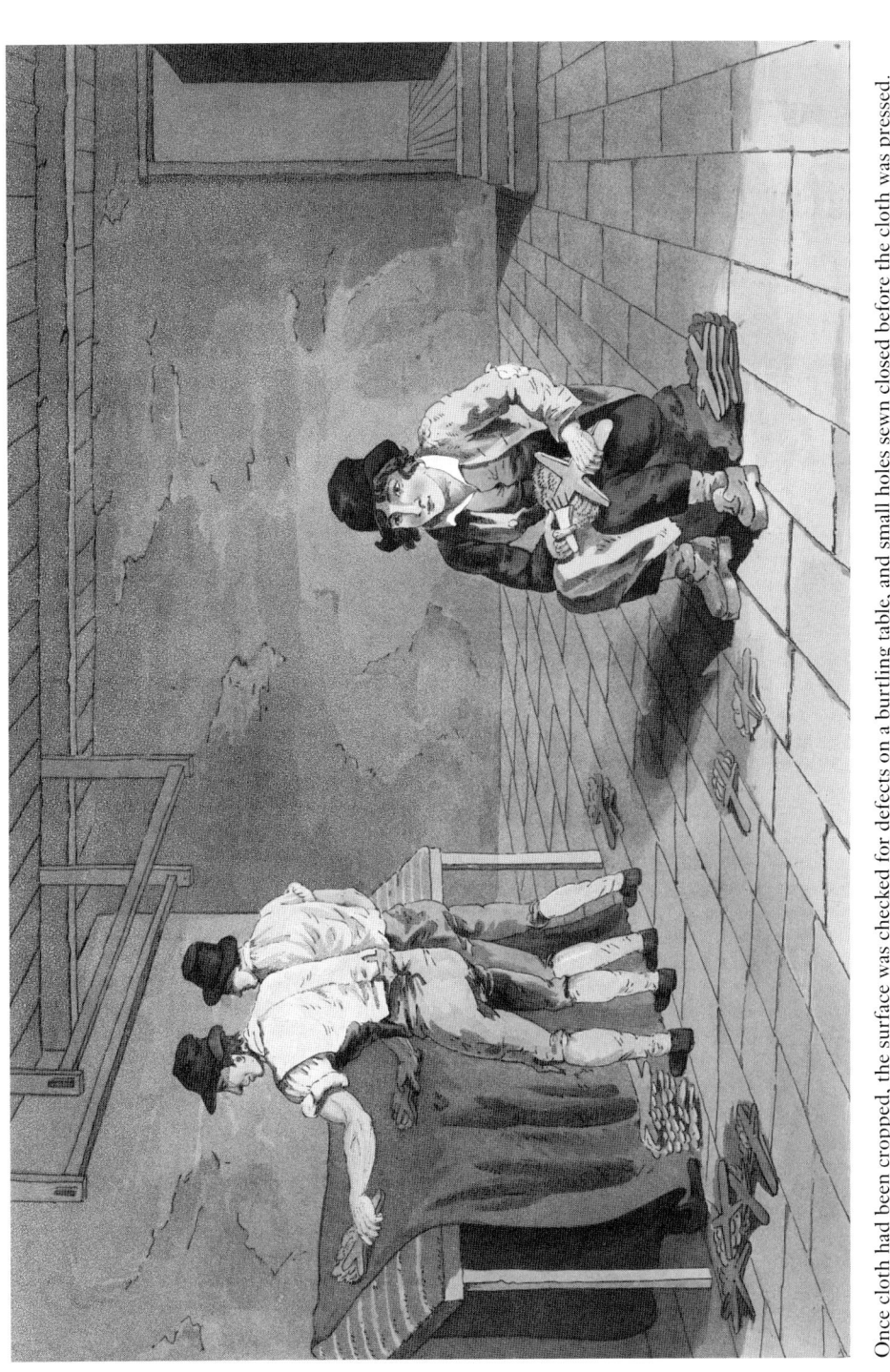

Once cloth had been cropped, the surface was checked for defects on a burtling table, and small holes sewn closed before the cloth was pressed. The men on the left of the image are working at the burtling table.

Lengths of cloth were sold at the cloth hall. Leeds at one time boasted three halls, two of which still stand; Huddersfield had one, which no longer stands; Wakefield had two, of which one partly remains; and Halifax had the magnificent Piece Hall. On the image, we see the interior of the Leeds Coloured Cloth Hall.

Cloth was taken to and from the hall by clothiers, who carried their wares on packhorses, as George Walker shows here.

Bean Ing Mill in Leeds was one of the first and largest factories in Yorkshire, depicted by George Walker, with ubiquitous child labourers heading off to work.

Georgian threshing machines were substantial pieces of equipment built into barns. They took away seasonal work form hundreds of families and were the target for destruction by Luddites.

Replacing the spinning wheel in the home was the spinning jenny. Its adoption had caused riots in the early 1770s. By 1812, many homes had these simple machines rather than a spinning wheel to make yarn.

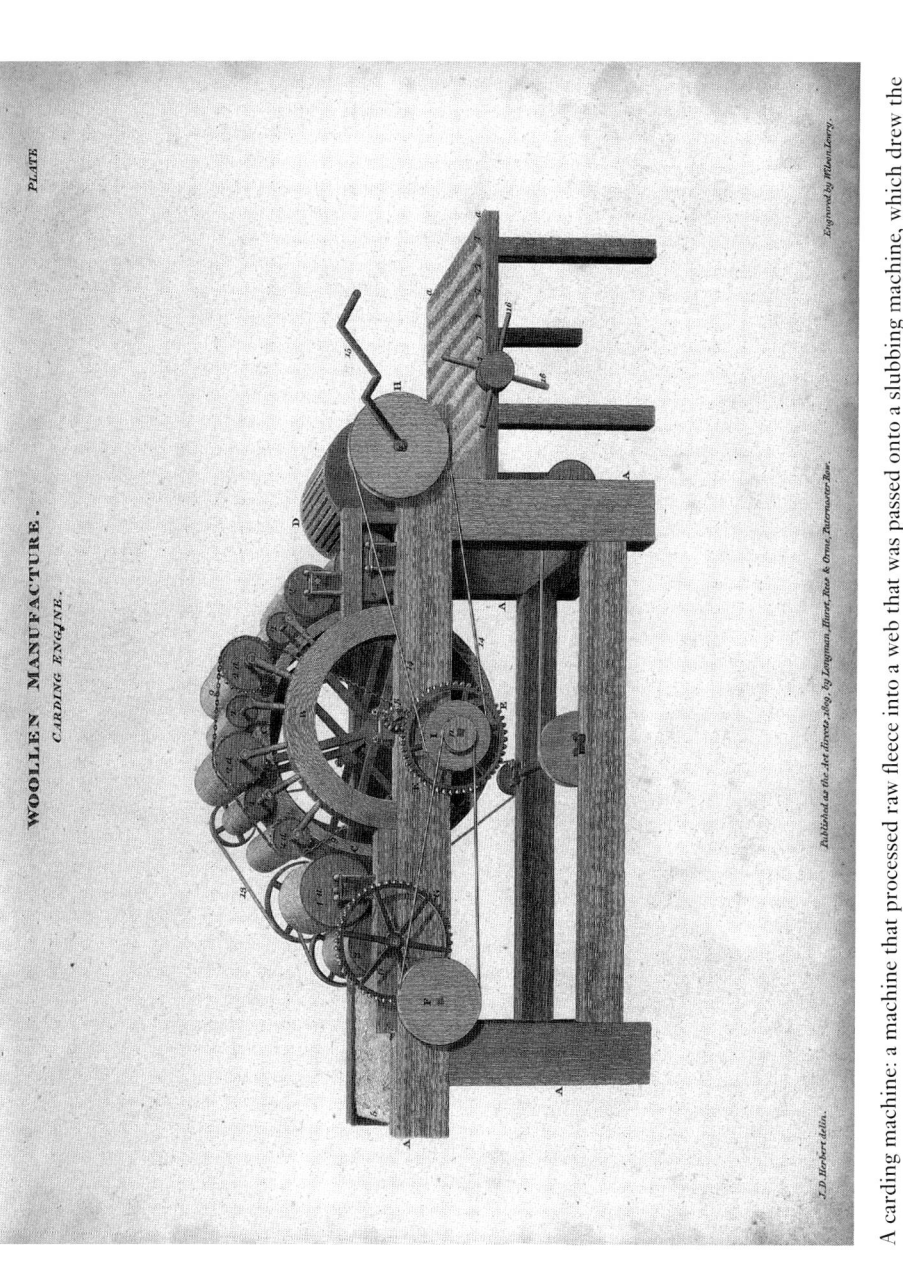

A carding machine: a machine that processed raw fleece into a web that was passed onto a slubbing machine, which drew the web into slubs, which were then spun into yarn. The adoption of these machines had provoked community outrage in the 1780s.

The target of the Luddites' fury was the gig-mill, a machine that used plates of teasels to raise the nap of the woven cloth. The machine would complete in a day what a skilled man had previously been able to undertake in a week.

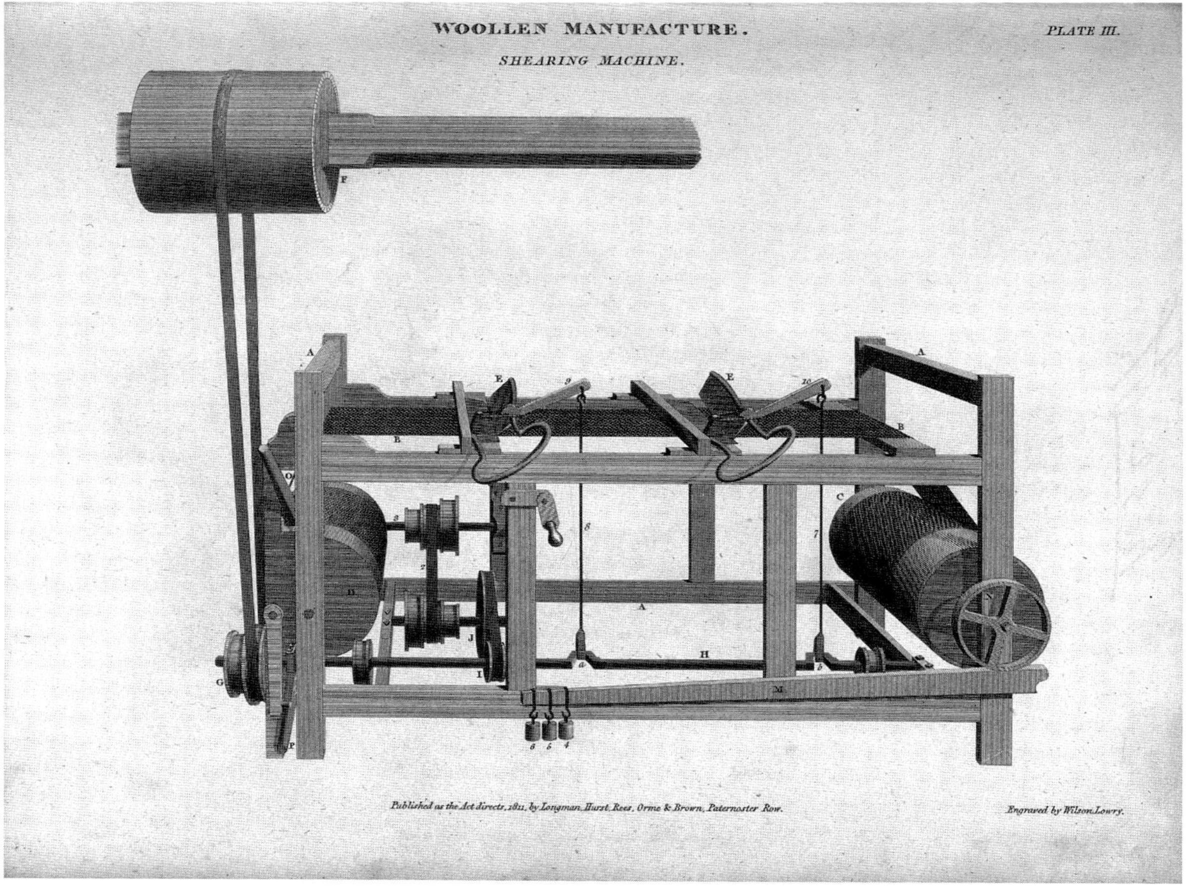

WOOLLEN MANUFACTURE.
SHEARING MACHINE.

PLATE III.

Published as the Act directs, 1811, by Longman, Hurst, Rees, Orme & Brown, Paternoster Row.

Engraved by Wilson Lowry.

The shearing frame, patented in Sheffield in 1787, replaced the skilled cropper with a machine. These machines were the target of retribution by the men rendered economically obsolescent by their adoption.

A slubbing machine processed webs of fleece into slubs, which were then sent to spinners to produce yarn.

Benjamin Gott: Leeds industrialist and bitter opponent of the Luddites.

Robert Bakewell, Unitarian cloth merchant and champion of the domestic system, the leading voice for making peace with Napoleon across the West Riding in 1801 and 1807–8. His business was destroyed by the trading conditions occasioned by the Napoleonic Wars. A friend of Thomas Jefferson, he was outspoken in his support for French Revolutionary principles, for which he was gaoled in 1793.

Milnsbridge House, home of Magistrate Joseph Radcliffe. Now semi-derelict, the house is one of the few buildings that remain today with a direct link to Luddism.

The Dumb Steeple at Mirfield. Originally positioned on higher ground, this was a rallying point for the Luddite attacks at Rawfolds Mill.

On Wednesday (the market day) at Barnsley, a disposition to riot manifested itself; the cause of complaint alleged, was the high price of provisions, particularly potatoes. In consequence of an express sent to G.W. Wentworth, Esq. the magistrate, who, knowing that the Wakefield Royal Volunteers were that day on duty, sent orders to them and the Wakefield troop of Yeomanry Cavalry to prepare immediately to set out for Barnsley. The latter commenced their march with all expedition, but were met on the road by a messenger, informing them that the civil power alone had succeeded in allaying the tumult. They immediately returned, and stopped the infantry, just ready to commence their march.[16]

This came a day after the smashing of threshing machines and the setting on fire of a barn full of grain at a farm at Carlton, near Barnsley, the property of James Stuart-Wortley. Not since 1791 had similar outrages been committed in the West Riding, when the home of James Wheat, Norwood Hall, was attacked, the barns, threshing machine and contents being set on fire.[17] Community anger at enclosure and the changing nature of agricultural work where machines replaced men now burst into life. The fire was judged not to be 'the work of a private incendiary, but of a mad combination that now exists against machinery' and the mob that attacked the farm, which numbered perhaps thirty, all had blackened faces.[18]

Matthew Tomlinson's diary entry of 19 April records:

In the course of the week had very winterly weather; on Thursday it snowed near all the day and since have had snowy frosts in the mornings; we get forward as fast as we are able with our seed-time; but the minds of the lower-class of people are so rife for plunder and revolt that I scarcely dare venture [?] my stacks to remain in my stack yard until I have put in my seed least they should be set on fire as was the case with the Blaydons of Royston on Friday night; all the stacks and premises were totally consumed; and also Mr Rimington of Carlton which had only burned a hole in one stack.[19]

The *Leeds Mercury* opined that 'to burn corn and destroy thrashing machines, is the sure way to convert scarcity into famine.'[20] Wortley received the deposition from a 10-year-old son of the local bailiff, who reported that 'a stout man' on a horse asked him on Saturday, 18 April, 'if Sir Francis Wood, Mr Volland, Mr Bingley and Mr Wilson of Vizett had not threshing machines'. The boy confirmed that they had. The boy recalled that the men replied, 'I will have them all pulled down … I do not care for Sir Wood or any of them,' concluding that the party rode off in the direction of Barnsley.[21]

A cold and wet spring was followed by an unseasonal hot and dry summer – potence of a bad harvest and continued famine. Desperate people with nothing to lose resorted to desperate measures. Rural Luddism went hand in glove with the breaking of mill machinery: the domestic system of production was primarily conducted away from urban centres. Weavers and spinners were embedded in the rural economy. Most clothiers' economic basis was divided between the woollen trade and market gardening: domestic outworkers divided their employment between loom in winter and field at harvest time.[22]

Even larger concerns like that of Joseph Rogerson of Bramley, who owned a steam-powered fulling mill, relied upon supplementary income from hay, wheat, barley and other crops. For many master clothiers, small-scale farming saved the family from the poor house.[23] With the concentration of processes in the production of cloth being centralised in mills – not all being urban – it meant that new stresses were placed on the rural economy. Many of the domestic system outworkers faced the double challenge from centralisation and mechanisation of the woollen trade as well as the loss of their agricultural employment with the spread of the threshing machine. Community and tradition simply could not survive these twin threats. The seasonal nature of the woollen trade and cloth production meant that agricultural labour for those not able to afford their own land was a vital income stream. Enclosure, land price increase and mechanisation of farming meant that a centuries-old traditions of seasonal employment patterns came shuddering to an end. A threshing machine, a technology dating from the late eighteenth century, it was reckoned could do the work of 200 men. Although five labourers were still required to work the machines, an edition of the *Farmer's Magazine* of 1812 observed that children could conduct some of the labour.[24] No consideration was given to the labourers made redundant, many of whom were likely to have been displaced from the domestic system of cloth production. Thus, agricultural machinery was as much a target as the machines in a woollen mill. Therefore, it comes as no surprise that a threshing machine within a barn was burned to the ground at Soothill, about 6 miles along the Dewsbury Road north-west of Lupset, where Tomlinson resided. It belonged to a corn dealer and farmer, Robert Wooler, of Rouse Mill on the Bradford road leading to Soothill.[25] Hostility to the Enclosure Act was commonplace across the West Riding. For example, Horbury Enclosure Act was passed in 1809, but the enclosure proper began during 1810, witnessing foot paths stopped up and field boundaries changed. In July 1811, four Horbury labourers were arrested for violently demolishing a stone wall and fence that had stopped up a road.[26] This act of destruction intimated at much wider tensions and grievances about a changing way of life as well as opposing the physical barriers that hedges and fences created as much as the symbolism of private property ownership that they represented.[27]

Writing to his employer, industrialist and politician Walter Spencer Stanhope, the Cannon Hall estate steward commented that there had been no further rioting in Barnsley, noting that the Luddites had been contained by 'the number of soldiers' in the area, commenting that:

> with the addition of the cavalry they would be quite able, not only to keep them off but to drive them away – at Barnsley there are foot and horse about 250 – also at Penistone and most of the villages near likewise, Sheffield and Huddersfield being not far distant would be more than equal to any number that can come.[28]

About troop movements, the *Leeds Mercury* noted that 'on Thursday 30th April 1812, a squadron of the 15th Light Dragoons marched into Leeds, whilst one troop each of the same regiment were also placed in Barnsley and Wakefield.' We suppose that Spencer Stanhope was behind the deployment of troops to defend Cannon Hall.[29] The steward added:

> Should any attempt be made, it must be to plunder the mills, for meal and flower [sic], as the millers are now all alarmed and dare not take up any. The threshing machines seem a plea for them – many are already taken down, and I hope others will do so till things are more settled.[30]

The steward was correct in his assessment: rural violence around Barnsley abated for nearly a month. The *Leeds Mercury* reported that 'In the evening of Thursday 7th May, a bean stack belonging to a Mr. West of Cawthorne, near Barnsley was set alight and almost completely destroyed.'[31]

However, across the Pennines, Saturday, 18 April 1812 was market day in Manchester. It was the first of three days of violence over the cost of food. The Scots Greys killed one protestor that day, and would go on to kill many others over the coming days.[32]

A day later, news filtered through to Earl Fitzwilliam from John Beckett that the weavers in Barnsley were to assemble on the common, 20 April, at ten o'clock for the purpose of raising their wages.[33] Such meetings had not been held in the West Riding since 1802! The same day as a panicked Beckett wrote to Fitzwilliam, William Clegg of the 33rd Regiment of Foot was billeted in Barnsley, at the Red Lion, and was interrogated by Magistrate Godfrey Wentworth about events he had witnessed. How and why Clegg was out of barracks and miles from the inn we know not, unless he was engaged as a semi-official spy. Clegg related that on the 17th, he left Barnsley to head to the home of his late mistress, Mrs Cotton, at Haigh Hall, and stopped for about an hour at the home of Widow Dansford, which was about a half mile from Darton. On leaving Darton on the Huddersfield to Barnsley road, he met three men with their faces blacked out going to Huddersfield 'to join the soldiers there'. A quarter of a mile further along the road heading to Barnsley, Clegg observed a body of 400 men, led by a mounted officer, 'marching in closed columns', wearing masks or had their faces blacked out. Clegg was spotted by the officer, whom Clegg described as an ex-soldier, who told him to go about his business or 'he would blow his brains out'.[34]

William Dawson, the Wakefield magistrate, informed Earl Fitzwilliam, that the magistrates felt it desirable to order the Local Militia regiments 'to more distant parts' and to rely on the regular Militia for local defence. He commented that Wakefield was a hotbed of Luddism, but felt the town was secure with the presence of the Royal Wakefield Volunteers and a troop of Hussars. Dawson reported furthermore that a Luddite had been killed in Middleton. An oath card had been recovered from the body and Dawson was in no doubt that nighttime secret meetings were being conducted. He added that the men who had been disciplined were being paid 1 guinea a week and those out of work were receiving 18s. a week. Ominously, he reported that arms had been seized around Wakefield, but felt confident enough to state that very few of the Luddites were acting out of political convictions. Rather he felt that the crisis the country faced was the high cost of living and the scarcity of food, adding:

> the cause of the prevailing discontent is not so strong as the voice of the people with them, that unless some very decisive measures are speedily adopted, these parts must soon submit to martial law ... allow me to say there is no punishment the lower order seem to dread as much as being sent to sea. If an act cd be passed to prevent any assembly of the people by day or night unless they could show it was for lawful purposes under the punishment of the unmarried men being sent into his Majesty's Naval Forces it might precent much mischief.[35]

On 26 April, diarist Tomlinson adds that 'most certainly there is great scarcity of grain in the land; I dare so no man now living has saw the [illegible] of the lower class of people more ripe for universal rioting and outrage.'[36]

As prices rose, discontent increased. A Luddite handbill boldly asserted:

> all the miners and colliers are ready to join us. – 3,000 men can be collected in a few hours.
> The poor cry aloud for bread
> Prince regent shall lose his head
> And all the rich who oppress the poor
> In a little time shall be no more.
> Take care you be not in the number of the oppressors.[37]

The threat was obvious and it was not long before violence broke out against those the starving masses believed were making money from hoarding corn and flour to make profit.

Chapter 14

THE REVOLUTIONARIES

Following the attack on Rawfolds, Luddism took on a new form and menace: the famine acted as a recruiting sergeant and Luddism evolved into an underground revolutionary army, the likes of which had not been seen since the execution of Colonel Marcus Edward Despard in February 1803 and the dislocation of the Black Lamp and United Englishmen. Revolutionary sentiment and ideals are hard to eradicate through legislation and many of those who participated with Despard took up arms once more. A direct link to the Black Lamp revolutionary group was uncovered in the debris following the attack at Foster's Mill. Magistrate Hay was a reactionary, right-wing Tory who sat on the magistrates' bench, who seven years later allowed the Peterloo Massacre to take place. At Foster's Mill he uncovered documents that stated:

> Liberty and Slavery are placed before you; on the wisdom of your decision is suspended not only your destinies, but the dearest interest of Posterity and the general happiness of the universe … will you tamely abandon those rights which have been purchased with the blood of your ancestors and submit to slavery … with its attendant scourges, war, fatigue and famine! Or whether you will boldly vindicate your claim to liberty and her similar attributes – whether you will longer behold with indifference the ravages committed on the fair face of Nature, and millions of your fellow creatures continually sacrificed in the prosecution of wars for the … gratifying ambition and avarice of a few who fatten on the Public Ruin and wallow in the public plunder – or whether you will manfully with the collected and Omnipotent voice of the nation, arrest the arm of devastation, and by substituting in its room the Olive of Peace.[1]

He also recovered an oath card, which read:

> I A. B. of my own free will and accord do hereby promise, and swear that I will never reveal any of the names of any one of this secret committee, under the penalty of being sent out of this world by the first brother that may meet me, I furthermore do swear, that I will pursue with unceasing vengeance any traitor or traitors, should there any arise should he fly to the verge of ——. I furthermore do swear that I will be sober and faithful in all my dealings with all my brothers, and if ever I declare them, my name to be blotted out from the list of society, and never to be remembered, but with contempt and abhorrence. So help me God to keep this my oath inviolate.
>   B. Sign.
>   You must raise your right hand over your right eye if there be another Luddite in company he will raise his left hand over his left eye – then you must raise the forefinger of your right hand to the right side of your mouth – the other will raise the little finger of his left hand to the left side of his mouth and will say What are you? The answer, Determined – he will say, What for? Your answer, Free Liberty – then he will converse with you and tell you anything he knows.[2]

This was the same oath as used by the United Englishmen a decade earlier. It must have been abundantly clear by now to the Crown that they were dealing not simply with machine breaking, but with a reborn movement to bring about revolution across the country, the aim of which was to sweep aside monarchy and Parliament. On 1 May, Hay wrote to the Home Office saying that he had found identical oath cards in use in Bolton, Oldham and Manchester, which had been the epicentre of the United Irishmen. Hay reported that one of his spies had attended a meeting of delegates, and 'was told that there were some Gentlemen in London who were at the head of this … Manchester was the centre of this part of the country – that regular delegates forwarded from other towns through this place to London'.[3] Clearly, as with the United Englishmen a decade earlier, Luddites were organised into oath-bound cells, and each cell sent a delegate to a regional committee, who then reported to the 'secret committee' in London. It seems, therefore, that the high degree of similarity between United Englishmen of 1795–1803 and Luddism indicates that Luddism was the United Englishmen rebranded. The United Englishmen destroyed factories and advocated revolution just as the Luddites were doing in 1812. Indeed, the degree of synchronicity between the two groups is reflected in a letter from Eliza Ludd to a Manchester special constable:

> Sir,
> Doubtless you are well acquainted with the Political History of America, if so you must confess that, it was ministerial tyranny that gave rise to that glorious spirit in which the British Colonies obtain'd their independance by force of arms, at a period, when we was ten times as strong as now!—if bands of husbandmen could do this, in spite of all the force our government was then able to employ – cannot such an action be accomplish'd here, now the military strength of the country is so reduced—Consider Sir, what a few troops there is at present in England,—remember that none can be call'd home; because that would [be] relinquishing the little we have gain'd to the fury of the enemy—little indeed to have coss'd so much money and such torrents of blood, yes British blood!———let me persuad you to quit your present post, lay by your sword, and become a friend to the oppress'd—for curs'd is the man that even lifts a straw against the sacred cause of Liberty.[4]

A further link to the Black Lamp is the signature A.B. on a letter to Magistrate Radcliffe: this is clearly a direct reference to the United Englishmen cum Black Lamp oaths, which stated 'I A B—on my own voluntary will and accord, do declare and solemnly swear'. The letter reads:

> April 27th 1812
> Sir,
> I thought it my duty as a Friend, to address you with a few lines upon the Perrilous situation of this Country; as you are the principle Magistrate for this District, they look to you, and only you, for some Redress; If this Machinery is suffer'd to go on it will probable terminate with a Civil War, which I could wish to be avoided, there fore as you are not intrested by Machinery and the Spirit of the People appears so resolute in the Cause, that if some measures be not adopted and immediately, it will be attended with great Distruction, and particular those who are our greatest Persecutors. With respect to this Watch and Ward Act, you are not aware of the additional, Oppression you are bringing upon your Tenants, and other Occupiers of Lands, and all for the sake of two Individuals in this District, which I am not afraid to subscribe their names, Mr Ths Atkinson, & Mr Wm Horsfall, who will soon be number'd with the dead, and summoned before the awfull Tribunal, and that God who will Judge every Man according to the Deeds done in the Body.
> And Jesus knew their thoughts and said unto them, every Kingdom divided against itself is brought to desolation; and every city or house divided against itself, shall not stand.
> A.B.[5]

About the oath-taking, one eyewitness reported:

> at the time the oath was so administered by Cookson and Eadon to the informant, they explained to him that his duty as a secret committee man, would be to attend all meetings when warned, or called upon, to collect money subscribed by the Luddites to defray the expenses of the delegates and secret committee when required, and to go when sent to collect information and carry on correspondence with other committees. The committee with whom this informant acted were the said Eadon and Cookson and William Thompson and Stephen Ritchinman both of Barnsley weavers, who were appointed to act as a secret committee for Barnsley. The informant further saith that it is also the business of the secret committee to twist in new members. That there are about 200 persons twisted in, in Barnsley, among whom, the informant particularized John Baxter, Commercial Inn, James Brown, publican, George Watson, linen manufacturer, Henry Tyne, hatter, Richard and — Bottom, gardener. That the informant knows a great many other Luddites by sight, but not by name. That the committee at Barnsley, do not admit Irishmen to be twisted in, for fear that they should betray the secret. The delegates (as the informant has been informed by the committee) from Leeds to Sheffield, and from Sheffield to Leeds, pass and repass weekly, but neither of those committees had any intercourse or correspondence with the Barnsley committee till about a week ago, when the informant opened a correspondence with Leeds for Barnsley, through the medium of Mr. Whittle, pattern maker at Leeds.[6]

The organisation into regional cells is remarkably similar to the Black Lamp. Fundraising reminds us of 'the Institution' of 1799–1805. It seems working-class trade unionism and Jacobinism collided.

Given the similarities between Luddism and the activities of the United Englishmen and United Irishmen less than a decade earlier, it comes as no surprise that links between the reborn United Englishmen, the United Irishmen (who had been reborn as 'Ribbonmen'), and France existed.

Enter Napoleon?

With unrest increasing in Ireland, largely from mass unemployment and starvation, Napoleon sought to harness this anger, by endeavouring to resurrect the alliance between France and the United Irishmen. To do so, former Royal Navy officer Luke Lawless was sent to tour Ireland to link with the Irish radical movement as a precursor to an invasion by the French to liberate Ireland from the British Crown. So seriously was the offer of French assistance to aid them in a revolution taken by the 'Ribbonmen', they started stealing roofing lead to melt down to make musket balls, and reports were received by Dublin Castle that the Catholics wanted to overthrow the Act of Union and British constitution.[7] It comes as no surprise, therefore, that in the immediate wake of Lawless's arrival in Ireland, Irish delegates toured England, gathering information for Lawless to send back to France and also for the Irish leadership to gauge support from England for a diversionary uprising. Ever since the 1790s, the Irish Republicans realised that they needed to foster revolution in England to keep the British Army 'tied down' if they were to stand any chance of success backed by the French. Rising industrial tensions created the ideal situation to exploit to further French and Irish aims. At the same time, genuine grievances about the lack of political representation, which had been a dominant feature of British politics in the 1790s, as well as community 'push back' against mechanisation created a radicalised working class across the north of England ready to rise in rebellion, even if Napoleon never landed. For many Jacobins who remembered and had taken part in the Despard plot, now was the time to rise. The old United Irishmen network was reawakened: Liverpool, Manchester and London, with large Irish populations, became key locations for the reawakened movement. Consequently, on 31 October an informant told the Crown that there was an underground movement 'now systematically preparing measures calculated for overthrowing the existing order of things'. The French, it seems, hoped to exploit social unrest caused by famine and the economic collapse in the woollen and cotton trades to recruit supporters to rise in revolution. The informant noted that whilst the bulk of the British Army was deployed in the Peninsula, Ireland and England were vulnerable to attack. The writer feared the presence of the French fleet at Bantry Bay was 'sufficient proof for how little dependence can be placed in blockading sea ports'.[8] Days later, the same writer noted that thousands were prepared to rise to aid the French.[9] A spy reported on 7 November that the French were making plans to invade Ireland.[10] This was of course perfectly true. Four days earlier, Napoleon had ordered agents be sent to Ireland, and reported that he was to begin organising an invasion force in February 1812 to be ready by March:[11] 30,000 infantry and 6,000 cavalry were to be readied to land.[12] On 11 November, reports were received that amongst the unemployed and starving the general feeling 'was for a revelaiton [sic] and nothing Else as nothing Else would do'. The cause of the revolution was reported to be heavy taxation, the national debt and the depressed nature of trade brought about because of the hated war. The spy added that 'Bonaparte knows he is doing the business and will finish it in short time and this is what he aims at' in driving the people to desperation in order to rally them to his cause in making them take action against the Crown.[13]

One of the key documents that reveals the truth about the nature and scope of Luddism is a letter sent by Ned Ludd to a Mr Smith of Hill End:

> To Mr Smith Shearing Frame Holder at Hill End Yorkshire.
> Sir
> Information has just been given in that you are a holder of those detestable Shearing Frames, and I was desired by my Men to write to you and give you fair Warning to pull them down, and for that purpose I desire you will now understand I am now writing to you. you will take Notice that if they are not taken down by the end of next Week, I will detach one of my Lieutenants with at least 300 Men to destroy them and furthermore take Notice that if you give us the Trouble of coming so far we will increase your misfortune by burning your Buildings down to Ashes and if you have Impudence to fire upon any of my Men, they have orders to murder you, & burn all your Housing, you will have the Goodness to your Neighbours to inform them that the same fate awaits them if their Frames are not speedily taken down as I understand there are several in your Neighbourhood, Frame holders. And as the Views and Intentions of me and my Men have been much misrepresented. I will take this opportunity of stating them, which I desire you will let all your Brethren in Sin know of. I would have the Merchants, Master Dressers, the Goverment & the public to know that the Grievances of such a Number of Men are not to be made sport of for by the last Returns there were 2,782 Sworn Heroes bound in a Bond of Necessity either to redress their Grievances or gloriously perish in the Attempt in the Army of Huddersfield alone, nearly double sworn Men in Leeds.
>
> By the latest Letters from our Correspondents, we learn that the Manufacturers in the following Places are going to rise and join us in redressing their Wrongs Viz. Manchester, Wakefield, Halifax, Bradford, Sheffield, Old-ham, Rochdale and all the Cotton Country where the brave Mr Hanson will lead them on to Victory. the Weavers in Glasgow and many parts of Scotland will join us the Papists in Ireland are rising to a[nd] so that they are likely to find the Soldiers something else to do than Idle in Huddersfield and then Woe be to the places now guarded by them for we have come to the easier Way of burning them to Ashes which will most assuredly be their Fate either sooner or later. The immediate Cause of us beginning when we did was that Rascally letter of the Prince Regents to Lords Grey & Grenville, which left us no hopes of any Change for the better, by his falling in with that Damn'd set of Rogues, Perceval & Co to whom we attribute all the Miseries of our Country. But

we hope for assistance from the French Emperor in shaking off the Yoke of the Rottenest, Wickedest and most Tyranious Government that ever existed; then down come the Hanover Tyrants, and all our Tyrants from the greatest to the smallest. and we will be governed by a just Republic, and may the Almighty hasten those happy Times is the Wish and Prayer of Millions in this Land, but we won't only pray but we will fight, the Redcoats shall know that when the proper time comes We will never lay down our Arms. The House of Commons passes an Act to put down all Machinery hurtful to Commonality, and repeal that to hang Frame Breakers. But We. We petition no more that won't do fighting must.

Signed by the General of the Army of Redressers
Ned Ludd Clerk
Redressers for ever Amen, You may make this Public March 9th or 10th[14]

The letter is militantly political, almost Jacobin (but for some millenarian expressions and the nationalistic observations about the 'Hanover Tyrants'). It is also remarkable for its exceedingly democratic tenor, for the democratic process it describes, and for the variety of discourse that it reveals to exist even in one region. Smith, who lived near Holmfirth, had all his dressing frames and shears broken on 5 April 1812. The letter also shows the transregional scope of Luddism as a revolutionary force. In May, Judge Dallas opined to the Chester Assizes that:

> But I fear there is reason to apprehend, that much of the character of these dreadful outrages is of a different description: the printed handbills, which have been circulated for some time past; the discourses which have been held; the doctrines which have been published; the hopes held out to the disaffected; and the threats made use of to the well-disposed; and lastly, and above all that which was before surmised, but will now distinctly appear, at least in point of existence, though not of extent, the secret oath or engagement binding equally to the commission and concealment of crime; this cement and consolidation of all conspiracy; this stamp and treason itself! All these, put together, denote, and too plainly, for prudence to disregard, the instrumentality of wicked instigation, working to the production of something more than [illegible] or partial mischief.[15]

For the Crown, revolution seemed imminent, and memories of the United Englishmen of a decade earlier must have gripped the imagination of those in power. Yet we ask, were the French really coming? Some Luddites thought so. When Joseph Barrowclough – a corporal in the Light Company of the Upper Agbrigg Local Militia –

was interrogated in July 1812, he confessed that the 'Lud System' began twenty-two years earlier, i.e. 1792, the beginning of the United Irishmen movement, and dropped the bombshell that the French were behind Luddism. In the interrogation, Barrowclough remarked:

> that it had been mentioned amongst the luddites that on the landing of the French, the French prisoners as well at Chesterfield, as at Plymouth and Dartmoor were to rise and would be joined by the luddites. Barrowclough says he knows where there is a French officer who was at Dartmoor barracks ... he was a General in the French service who had escaped or broke his parole but had been taken again.[16]

He added that of the four local commanders engaged in organising the arms raid, three were French. A remarkably similar story had been reported to the Home Office from Hull that Luddites were sent:

> to different parts of the Country, and especially where French Prisoners are many to some thousands, are already sworn in, to rise on a certain day, appointed in all parts of the Kingdom ... the Luddites mean to rid themselves, of all their Enemys. They reckon on 50,000 French Prisoners, as helpers.

The writer noted that a sign that the revolution had begun was the stopping of mail coaches, and that Lords Castlereagh and Liverpool would be assassinated.[17] How true this all was we can only guess, but the Luddites themselves seem to have believed that the French were coming to help them in bringing about a revolution in England. This aspect of Luddism needs further research in French and English archives.

Such thinking may have been desperately naïve, yet the threat of an uprising in 1812, led by French officers on parole who planned to march on the large POW camps with armed Luddites, free the prisoners and occupy the ports preparatory to a French invasion, forced the government to disperse prisoners to locales that were more distant.[18]

For the Crown, revolution seemed imminent, and memories of the United Englishmen of a decade earlier must have gripped the imagination of those in power. As April began, news filtered to the Home Office that the disturbances in the West Riding were more than industrial unrest.

Chapter 15

THE REVOLUTION BEGINS

On 6 April, Ralph Fletcher wrote to the Home Office: he was a worried man. The Luddites in Eccles, he was informed, had seized 183 firearms in the space of two weeks, and they were pledged 'to put the great man down who had [illegible] them under foot for so long'. Was this a threat against the King or Spencer Perceval? Either way, the Luddites in Lancashire were arming themselves and 'were determined … to seize the arms and ammunition belonging to the Local Militia'.[1] Arms raiding arrived in the West Riding seemingly from Manchester. An informant in Manchester, Humphrey Yarwood, reported that 'something further than the destruction of steam looms or machinery was intended';[2] likewise, Thomas Wood of Mottram stated 'that there was to be a revolution, and that all who are not for it would be killed; and those that were for it, were to take the oath'.[3] Across the Pennines in Barnsley, Thomas Broughton informed the magistrates that 'the Luddites have in view ultimately to overturn the system of government by revolutionising the country'.[4] Citizen Bent reported to Ralph Fletcher that he had met a delegate from the Irish radical Ribbonmen, Patrick Cannovan, in Stockport in the middle weeks of April. This group was the heir to the United Irishmen of 1791–1805. Cannovan proceeded to relate to them his travels in Scotland and Ireland and dealings with underground committees in Belfast and Glasgow, and that a secret committee in Dublin pledged their support for fellow committees in England and Scotland. The Irish plotters hoped to take Dublin Castle in the planned uprising. Bent noted: 'the committee at Glasgow said the ad'on amount of the different towns in Scotland the number attested was about nine thousand seven hundred and that they was determined to persevere in the cause.' He added that the committee in Belfast were in overall command of what was being planned and that:

they would soon make the government wish they had granted them their emancipation ... Ireland was determined to have ... or lose all that was dear to them and all the Cartherlicks [sic] in Ireland was of the same way of thinking ... the Committee at Dublin and is constituents in England and that the Catherlicks of Ireland would do all in their power to shake off the yoke.

The Committee of Dublin 'assure the Citizens in England that there is not a town of [illegible] five score in Ireland [illegible] who will come forward with men & money to support the cause to the uttermost of their power', and continued that the Irish would 'do all in their power to keep good understanding with the Citizens of England and Scotland and do all in their power to forward them some [arms] but arms was difficult things to get as government had taken their from time to time and had scoured the country completely of them'. Bent informed the Crown that 'eighty-two thousand enrolled of Carterlicks [sic] all ready and a few protestants also and that the Kingdom was readyer to shake off the yook [sic] themthe [sic] have been for the last century'. Bent added, moreover:

> the citizens of London ... been informed that a delegate would go to Dublin by the way of Glasgow and was returned would go to London by the way of Birmingham and return by Derby and take the different towns in his way to establish the business with them.[5]

If the evidence is credible, the Catholic majority in Ireland, despite the failure of Robert Emmet's rebellion less than a decade earlier, were once more planning to rise in rebellion. The French government had supported Emmet's goal, and the goal of an independent Ireland since the 1790s, as the author discusses in *French Invasions of Britain and Ireland 1797–1798*.[6] For the Irish, home rule was the goal. For the French, it would create a new ally to carry the fight against the British Crown. As had been part of event planning for Emmet's rebellion, a rebellion in Ireland relied upon a diversion being carried out in England, to allow the French to get boots on the ground. This had been the task of Despard and United Englishmen, and now the task had fallen to the Luddites, amongst whom no doubt were many thousands who had participated in the failed Despard plot.

Religion, politics and industrial grievances coalesced, and, as in the 1790s, external forces hoped to shape the unfolding events in England to their advantage. Just as in the 1790s, France hoped to exploit industrial and social unrest to their advantage. If a revolution was to take place, the revolutionaries needed arms, ammunition and men.[7]

Arms were stolen from farmers and private householders: most famers possessed at least one musket for self-defence and to 'lamp' pigeons, rabbits and other pests; Gentlemen owned pistols and epees; others owned blunderbusses and similar weapons to guard against burglars. Arms raids had been a notable feature of the Irish rebellion of 1798, and was a practice that spread into the West Riding from Manchester, and may have been led by former United Irishmen. Luddism took on a new and troubling form: collecting arms by whatever means they could. By May, the north of England was virtually under martial law. General Maitland, who would rise to fame at Waterloo, commanded some 7,000 men in and around Manchester, of which 1,400 were mounted troops, including the Scots Greys. General Dyott headed a force of 4,000 in the midlands and General Grey commanded a force approaching 2,000 in the West Riding. The force was considerably augmented by the regular Militia being mobilised, as well as the Local Militia and Yeomanry, which in the West Riding perhaps totalled 12,000 men, and a similar number in Lancashire and Cheshire – in all, perhaps 35,000 men, who were augmented by an ever-increasing number of auxiliaries in the form of special constables and volunteers under the 'Watch and Ward' legislation. Maitland was in overall command of a combined army of perhaps 50,000 and set out to overawe and overwhelm those creating disorder. When he took up command, he marched all his troops, some 7,000, through Manchester in full regimental order in a show of strength that took three days to complete. A large detachment of the Stirlingshire Militia, led by Captain Raynes, was tasked with harrying clandestine Luddite activity. Moving constantly around the hill country, Raynes and his men sought out, attacked and arrested any gangs of men out and about after night had fallen. He proved remarkably adept in forming the first effective commando unit in the British Army. Maitland's aggressive policy of military pacification was supplemented by the detention of suspected Luddites. The highly aggressive interrogation methods used by magistrates such as Joseph Radcliffe of Huddersfield, John Lloyd of Stockport, and Joseph Nadin, the Manchester deputy constable, more than likely included torture. General Maitland informed Henry Addington, now Lord Sidmouth: 'We are shutting our eyes to an evil ... from dread of trying totally to extirpate it.'[8] The Oldham diarist Rowbottom remarked:

> last night Joseph Nadin Deputy Constable of Manchester arived at Midleton attended by a Large party of Scotch Greys and about one o clock this morning Broke into several Houses Secured people in their Beds he was provided with several post Chaises in wich he Emediately put his prisoners and drove off for the New Bayley.[9]

Terror was the order of the day. Raynes would be deployed in the West Riding, as we shall see, where he continued his trade in 'fear and terror'. A troubled Major William Gordon of the 2nd Dragoon Guards reported:

> The Rioters are collecting arms by force – last night in the neighbourhood of Lockwood, (2 miles from hence) about twenty of them entered a house and demanded the arms (a Gun & pistol) which they knew the person had – he at first refused to deliver them – they then threatened to destroy his house & put him & his family to death if he resisted – Several other attacks of the same description have been made within these few days. ... feel under the necessity of reporting that I conceive it absolutely necessary a much larger force should be in this neighbourhood and that a temporary Barrack should be found in the towns for the accommodation of the Troops, Cavalry in particular, for our arms are not safe which the men are with their arms, in addition to which, they may with ease be prevented turning out, in case of a sudden attack and which we are always liable to in this place – I can assure you Sir this requires immediate attention–
>
> The Depot of the Local Militia is also in this town, which I conceive extremely dangerous, there are seven barrel of Ball Cartridge, and about 40 Stand of arms complete, which alone require a strong guard to protect it, independent of the danger arising from the powder lying in the middle of the town, at all times liable to be destroyed by fire, and which they will endeavour to do if they are prevented taking possession of it.[10]

Joseph Scott, magistrate of Woodsome, near Huddersfield, opined to the Home Office that:

> the disturbed and alarming state of this part of the country ... his Majesty's government ... to take such prompt and decisive measures ... in order to depress a spirit of outrage and rebellion against the laws which threaten the security of all property as well as the person safety of every peaceable and loyal inhabitants ... we feel it our duty most particularly to request the attention of his Majesty's Government to the forcibly seizing of firearms by a band of desperate men, who surround or [illegible] upon houses in the night, and threatening death and destruction in case of resistance: every night for the past week has been marked by many acts of this sort, which too [illegible] indicates the approach of some divisive movement on the part of this numerous and formidable band.[11]

Days later, Magistrate Radcliffe from Milnsbridge reported twenty stands of arms were taken by the Luddites in the previous few days.[12] The *Leeds Mercury* reported on 9 May 1812:

> I am sorry to inform you that the Luddites have been very active in collecting arms this last week, and have been too successful.—They proceeded to people's houses, in the townships of Almondbury, Wooldale, Farnley, Netherthong, Meltham, Honley, and Marsden and many other places in this neighbourhood; they entered the houses by about 20 or 30 in a gang, and demanded all the arms in the house, on pain of instant death. By this means they have obtained possession of upwards of 100 stand of arms since my last letter to you, and not one night has passed without some arms having been so taken.[13]

As well as arms raids, Luddite attacks continued. On the night of Sunday, 10 May 1812, a barn containing a threshing machine at Rouse Mill, Soothill, near Dewsbury, was almost completely destroyed in an arson attack.[14] On 11 May, the postmaster of Leeds reported to the General Postmaster: 'Last night a barn and its contents at Birstall were set on fire; a threshing machine it is thought was the object of dislike.' This may or may not have been the same incident as the Soothill arson: the two villages are about 3 miles apart. The postmaster continued that 'no threatening letters [were] received', but blamed the 'stubborn, discontented Body' of croppers. He thereby clearly placed the incident within a Luddite framework.[15]

The death of Spencer Perceval

Amidst the gathering storm of violence in the north, an event like no other before or since sent shock waves through the country. In the early evening of Monday, 11 May, as he walked through the lobby of the House to attend a session of evidence on the Orders in Council, Spencer Perceval was shot through the heart by John Bellingham – a moment captured by several sensationalist contemporary prints. Reports of the impact of the assassination on the 'public Mind' reached parliamentarians quickly and linked the murder to the prevailing distress, as did a correspondent from Wolverhampton:

> Every serious well-disposed person is struck with horror; but I am sorry to say that numbers of a quite different description have been shewing marks of rejoicing, by firing Guns till near midnight, & the greater part of this Day! Boys in the streets are taught to exclaim—now the great Man in the Parliament House is dead, we shall have a big Loaf! My Ears are assail'd as I pass along the streets with declarations of distress, & almost threats; and I have too much reason to dread that it cannot be long before some serious Event must take place, as the lower classes seem quite ripe for it.[16]

Celebrations at the death of Perceval broke out across the country. In Wakefield, a diarist tells us that some of his townsfolk felt that 'Bellingham has done a great thing and a serviceable thing to his country'.[17] In Bolton, Ralph Fletcher, the prominent and virulently anti-radical magistrate, reported:

> The Loyalists here cannot accede to what is stated in the Public Prints— viz that Bellingham had no political motive for committing the foul deed. We here, from the general language of the disaffected and from some secret Information, of a Revolution ... expected to have taken place early in May, cannot refrain from entertaining an opinion that Bellingham's motives were revolutionary.[18]

In Nottingham, the news of Perceval's death was:

> received with the greatest Joy by the Populace here & before the Magistrates were aware of their Intention attempted to be celebrated by many noisy testimonies of their exultation such as shouting making Bonfires & in one Instance carrying a Flag & a Drum.[19]

Attempts to brand Bellingham as a Jacobin, or a Catholic, or an infidel, or a speculator, were part of a process through which loyalists derived their own meanings from the assassination of Perceval. The assignation emboldened the Luddite and radical cause. An anonymous letter to the Prince Regent on 17 May urged 'bread or blood' and told the Regent to adopt Burdett as his adviser: 'If you do not you shall share the same fate that Pervical [sic] has done.'[20] In Wigan, an examination of a man involved in an open discussion in a public house about Perceval's murder confirmed that the discussion had revolved around the oppressive nature of wartime taxes and that there had been general approval of Bellingham's actions. One Mr Atkinson 'approved of the murder of Mr Percivall [sic] and said that a subscription for Bellingham's wife and family would be a good thing'.[21] A placard posted up in Hull read: 'Civil and Religious Liberty. It is hoped that the friends of Civil & Religious Liberty will enter into a subscription to support Mr Bellingham in his Trial for shooting Mr Percival, the Enemy of England. An Englishman.'[22]

The same day that Spencer Perceval died, Citizen Bent reported:

> regular correspondence to and from Ireland, Scotland & many towns in England & particularly those in Yorkshire, Nottingham, Leicester, & Cornwall ... friends in the sister kingdom are doing well & only waiting

for England & are ready to start at the same time as Ireland, & by that means the business is to be carried on ... they have more than 400,000 men who can be depended on [illegible] what soldiers come over to join in the cause and that the delegates from Ireland suggested to the Manchester citizens to be as careful as possible.[23]

A delegate from Huddersfield to the Stockport assembly reported to the gathered delegates that the 'croppers and shearmen have been twisted & some sworn on the same way as last appeared', clearly an allusion to the United Englishmen of a decade earlier. The delegate continued, 'Our town hath done all in thur [sic] power to do away with such business as breaking & burning machinery a attempting to take mans lives.' Evidently, machine-breaking Luddites were being co-opted into the insurrectionary plan, although in Manchester, 'The weavers have stopped twisting in at present, as there is a breach between them & the spinners, tayllors & shoemakers.' The difference of opinion was the aims of the 'business', which was split between 'peace & parliamentary reform', and redressing industrial grievances. The Irish weavers in Manchester were at loggerheads with their English counterparts. A 'dissenting preacher' led 'the spinners, taylors, shoe makers, Brick layers, fustian makers, joiners & many others' in favouring political reform, noting that in Huddersfield, Saddleworth, Hallamwood, Stockport, Denton and Manchester, the trades agreed to petition Parliament for political reform.[24] Bent concluded that the Luddites and Ribbonmen would 'Ruin this Kingdom if these meetings is not prohibited ... this must be Looked after before it is too Late all the Manufacturing towns is on this plan and many of the viliges also.'[25]

One commentator from the period remarked all too correctly that:

> Jacobinism having almost totally disappeared from the educated classes has sunk down into the mob: so that since the year 1793, our internal state has undergone as great a change as our foreign relations ... young men of ardent mind ... became enthusiastic disciples of a political faith ... their talk was not merely of the rights of man, but of the hopes and destinies of the human race ... the populous were incapable for entering into such views: they beheld nothing ... finding them hostile to the war regarded them as men who preferred France to England, and therefore as enemies to their country. That this was the feeling of the populace twenty years ago is notorious to every one ... where riots broke out, Church and King was the cry of the mob, and their fury was directed against whom they considered as the enemies of both. Time passed on. ... Every topic is made subservient to the same conclusion that things are bad and must be changed; that corruption must be cut up by the

root ... the famous text in Ezekiel is the watch-word of the Luddites, was current among the manufacturers of the North, more than seven years before they made any public manifestation in serious spirit.[26]

By the end of April, Bent reckoned that in Staffordshire, '7,000 men sworn in, as such all will do their duty when called on & they have 2,680 guns, pistols and swords & others are providing themselves with pikes'. He added that in London, 14,000 had been twisted-in 'chiefly amongst the Spitalfields weavers'.[27] A concerned Francis Foljambe wrote from Wakefield on 29 April that 'nothing but a considerable powerful military force will be able to quell the strong & bad propensity to plunder & insurrection that may I fear infect different ranks in society & threatens serious evils as not only smashing mills &c are not the objects of their [illegible] attacks.'[28]

At the start of May, the Crown introduced legislation to make soliciting oaths punishable by death. The *Leeds Mercury* tells us that in the 'early morning' of Sunday, 10 May, a group of up to 100 men moved down Kirkgate in Wakefield and smashed the windows of the middle-class residents' homes and that 'In the evening of Sunday 10th May 1812, the hot-house belonging to a corn factor called Tootal were attacked at Wakefield. 300 panes of glass were broken.' Tootal was an obvious target; his warehouses contained thousands of tonnes of corn yet to be milled into flour. The paper also reported:

> William Cartwright had sent 11 pairs of shears, used in his shearing frames, to be sharpened at a grinders in Wakefield. On Friday 8th May 1812, they were taken to a field at a distance, along with 2 pairs belonging to someone else, and broken.[29]

Six days later, Earl Fitzwilliam noted to Richard Ryder at the Home Office that 'there is an evil spirit pervading many districts of the Country & much bad intention in several individuals ... a description of outrage no one can foresee where it is to happen'.[30]

Chapter 16

ARMING THE REVOLUTION

At the end of May, Sir Francis Lindley Wood, acting as Vice Lieutenant for Yorkshire in the absence of Earl Fitzwilliam, informed the earl that 'I am entirely disposed at present to the think that a liberal subscription amongst the more opulent for the relief of the lower order of manufacturers distressed by the high & increasing prices of provisions would have a very good effect on the public mind.' No doubt the idea was to fund public soup kitchens for the poor and unemployed as had occurred in 1799–1801, yet the plan came to nought. Letting the market set the prices of food condemned thousands to starvation while the merchants and middle class could profit from the situation. Wood also noted, 'I fear that the taking of fire-arms in the night still takes place occasionally in the neighbourhood of Birstall & Huddersfield & that the populace at Leeds are in a very unquiet and inflamed state.'[1] In order to reduce the number of firearms the Luddites could seize, the magistrates ordered their own arms raids, instructing constables to seize arms.

In Netherton, near Ossett, beer and firearms had been demanded with threats of violence on 26 May from the local landlord, and Netherton was attacked again in June when:

> several person at Netherton, near Horbury, had been robbed of their fire-arms; but one instance (the particulars of which have since come to our knowledge,) is of so daring and atrocious a nature, as to require being stated somewhat in detail. Mr. Abraham Lees, an inoffensive old man, who lives at a lone house in Netherton, about two miles from Wakefield, was visited by a party of those nocturnal depredators about twelve o'clock on the night of Wednesday the 3d instant. Incapable of making any resistance, he delivered up his fire-arms; they then demanded his money, and threatened him with instant death if he hesitated; upon this threat he gave them a guinea note and some silver, which was all the

money he had in the house ; they then insisted upon having the keys of his drawers delivered to them, which he was under the necessity of complying with. They then ransacked his drawers but not finding the treasure they expected, they behaved in so violent a manner as to excite an apprehension that murder was intended, and Mr. Lees, on his knees, begged for the life of himself and his sister. The intimidation created by this outrage was so strong, that Mr. Lees has left his house and gone to reside in a neighbouring town for security.[2]

Two days later, the *Leeds Mercury* tells us that the home of Thomas Milnes, who lived at Storrs-Hill, Horbury, was raided:

about seven or eight, undisguised, went about midnight to the house of Mr. Thomas Milnes, Storrs-Hill, in Horbury, and rousing him from his sleep, demanded entrance. Mr. Milnes not appearing inclined to obey this mandate, they threatened if he did not instantly open the door, they would immediately force it Mr. Milnes finding he could make no availing resistance to their demand, gave them admittance.— They then insisted upon having his fire-arms; but on being satisfied that he had none, they demanded money and refreshment; he gave them some silver, and bread, cheese and beer. They then requested that he would allow them to take some to some poor fellows who they said were watching at a distance; with this requesation he thought it also prudent to comply, and they then civilly took their leave of him. On Sunday night these depredators made a further attack on several houses at Netherton, (a place in the immediate vicinity of Horbury,) where they succeeded in obtaining seven or eight stand of arms; and upon this occasion they behaved with peculiar atrocity, by wantonly firing several musket balls into one of the houses. The success of these nocturnal depredators on this occasion is the more remarkable, as on the day before, (Saturday) the Chief Constable of the District, and the Constable of Horbury, had received directions to receive the fire-arms of such of the inhabitants as were disposed to give them up, and which they carried into effect the same day, most of the inhabitants readily giving up their arms to the custody of the Civil Magistrates, but some few refused. The Constables were much hooted and abused by the populace while they were executing this duty, and one of the mob had the effrontery to take from his pocket a handful of musket balls which he threw into the air, ex-claiming 'Here are hailstones for you.' It is said there is a person in Horbury employed in crafting these leaden messengers of death. Every article of lead, such as pumps and water-spouts, &c. which can be readily conveyed away, are constantly disappearing. The glaring violation of the laws of society and of private property, evinced in these nocturnal visits, though an evil of great magnitude, is, as it were, lost in the contemplation of the more atrocious purposes for which these instruments of death are collected, and which the imagination almost sickens at the thought of. It is probable that the offenders may deceive them-selves with the notion, that as they do not actually break into the houses, their offence is not a capital one; but they ought to know, that to obtain property of any kind by threats of violence, is an offence equally penal, and will subject them to the punishment of death.

On Thursday fe'nnight, the shed, adjoining the barn of Mr. Robert Waltshaw, of Horbury, was maliciously set on fire, but was fortunately discovered in time to prevent its communicating to the barn.

On Thursday night last the same system of depredation was pursued at Osset [sic], about a mile from Horbury, at half-past twelve, a party of men, consisting of about twelve persons, surrounded the house of Mr. Butterfield, and demanded his firearms, threatening him with instant death if he hesitated; at two other houses they fired two musket balls through the door. This lawless banditti then went down the common, where they entered every house likely to contain arms, and insisted upon their being delivered up, threatening to shoot the owners if the least delay was manifested. These depredators were armed with muskets and pistols. They obtained on this occasion about six stand of arms.[3]

Saturday, 30 May witnessed the special constables of Horbury and District begin to collect firearms from members of the public who were prepared to surrender them. While doing so, the *Leeds Mercury* reported that the constables were openly mocked, 'hooted and abused'.[4] In Dewsbury, a food riot turned to violence, as the *Leeds Mercury* reported:

> we are informed, that an affray of some hours duration, took place between the military and a number of the inhabitants at Dewsbury, on Wednesday night, in which two of the populace were bayonetted, but we are happy to say, not mortally. The particulars of this unfortunate encounter have not yet reached us.[5]

Another raid for arms took place on 31 May, when guns were forcibly seized from David Stephenson, Joseph Shaw, Morrit Mathews and John Burgin: the latter refused to hand over his firearms and was threatened with violence if he did not do so and 'fired thro the door' in an act of intimidation. After taking Burgin's firearms, the Luddites moved on to the home of William Dickinson.[6]

That day, diarist Tomlinson wrote: 'felt myself unsettled and uneasy as the Luddites or plunderers are entering into houses in the night and demanding arms and what else they choose,' and noted, 'on Thursday night they set fire to Robt Walshaw's threshing machinery at Horbury Bridge,' ending his diary entry with, 'I much expected them coming to my house last night for my guns.'[7]

Weapons and ammunition were seized from the home of Mr Moorhouse at Long Haigh, near Netherton, on 3 June, and on Saturday, 6 June, firearms were seized from a Mr Hemsworth of Woodkirk, as well as John Boyle and Isaac Rhodes of nearby Haigh Moore. In the same deposition, we find a reference that at 10 p.m. on Saturday, 6 June, 'a number of men' armed with muskets were seen to be drilling on the edge of Soothill Wood in the Parish of West Ardsley. A Mr Hemsworth of Woodchurch later deposed that he heard drilling at the same location between 1 a.m. and 2 a.m. the following morning at the same location.[8] A farmer from Shitlington (Sitlington) reported to the magistrates that between 'twelve and One o'clock' in the morning he was awoken by a group of men banging on his door. Upon opening the door, he was faced by a group of men pointing pistols at his head and demanding that he hand over any firearms he may have. On being told that he had no firearms, the group demanded money: he handed over 'a guinea ... and about four shillings in coins'.[9]

A combination of famine, industrial unrest and pestilence made the government fear revolution was at hand by early June:

> Wakefield June 7th 1812
> My Lord,
> I inclose to you two most material Depositions which are in the originals signed by most respectable Individuals, but who state that they would be murdered immediately if their Names became known. Mr Woods the Magistrates & Mr Foljambie [sic] the Deputy Clerk of the Peace know the Men & their Handwriting. – In consequence of a Letter I rec'd from Mr Bolland this Morning I have appointed a Genl Meeting of Lieutenancy & have fixed it for so early a Day as Thursday next in Consequence of the alarming State of this Neighbourhood, the further Seizures of Arms are expected every Night in the adjacent Villages. – Under these Circumstances I should be happy if your Lordship could possibly communicate to me at Wakefield on Thursday Morning your opinion what general Steps can & ought to be taken to put a Stop to these Outrages which are taking the direct Road to an open Insurrection & if you think it expedient to see the Secretary of State on these Matters on Tuesday I shd be very glad to be prepared on Thursday with the Result of your Deliberation thereupon.[10]

Wood reported to Fitzwilliam the ominous news that the Sheffield Militia Depot arms raid was likely to be repeated.

> I have heard this morning from a medical man that the arms are to be found if searched for in the villages, that the Luddites openly say they are <u>not</u> collecting them from individuals because they can <u>have</u> them from the Local Militia Store rooms when they please & when they are ready for action.[11]

The fear of arms raids and a general uprising led to the West Riding magistrates being called to assemble and discuss the imposition of martial law. John Pemberton Heywood, magistrate and barrister of law in Wakefield, was against non-imposition.[12] Grey and Wood both desired the law strengthening to aid the magistrates in prosecuting the troublemakers.[13] An eyewitness to the events wrote:

> have every night fully expected the luddites coming for my gun as they have been very active in the last week; at some places they behave very ill indeed demanding money, meat and drink with a brace of pistols placed at the head or breast of the mother of the house; at Wm Morres they practised these abuses and dragged the servant girl out of bed onto the floor; what will be the end I know not.

Our writer, Matthew Tomlinson was clearly a scared man, like many hundreds if not thousands of well-to-do townsfolk in Wakefield and area. He added that the Luddites formed companies and had assembled guns and ammunition for more than 800 men.[14]

Despite the blustering of the magistracy, in Elland, merchant Joseph Woodhead reported that while on his way to Woodman House on the evening of 16 June, 'accompanied by some ladies, he was accosted by some persons who had a gun in his hand in the town fields of Elland and, "advance friend and give the counter signs or damn your blood, I'll blow your Brains out".' Woodhead added that he became aware that the challenger was not alone, and was accompanied by other armed men. From the darkness, Woodhead reports that a voice said, 'Let them pass'. Woodhead and the women carried on, 'and having walked 100 yards heard around 6 gunshots – the first shot passed over their heads.' Woodhead did not record what happened to him after that. The next day, Woodhead was informed that shortly after the incident in Elland, the home of James Astley, an excise officer, was raided by fourteen men. In the attack, Woodhead reported that Astley suffered windows of his house broken and other threats, and in response, he gave the men three pistols.[15]

Woodhead added that a man called Smith had been similarly raided. Smith reportedly told the raiders he had got rid of his gun; in reply, the Luddites told him they expected him to get them one, and would call again in a fortnight. Upon demanding something to drink, Smith gave them milk. Woodhead comments that they asked Smith if he knew of anyone else with arms in the vicinity. Smith told them that a Miss Cartledge at Woodman House had a gun, but this had been surrendered to the military. The men pledged to 'make her pay' for this, and Woodhead reported that lead was stolen from the house of this Miss Cartledge that night, including 'the leaden parts of a water pump', presumably for use in creating bullets.[16] Our diarist Matthew Tomlinson records on 14 June:

> Several acts of outrage have been committed round about us, the military have been active in collecting the arms of the surrounding villages, some have, others have not given them up; no one has yet been to demand my piece, but have expected the Luddites coming every night for a fortnight back – the spare money which I have by me I am necessitated to bury in the field for I am determined that I will not give up my money to a gang of ruffians who [are] only bent on plunder.[17]

The arms raids and nocturnal drilling came to the attention of Sir Francis Lindley Wood, the acting Lord Lieutenant, who opined to Earl Fitzwilliam on 17 June:

> It was stated on the 11th that in the whole Neighbourhood of Huddersfield & Birstall the Arms of the peaceable Inhabitants had been swept away within the last Month by Bands of armed Robbers – that the Watch & Ward Act could not, except in two Places in the District, possibly be carried into Effect, the disaffected outnumbering by every Degree the peaceable Inhabitants; that the well-disposed could not & would not join in any armed or civil association but lay entirely at the Mercy of a Banditti with Arms in their Hands; that, except the very Spots which were occupied by Soldiers, the Country was virtually in Possession of a lawless.—On the Friday subsequent to our Meeting of the 11th, a partial Robbery of Arms took Place near Netherton, on the 12th strong Patroles of the 15th Light Dragoons were sent out both on the North & South Banks of the Calder—they report that in the ill-affected Villages they found the People up at Midnight, that they heard the firing of small Arms at short Distances from them throughout the whole Night to a very great Extent & had no Doubt but that it proceeded from Parties at Drills—& this Part of the Report is entirely confirmed by the Farmers & Men of Property throughout the Country.
>
> Under all the foregoing Circumstances I beg to state my entire Conviction that the Arms & Ammunition now collected by the Depredators will first be employed in enforcing their alarming System of Terror & Robbery, [next] in ye Assassination of the Magistracy & others

whom they may chuze to mark out for Destruction, & lastly, will end, as the same Course of Outrage ended in Ireland, in open Rebellion against the Government of the Country.—The similarity of our present State to that of Ireland strikes everyone who witnessed the [transactions] of 1797 & 1798 in that Country, & in this close Similarity we are unfortunately distinguished from the more open, riotous & unorganized Proceedings in Lancashire & in Cheshire.—We fear greatly that there will be a further Resemblance in the Circumstance of the Magistrates speedily feeling themselves unable to render any Service to their Country, & on that account declining to act as they did in Ireland, or to expose themselves to Danger without a Prospect of any commensurate Advantage from their Exertions.[18]

The allusion to the events in Ireland in 1798 are incredibly telling about the level of disaffection then existing in the West Riding and the very real fears that the magistrates felt about losing control of the situation. The country was reaching a revolutionary moment, unless the Crown took strong and decisive action. Wood feared that:

the Rt. Honble Secretary is by no means aware of the full Extent of the Outrages committed in the Country, particularly in the Wapentakes of Agbrigg & Morley, of the total Insecurity of the Persons & Property of the well-affected Inhabitants therein, & of the rapid & extending Organization & drilling of the rebellious.[19]

A day later, he reported to Fitzwilliam that the magistrate had 'grown hopeless from their past experience of gaining such information' about the arms raids.[20] The same week, Fitzwilliam was informed of the crisis in West Yorkshire, the *Leeds Mercury* reported:

These dangerous outrages on the peace of society, and the property of individuals still continue, and with which is combined a spirit of indiscriminate plunder, and in some cases the demand of arms is only the ostensible pretext the real object being to obtain money. On Saturday morning, about one o'clock, the family of Mr. Barraclough was roused from sleep, by a party of men, who demanded fire arms, this demand was immediately complied with, and a piece was given to them out of the window, but not content with this, they insisted that the door should be opened to them, which was done, having obtained admittance, they insisted upon having the keys of the desk and drawers, which they completely ransacked, but without finding any money, disappointed in the search, they proceeded to the bed-room of Mr. Barraclough, and insisted upon his giving them all the money he had, he gave them about

20s. in silver, and having helped themselves to a large loaf, a piece of cheese, and some butter, they took their leave; one of the party almost immediately returned, and brought back the piece, saying they had no occasion for it. The same night a robbery very similar in its circumstances, took place at Kirkburton, near Huddersfield, but in which the robbers, were not so ceremonious as to ask for admittance, but broke into the house, and two of them entered the bedroom of Mr. Savage, and each presenting a pistol to Mr. Savage and his son who slept in the same room, demanded his money and keys, he gave them about 23s. and they proceeded to examine his drawers, but did not meet with the treasure they expected; Mr. Savage having fortunately been disappointed in receiving a very considerable sum of money; which was to have been paid to him the preceding day.[21]

As well as arms raids, assassination was still on the Luddite agenda: William Milnes was a special constable for the Huddersfield area. He lived in Lockwood, near the Huddersfield. Between 11 p.m. and 12 a.m. on Monday, 15 June 1812, his house came under attack. The *Leeds Mercury* reported:

About twelve o'clock on Monday night last, three musket balls were fired thro' the windows into the house of Mr. Wm. Milnes, who is a Constable at Lockwood, near Huddersfield; the windows were then broke to pieces with large sticks, and the persons who committed this atrocious act, immediately made off. It appears Mr. Milnes had incurred the displeasure of the Luddites by the vigilant discharge of his duty as a Constable. Similar depredations have also been committed at the house of an Excise Officer at Elland; he had several pistols in his house which he was compelled to deliver up. —These atrocities have become so common in this neighbourhood, that they now excite little attention.[22]

In the midst of the arms raids, food was scarce and costly. Horbury, close to Wakefield, was also the scene of rioting over food:

On Wednesday 17th June 1812, Benjamin Byrom, a hawker of potatoes & onions had set up his cart at Horbury on market day. At some point during the day, a crowd gathered and set about upsetting the cart, tipping the contents into the street.[23]

The Wakefield press reported that 'a few huzzars making their appearance, tranquillity was soon restored. Warrants had, we understand, been issued against some of these miserable wretches who were engaged in this culpable outrage.'[24]

The trial was reported:

BETTY WOOD (aged 60), MARY ELLIS (aged 24), and MARY WRIGHT (aged 20) were charged with Highway Robbery, in putting in bodily fear, and stealing by force and violence from the person of Benjamin Byrom, a quantity of potatoes and onions. This case may be stated in a few words.
On the 17th of June, Benjamin Byrom, a hawker of potatoes, went with his cart to Horbury, where a number of women and children made an assault upon him, and threw his potatoes into the street; some of the rabble run away with a few of them – but nothing of this kind was proved against the Prisoners. The law in this case, as stated by the Judge, ought to be known. If the intention of the mob is to steal, or to convert to their own use, any part of the property, every person in the mob is answerable for the acts of that mob; and if property is taken away, every individual in the riot may be prosecuted for the robbery, and may be capitally convicted, as the case may be, though such individual may have taken no part of the property. But if the intention of the mob is to destroy the property, and a few in the mob deviate from such intention, and steal part of it, their acts affects only themselves, and does not implicate any other person. The Jury, without hesitation acquitted all the Prisoners.[25]

The Reverend Dr Martin Naylor opined in his editorial of the 19th that:

We are sorry to hear from various quarters that the misguided people who call themselves luddites, continue to make nocturnal visitations, to demand arms and ammunition, and in many instances, advancing to a greater pitch of audacity and impudence to demand money, which they have frequently obtained. They are also engaged, almost every night, in one quarter or another, in exercising themselves in the use of arms, in which they are reported to have attained no despicable degree of proficiency. A party of them so occupied were surprised, a few evenings ago, but a patrole of the 15th Light Dragoons, but on the latter advancing, the Luddite troops marched quick step into Soothill wood, on the skirts of which they were drawn up and left the ground of action undisputed to their adversaries.
On Friday night at Mr Barraclough's Crigglestone, a part after firing two or three shots through the door, gained admittance into the house, where they behaved in the most outrageous manner, took away a gun and betwixt 20 and 30 shillings in money. They also devoured or took away the principal part of the eatables in the house.[26]

Naylor concluded by telling his readers that the home of D. Coope of Horbury had been shot at by Luddites.[27] The *Leeds Mercury* adds some more details:

depredators visited a number of houses at Osset, where they got from eight to ten guns ; they also demanded, and in some cases obtained ammunition. Some delay having occurred at one house, they fired several balls through the door.

On Saturday night, about ten o'clock, a number of men, with muskets, were seen performing the military exercise, at the skirts of Soothill-Wood, in the parish of West-Ardsley ; and about two o'clock on Sunday morning, 47 of them, all armed, passed through the village of Gawthorp, near Osset, where they obtained some guns, and several sums Of money, which they are now in the habit of demanding. About half past twelve o'clock the same night, a number of these people knocked at the door of Mr. Israel Rhodes, of Lee-Fair, and demanded his gun, which he was obliged to surrender into their hands. They then proceeded to another house in the neighbourhood, and took from the family a gun; and afterwards to the house of Mr. Leathley, of the same place, and extorted from him two muskets, a pistol, and a guinea.

Several parties of the same description of persons have also been active in collecting arms in the neighbourhood of Holmfirth, almost every night since our last; but they have not demanded money as in the neighbourhood of Horbury and Osset.[28]

The Gentleman's Magazine adds that:

the malcontents in the Western Part of Yorkshire, hold nightly watches on the tops of the hills, lighting beacons or making some other sorts of signals; and when the cavalry are proceeding to surprise them, rockets are thrown up to give notice of their approach.

The magazine informed its readers in London furthermore that 'there has been great destruction of farming machinery and nightly depredations of upon every building that has lead upon it,' noting, 'the system of stealing arms and lead in the neighbourhood of Wakefield and Huddersfield still continues and that assemblages of between two and three hundred men have been seen out different nights in remote places going through military exercises.'[29] The inference here is that this was an underground army, and that revolution was imminent. On 16 June, the Home Office received reports that the Irish weavers in Denton, Rochdale and across the north west were arming themselves for a rebellion, and had begun raiding farms and houses for arms. The report noted: 'It is said that they number near 40,000 strong in Lancashire and 100,000 in Yorkshire' with 40,000 in London. The report concluded, 'I do think they will attempt something.'[30] Reports came in during June of pikes being made in Sheffield and that the uprising was to take place at the end of September or early October to coincide with the opening of Parliament.[31] On 17 June, a spy reported to the Home Office that the signal for a rising in the north would be the stopping of the mail coaches as well as signal rockets. The goal was to topple the government and replace it with a republic whereby every adult male had the vote and bring about a reduction in food prices and rise in wages.[32]

It is undeniable that many thousands saw revolution as the only legitimate option left to them in order to safeguard community and tradition and to bring about real change. A writer who called himself 'Thomas Paine' sent a threatening letter to Richard Wood of Manchester:

> you have been the cause of much bloodshed; you convened the people and did not meet them: you are therefore marked for punishment. Your childish excuse of Stairs! You might have adjourned to the Square called St Anns or to a field. The fact is; that there is a regular, general, progressive organisation of the people going forward. They may be called Hamdenites, Sidneyites, or Paineites. it has fallen to my lot to unite many thousands. WE for I speake in the name of multitudes. I say we deny and disavow all, or any connection with machine breakers, burners of factories, extorters of money, plunderers of private property or assasans. We know that every machine for the abridgment of human labour is a blessing to the great family of which we are a part. We mean to begin at the Source of our grievances as it is of no use to petition, We mean to demand & command a redress of our grievances. We have both the will & the power. What? must the industrious artisans or the humble cultivators of the soil, be always robb'ed of the rewards of their labours? must they be forever doom'd to behold their helpless infants unfed, uncloathed, untaught. in short deprived of every comfort that makes existance worth holding? must they see the Vultures of Oppressions legally robbing them to pay Sinecures, make loans, to other nations virtual fleets & armies: To give extravagant establishments to all the branches of what are called the ROYAL FAMILY, when other paupers are obliged to exist on 3 or 4 shillings p week? no not long. Tell Mr Ottiwell Wood, that his character has travelled farther than his feet, that he is much esteemed & respected by our Society & if ever we have an opportunity we will reward him, request him to accept our best wishes for all his families Happiness & Comfort.[33]

The letter was countersigned by 'Hampdenites', i.e., members of the Hampden club founded by Major Cartwright for political reform. Therefore, we are seeing a convergence of political reform, radical millenarian religion and industrial grievances all rolled into Luddism, which for almost 200 years has been compartmentalised as mere machine breaking. Revolution was in the air, and the Crown sought to destroy the hopes and desires of the working man in what amounted to a civil war between the haves and the have-nots to keep the rich oligarchs in power, and above all to keep the rich very rich indeed at the expense of the working man.

In Rastrick on the night of Saturday, 20 June 1812, Luddites were again out conducting arms raids. Several homes were raided, including the home of a John Oldroyd, from where was obtained a horse pistol and three guns from the gamekeeper of Magistrate Armitage.[34] On the night of the 29th, 'Cookson Stephenson & his family were asleep in their beds when they were roused by a loud banging at the door. From the safety of his bedroom, Stephenson enquired who was there, and the reply came "General Ludd".' Stephenson opened his door to ten armed men who were in disguise who demanded his pistol, which was handed over. The same group took another six firearms in the neighbourhood the same night.[35]

In his diary of 21 June, Tomlinson recorded:

> The plunderer still continues to practice their insults upon the honest industrious men of the community, but in the general do not meet with much plunder, as most people are upon their guard and do not keep much money in their houses. Last week two of these villains with capes over their faces about midnight demanded admission to the house of David Coope in the West-Field; he had resolution enough to repulse them; they stopped about ½ an hour and fired 9 shots into the house.

He concluded, noting that '36 rifle men were marched into Horbury and quartered there, I hope we shall have harmony again restored.'[36]

The Reverend Ralph Fletcher wrote from Bolton on 23 June that 'the Huddersfield luddites ... have 300 stand of arms in one depot and 225 stand in another [sic] in another also 9 blunderbusses and a vast [illegible] of pistols.'[37] The Luddites needed arms, as we have noted, both for self-defence, and also for offensive action against the Crown, about which Major General Stevenson reported to Henry Addington:

> I am sorry to say the Civil Power is parelized & the Democratical Party know it. They govern the Country by a System of Terror and make no hesitation in declaring their intentions of destroying such a Person or such a property if any Informations are given by the Inhabitants, and they have in several instances carried these threats into execution, the Magistrates are afraid to Act.

He continued:

> these Republicans (for such is their object) meet 2 or 3 times in the Week on the Moors at 12 O'clock PM & generally Drill their Troops two Hours, the Magistrates say they have no other power than to recommend to the People to go quietly home. I have offered to march some Troops & take these people, but they say the Law will not authorize them – These Republicans are organized &, have regularly their Centinels on Duty, & demand the Countersign & [illegible], they have the regular System of War, should it unfortunately be true that, the Civil Power can only give good advice, instead of Proving the Protection of the Law, it, will prove the Cradle of the Rebellion, the Country is armed & should be disarmed, this measure would force the Rebels into Action before, they were ready, shd they resist, we shall know their strength and if they could not make resistance, would prevent the Rebellion breaking out, the Military Force of England is weak when compared to the Armed & well Drilled Population of England. Your Lordship will recollect that this year the, Services of most of the Local Militia expires, & that whole Regts of well disciplined Men are let loose – the Halifax Regt which I inspected last week, are as firm a Regt & as well disciplined as the Troops of the Line, above 700 of them have served their term, & will not re engage, their Officers have [tried] it, the Non Commiss'd Officers say the Men are all Luddites, & will join those disturbers of the Public Peace, your Lordship will receive some reports from the Neighbourhood of Halifax, of a serious nature – here I am obliged to Barrack Troops in the Villages around this place, my head Quarters here is in the midst of these Redressers – I could have reengaged many of the Local if Authorized to have paid them the £2. 20*d*. on the day previous to the Expiration of their Drill, indeed my Lord it is necessary that Lieut Genl Grey should have discretional Powers, to enable him & his Generals to avail themselves of any favorable occurrences. The Local Militia shd have a longer term of Service, & the Age extended to 45 – the Volunteers shd be disbanded or obliged to do the Duty if Piquit with, the Regular Forces in every Market Town, the late Lord Melville told me that, was their duty, & called them Armed Constables, at present they are useless & expensive &, have only entered into that association to avoid the Militia.[38]

This evidence is damning. Recruited from the same population as the Luddites, the Halifax Local Militia were far from reliable, and so too we must consider the Upper Agbrigg Volunteers, whose precursor unit had mutinied a decade earlier. In July, the theft of arms increased. The *Leeds Mercury* reports that on the evening of 3 July 1812, arms raids took place across the West Riding. Magistrate Walker, writing from Milnsbridge, informed Fitzwilliam, 'I have lived in a state of the most absolute tranquillity, undisturbed by anything more than the vague reports of distant depredations and nocturnal visitors, the greatest part of which that I have been able to trace to any reality.' Walker was basically saying the reports from magistrates were exaggerations, but darkly warned that 'a number of neighbouring gentlemen, all strongly implied with an apprehension of a great political danger', but added, 'tho' not one of them could give any very convincing reason for their fears'. He did acknowledge that 'there can be no question of a <u>great</u> quantity of arms having been taken away at different times.'[39] In his last diary entry for June, Tomlinson reports:

> the Human Devils still continue to make honest men afraid; the last Tuesday evening, eight of them entered into the house of John Taylor of [illegible] and after demanding a candle and his keys, took the amount of £49. The same night they (the 8 men) went to the house of James [illegible] (the father of our servant girl) broke the doors in two, six of them seized him while the other two with a candle took his money to the amount of 200 pounds: we have yet escaped, but I do not intend them to have two hundred pence come when they will.[40]

Fear and defiance gripped the West Riding. Revolution was in the air. The Luddites has assembled an army that numbered several thousand: yet where was all this heading? Who was the leader? What were their aims? It is undeniable that community anger had boiled over into vengeance, but what now? It must have been painfully obvious that by the summer of 1812 Napoleon was not coming, and whatever plan for a revolution in Ireland was 'dead and buried'. The French were not coming, yet the idea of a revolution was not yet dead and buried. Momentum had grown throughout the summer, and seemingly, now like a rudderless ship in a storm, without a clearly defined set of aims, objectives and leadership, the arms raids continued.

The government now sought to diffuse the situation through legislation.

The Crown strikes back

The assassination of Perceval had two immediate effects.

Firstly, the Prince Regent invited the 2nd Earl of Liverpool to form the new administration. Liverpool appointed Henry Addington, Viscount Sidmouth, as Home Secretary. His appointment marked a turning point in the Tory government's response to Luddism. Before May was over, a Special Commission sat in Lancaster and Chester, resulting in twenty-eight convictions in Lancaster, of which eight defendants were hanged and thirteen were transported. Among those executed was Abraham Charlson, a 16-year-old boy who cried for his mother, and a 58-year-old mother charged with stealing potatoes to feed her family. At Chester, forty-seven Luddites were tried; twenty-nine were convicted, of which fifteen were sentenced to death and eight to transportation for life. Most charges were for administering illegal oaths and not machine breaking. The executions had an inhibiting effect on the Luddites in Lancashire and Cheshire. The Crown's attention now shifted to the West Riding. Lieutenant General Thomas Maitland, who had held commanded in Lancashire, was given command of the troops in the West Riding over General Grey, who was judged to have been ineffective, according to Magistrate Radcliffe. Under Maitland's command, thousands of troops converged on the West Riding, with hundreds of men garrisoned in Halifax, Huddersfield, Leeds, Sheffield and Wakefield. Maitland would stop at nothing to wrest control of the Riding from the Luddites and was prepared to use torture, intimidation and kidnapping to instil fear amongst the Luddites and all those who questioned the Crown. Rather than have the soldiers under his command operate as 'text book soldiers' marching around in obvious detachments, Maitland authorised the formation of, in essence, units of 'storm troopers' or 'shock troops', operated under the cover of darkness with blackened faces in the manner of the Luddites. William Wilberforce was a vocal supporter of Liverpool's new administration and Maitland's hard-line tactics, and was pilloried by the radical William Cobbett for caring more about slaves in the Caribbean than the starving working classes in Yorkshire, which was largely true.

Secondly, the assassination ended the government's will to stand against a flood tide of petitions against the Orders in Council, which had been brought into Law at the behest of Perceval's administration. It was he who also rescinded the apprenticeship laws in the woollen trade and legalised the use of gig-mills.

Walter Ramsden Fawkes had informed acting Lord Lieutenant of the West Riding Francis Lindley Wood that the insurrection in Sheffield would be 'tranquilised by the suspension of orders in council, but I do not find the same opinion entertained at Huddersfield, Leeds or Wakefield'.[41]

The hand of the government was forced: if catastrophe was to be averted, then the government had to do more than suppress its own people. It had to take direction to end the conditions that caused the crisis in the first place – a crisis of its own making. Parliament apparently listened: the Orders in Council, which closed American ports, were rescinded on 23 June, heralding an increase in trade and employment.[42] The *Leeds Mercury* triumphed:

> It is with unfeigned joy that we congratulate our readers on the most beneficial Victory which has been achieved during the present war – a victory over what may justly be considered as the most dangerous enemy this country ever had to contend with – THE ORDERS IN COUNCIL … The country must feel themselves deeply indebted to that rising Statesman, Mr. BROUGHAM, for his indefatigable services, in exhibiting to the view of the Legislature, with such irresistible cogency, the ruinous consequences of these Orders in Council.[43]

The government's tactic worked. Celebrations broke out in the north and the midlands at the news of the reopening of American ports. General Maitland explained, days after the Orders had been rescinded and a week since he feared total insurrection, that:

> I can have no doubt, whatever may be, the ultimate result, of the late Measure, of His Majesty's Government, in suspending, the Orders in Council, that its immediate Effect, by stimulating, the Expectation, of the Manufactured Commodities, on hand, and consequently opening the Door, to the increased employment, of our Manufacturers, will be most salutary. And this, should we be fortunate enough in addition, to have the benefit, of a full Harvest, will I apprehend go far, indeed least to stop, the propagation, of the Mischief, further than it may, present have gone. But I own, I have many doubts, whether it will, have the effect, of bringing back, those who are already implicated in these transactions, and who are engaged, in these Revolutionary designs. My opinion in truth is, looking on the one hand, at the State, of the Magistracy, and on the other, at the length, to which the thing has gone, that nothing short, of a Legislative Measure, upon the Subject, will be adequate, to restore the Country, in a short time, to a state of Internal tranquillity, and Security.[44]

Sir Francis Lindley Wood expressed a similar degree of caution, noting:

> I have not heard of a single outrage – so great an immediate effect is in no doubt & identifiable to the repeal of the Orders in council – I am however not sanguine enough to hope that this tranquillity will continue if trade should experience any material check.[45]

The Crown was cautiously optimistic that the worst was now behind them. However, the rescindment came five days too late: on 18 June 1812, the United States declared war on Britain, and American ports remained firmly closed to British commerce.

Chapter 17

ARMS RAIDS CONTINUE

By the end of June, the West Riding was flooded with troops. The 2nd Dragoon Guards had 277 men in the barracks in York, 57 in Halifax, 98 in Huddersfield, and 59 in Bradford, with smaller detachments at Hull, Dobcross, Scarborough, Hunmanby, Driffield and Tadcaster, amongst other places. The 15th Light Dragoons had 134 men in Sheffield, 152 in Leeds, 111 in Wakefield, 59 in Barnsley, and 27 at Milns Bridge. Some 287 men from the South Hampshire Militia were billeted in Wakefield (making 398 soldiers garrisoned in the town); 209 men from the South Devon Militia were in Sheffield and 109 in Barnsley; 570 men from the West Kent Militia were in Leeds, with a further 60 at Milns Bridge. Also, 183 from the Cumberland Militia were in Halifax, 300 in Huddersfield and 151 in Bradford.[1]

Despite rescindment of the Orders in Council, any hopes of an immediate end to Luddism were misplaced. F.L. Wood ordered that in consequence of the 'danger in which the persons & property of the respectable inhabitants are placed', a military detachment of one officer and twenty-five to thirty soldiers was sent to keep the peace.[2]

To aid the magistrates, hundreds of special constables were sworn in across the Riding to begin a huge manhunt to find the stolen arms and apprehend Luddites. In West Ardsley, 21 special constables were sworn in, 14 in Batley, 31 in Crigglestone, 47 in Dewsbury, 44 in Horbury, 76 in Holmfirth, 31 in Huddersfield backed by an Armed Association of 160 men, and 73 in Mirfield, to name but a few places that rallied to the anti-Luddite cause.[3] The magistrates were armed with new legal powers: on 9 July, Parliament wrote into law the death penalty for administering an oath and transportation for life for taking one. A three-month amnesty was offered to swear allegiance to the Crown for any who had taken an illegal oath. This legislation had an immediate response, with hundreds coming forward in Stockport and Manchester to take the Oath of Allegiance.

The same day as the magistrates made grandiose plans, at Stainland, near Halifax, the homes of Benjamin Dyson and William Mellor were raided and a gun and a sword were taken from each house. Over 20 miles to the south at Whitley, near Sheffield, ten men raided the home of a carpenter called Megson. The press reported that Megson and his family were locked in a back room while the house was searched; four guinea notes and some provisions were taken, though the men did not demand firearms.[4] The arms raids were highly orchestrated and of military precision, as the correspondent to Earl Fitzwilliam remarked:

> the precision, intrepidity and dispatch with which the armed banditti regularly searched a populous village, a mile in length, for arms and took away six or seven without attempting to touch other property, firing repeatedly into houses and individuals who offer the least resistance with a promptitude and apparent discipline that no regular troops could exceed.[5]

Unsurprisingly, those who acted for the authorities or who were presumed to be providing information to them also came under attack. Shots were fired at Allun Edwards of Huddersfield, who 'rendered himself obnoxious to the incendiaries by the vigilant discharge of his duty' as constable of the watch. The colonel in charge of troops in Leeds was also targeted by the Luddites for assassination.[6] The West Riding magistrates agreed unanimously on 11 July to begin hunting for caches of arms and to ensure that the 'the system destroyed & the robbers delivered over', and sought powers to make the nighttime meetings that had characterised working-class resistance to the state to be made illegal.[7] Spies were deployed in an effort to break the Luddites:

> Sheffield July 11th 1812
> My Lord,
> Since I had the honor to address your Lordship on the alarming spirit which still seems to exist in this prt of the Country, I have again seen the person who gave me the information I then forwarded to your Lordship. At my request he has of late mix'd frequently with the Luddites, and by an appearance of zeal in their cause has so far gain'd their confidence, as to be elected a Committeeman — It is probable, he will in that capacity become acquainted with their most secret plans; and he is desirous of introducing some intelligent man to their assemblies, who may assist him in their detection — If therefore your Lordship should think proper to order a Police Officer in disguise, (for it must be a stranger) to be sent down for the purpose; I have no doubt great use might be made of this person in apprehending those most active at the nocturnal meetings

which are held in the neighbourhood of Barnsley, and lead to a full discovery of their plot.—

This person has given me various information respecting individuals but which it would be an unnecessary waste of your Lordship's time in me to recapitulate.[8]

Two days later, on 13 July, at Rastrick, near Brighouse, it was reported that, on 12 August:

the night on which an attack was made at Clifton, one shot was fire thru the door of a public house, and [illegible] thru the door of a warehouse. The windows of Mr [illegible] have all been shot thru. Guns have been frequently heard in the immediate [illegible] at different parts of the night supposed by the inhabitants tho' to be signals. Mr Greenwood warehouse was in June last robbed of arms, stated that his neighbours opened their door, and closed them again without searching him any afterance [?]. A sword taken from Mr Greenwood was found the next morning in a hedge near Elland.[9]

In the early hours of Tuesday, 14 July 1812, a group of up to thirty Luddites conducted a number of raids for arms in the village of Clifton in West Yorkshire. The raid was particularly audacious, as Clifton was the home of Sir George Armytage. The Luddites chose to start their raids at one of the ends of the village, at the home of Abraham Fairburn, a cardmaker. The attack was delayed because:

having lost the hammer they had previously provided, they furnish themselves with another, which they had burst open a Smith's shop to procure. They assault the door of Mr. Ab. Fairburn, near one end of the village—demand his gun—Mr. F. denies the possession of such an article (it belong to his son)—they persist in their demand, repeatedly assuring him, that they certainly know he has a gun. Mr. F. continues steady—they call for enoch (the great hammer.) The door is assaulted by two violent strokes, (the marks of which are visible enough) Mr. F. opens the door; a number of men present themselves before him, apparently armed with guns, in the military attitude of 'making ready'. Mr. F. still declines to deliver up his son's piece; invites the robbers to search his house for a gun themselves.

They become impatient, one of them presents a piece to his head protesting that if he, Mr F did not instantly produces gun, his brains blown out. — Mr F retires, they charge him to bring no light. He resigns the gun. They load it, bidding good night, and, having fired a piece as in triumph, offer a single, retire.[10]

The home of cardmaker John Wilkinson was also attacked. Wilkinson was ordered to hand over his guns or 'they would blow his brains out they immediately called for Enoch, told him to strike, which one of them did & broke the door open'. The mob rushed inside, and Wilkinson handed over his six firearms.[11]

The Luddites next appeared at the home of Joshua Goldthorpe, another cardmaker. Joshua Goldthorpe senior was in bed, and was woken by shouting and banging on his front door. He got out of bed, went to his window, pulled the curtain and shouted, 'What do you want?' He peered out to see fourteen or fifteen guns pointing up at him. The assembled men outside his house demanded that he was to hand over any guns he had on the property; Goldthorpe said he hadn't any in the house, and shouted for his family. The men outside levelled more threats that if 'he did not put up his stash they would blow his brains out'. Joshua senior went back to the window but was warned that if he looked out again, 'they would blow his brains out', and followed this up with a shot in the air.[12] Undeterred:

> Mr. G. called up his young men, one or two of whom despising their threats, boldly went out, and bid them blow away. They presented their guns and threatened instant death to young Goldthorpe if he did not directly proceed with them to the workshop, at about a quarter of a mile distance, and get them the guns which they knew were in the shop. They guarded him to the shop, received two guns, returned with him to the house, ordered him to bolt the door and keep within, and wished him good night.[13]

When the Luddites returned, they noticed a light at the nearby Black Bull Inn, which caused some alarm.

At the Black Bull Inn, the publican, George Pratt:

> was alarmed in bed by a great noise at the door of his house when he got up and went down stairs into the parlour, a number of persons outside of the door called out 'put that light out'. In his sworn statement Pratt tell us that Luddites then called of him to the door and said to him to deliver your guns.

Pratt notes that he had left a candle burning inside and went to snuff it out. Returning, the voices demanded his gun. Pratt protested that he was not dressed and he could not see in the dark. A voice said, 'No clothes, no light, fetch your gun.' Pratt complied, and opening the front door was ordered to deliver the gun up to the men butt end first. One of the men said that he would get it back and Pratt asked, 'When?'

The reply came, 'Very soon.' After wishing him goodnight, one of the men went to the window of the parlour, where Pratt's wife and child were, and asked them if they were alright, apologising for the shots fired earlier.[14]

On the same evening, the Luddites raided the homes of William Earnshaw and Crispin Wilkinson in a similar manner, procuring a gun from each of them. The Luddites also appeared at the home of William Armitage, another cardmaker. Armitage told them his gun was in his workshop, and the Luddites went with him to fetch it. It seems the Luddites knew Armitage had two guns, which Armitage reports startled him, and in his sworn testimony, stated one firearm belonged to his uncle and noted that the Luddites had returned it. He continued that he was ordered back into his house and one of the Luddites asked him if he had got the Enoch and the gun that had been found nearby recently. He said he had not, and the men wished him goodnight and left.[15]

In Leeds, Luddites broke into the premises of Fretwell and Cockshott by dismantling part of the roof and 'proceeded to a small barrel, containing about 14 pounds of gun-powder, wrapped up pound papers, which they took and got clear away with'. Yet the Luddites were not getting away undetected by the Crown. The Reverend Dr Martin Naylor gleefully reported through his newspaper that Abraham Armitage, Robert Filton, George Beaumont, Benjamin Chadwick, John Taylor and Benjamin Hinchliffe had been found guilty of breaking and entry, Samuel Haigh was found guilty of conducting arms raids and George Brookes was charged with assaulting an excise officer. Sadly, the Reverend lamented that Luddites had stolen three firearms in Clifton, and:

> in consequence of a rumour that arms were concealed under the floor of the gallery of the Methodist chapel at Nether Thong, formerly used for the depositing of brushes &c, but lately disused, a part of civil officers aided by some military, went and searched the place.

Five men were arrested and taken before Magistrate Radcliffe. Amongst the witnesses against the men 'were Mr Parkin of Thong, late a preacher amongst the Methodists and Miss Woodhead of Hay, near the same place, whose father at present officiates as a Methodist preacher'. Due to lack of evidence, the men were released.[16] We wonder if the arrested men attended the chapel? Did they really hide stolen firearms in the chapel? Perhaps so, as it would probably be the last place the authorities would search. We know many Luddites were

Methodists, so hiding the stolen firearms in your place of worship could have made a lot of sense to them.

Magistrate Walker informed Fitzwilliam on 18 July that that 'lights continue to be seen on the hills which seem answered by opposite ones in various directions three or four nights in a week from Dewsbury towards Bradford, Halifax & Huddersfield'.[17]

Days later, an anonymous report was delivered to Fitzwilliam – likely from 'Citizen Bent' – by a government spy, who reported:

> the gentlemen at Manchester hold meetings for the district that there is a considerable fund and many depots for pikes ... all information is conveyed from town to town by the delegates who are allowed 5/ or 5/6 per day and coach hire if necessary ... the Union extends from London to Nottingham and from thence to Manchester and Carlisle .... only some of the trades have taken the first oath.[18]

The same day, Major General Maitland reported to the Home Office:

> that Boxes of Pikes are frequently imported from Birmingham into Yorkshire and there concealed: It is further, stated they are completely prepared with quantities of Crow feet to impede the Action of Cavalry, and that is generally stated that their numbers are extremely great, and that they have communication with Scotland: A number of Delegates too, are represented to have gone into Yorkshire to meet a Congress.[19]

However, in contradiction to Maitland, Earl Fitzwilliam reported to the Home Office that:

> having yesterday had occasion to converse with different persons, I have the satisfaction of reporting that I am very confident the country is not in that alarming state it has been supposed to be. That there is combinations for mischievous purposes, there can be no doubt: most recent events corroborate that belief – the sweeping off every gun at Clifton proves a system of enquiry, and means of information: the manner in which the business was done, proves also a great degree of tactic in execution: but it goes no further than in the execution of robbery: it shews no symptom of preparation for resisting men in arms, military bodies – the very means they seem desirous of obtaining, that is guns, will never render them formidable against firelocks .... Though no resistance was made to them at Clifton, though every inhabitant yielded instant obedience to the demand of his gun, they fired into several houses. Again a party of them passing lately late at night through a village, upon a man saying they were Luddites, instantly a ball was fired at his head.[20]

He added:

> the reports of nocturnal training and drilling, when one comes to close quarters on the subject, and to enquire for evidence of fact, dwindles down to nothing; they are the offspring of fear, quite imaginary, and mere invention.
>
> I do not mean to say, that parties of Luddites have not been met travelling from place to place, and perhaps marshalled in some degree of order, but that there is no evidence whatever, that any one person has yet established the fact of their having been assembled and drilling in a military way – as far as negative evidence can go, I think, the contrary seems established.[21]

As an afterthought, he added:

> Nevertheless combination indisputably exists, very formidable to property and persons: most probably entered into originally for the destruction of that species of property, machinery in manufacture, and afterwards directed against the persons of the proprietors of that species of property as one means of its destruction, through the medium of intimidation. This is a very serious evil.[22]

Writing from his home at Lupset, near Wakefield, Matthew Tomlinson tells us:

> we are now [illegible] more peaceable concerning the plundering business; the soldiers seem to over awe the villains; the last week many have been taken into custody, two Bow Street Officers were from London in disguise and went amongst the people as Hawkers of Muslin and became acquainted with the Luddites; were sworn in and got to know who many of the way and where their arms were concealed and then got them secured by pickets of our soldiers; and I hope will break their confidence.[23]

Tomlinson was sadly mistaken. About 11.30 p.m. on Wednesday, 23 July 1812:

> Hinchcliff, was taken from his bed and compelled to accompany a party of these ruffians, who said they should take him to some particular place they mentioned; but on a horse being heard in the rear of them, they made off: but not without firing at Hinchcliff, by which some shots were lodged in one of his eyes, which occasioned its loss, and otherwise much injured his head.[24]

John Hinchcliffe was a professional singer and the parish clerk of Holmfirth, and was in business as a clothier. His sworn statement tells us he had been approached in May by John Schofield, a cropper, who had offered to 'twist him in' since the Luddites needed more men in the Holmfirth area to rise and overturn the government, and had informed the Reverend Keeling, the parish priest, who in turn had passed the intelligence to the parish constable, John Blythe. In consequence of the arrest of Schofield, Hinchcliffe tells us he had been woken from his bed by intruders who believed he had given evidence against the Luddites, who stated, 'You've been giving information against someone at Thong!'[25]

General Maitland proposed 'shock and awe' tactics to subdue the West Riding. 'My own feeling upon this subject is, that it will be advisable unless it assumes a very different appearance, to add considerably to the number of Troops in the West Riding.' He continued:

> by increasing the number of Troops we adopt the only measure that will give additional confidence to the Magistracy and Peace Officers, without which we can never expect tranquility.
>
> By employing Officers of High Rank, I have no hesitation in stating to Your Lordship, we take the best means of inducing the Magistrates to be more active, than they otherwise would, and with the two Measures combined, I have not a doubt, we will in a very short time, get the West Riding into a similar State of tranquility with the other disturbed parts of the Country.[26]

Chapter 18

LADY LUDD

In order to ascertain the true scale of Luddism, Wakefield magistrates the Reverend William Wood, John Naylor and Colonel Smithson began an information-gathering exercise. In Horbury, they did not think any inhabitants were suspected of Luddism, but special constables reported the village included many men of bad character. The special constables had learned that two public houses at Horbury Bridge were suspected of entertaining Luddites, that at Thornhill, nocturnal secret meetings had taken place, and arms had been seized and 'outrages committed'. At nearby Shitlington the constables reported again that Horbury Bridge was a place of meeting for the Luddites, and that the Luddites had crossed the river Calder on three ferry boats at night to commit arms raids. The Reverend Wood suggested that a military guard should be placed at Horbury Bridge, the ferry boats prevented from operating at night, and lamps lit, to stop communication across the river Calder.[1]

Tensions were still high in August. Luddism was not yet quite silent. Despite the abundant harvests that had been reported by the press, the price of corn in the West Riding remained high.

What had been a hot dry summer now turned very wet indeed, as diarist Tomlinson tells us in his entry for 2 August:

> We have had another rainy [illegible] week, not one day without rain. It has often agitated and perplexed me muchly when the mornings appeared promising we shook out the hay, and laid it broad upon the widening lawn; perhaps before we had accomplished our intention, the clouds gathered round us, the misty dew drops descended and put us in redoubled motion to do what we had undone before the broad bright drops incessant follow from their black abodes.[2]

Unable to dry hay would result in a lack of forage for animal feed over the winter. A wet harvest meant it was far more difficult to thresh the barley and wheat. It meant less bread, it meant higher food prices. It meant poverty and starvation for the poor.

Somewhere between the hours of midnight and 1 a.m. on Sunday, 2 August, the home of Edward Wright of Armley, near Leeds, was raided by Luddites. They were looking for arms. The Luddites told Wright that General Ludd had sent them for his musket, which Wright duly handed over. The Luddites also told Wright that they knew where to find all the arms in the village and were in consequence determined to collect them before the constables took possession. When the Luddites left Wright's house, they fired six or seven shots in celebration. Yet no other arms were taken from Armley. The raid on Wright's house was all the more audacious as a party of troops was stationed nearby guarding a gig-mill from an attack by Luddites.[3] Perhaps this explains why only one house was looted for arms.

The bad weather continued from July into August; 'there was not one fine day all last week,' Tomlinson wrote on 9 August. 'We have had 3 weeks of unsettled weather and scarcely one fine day,' noting, 'I certainly have fared very badly, some of my good neighbours have had some of their fodder totally failed.' He concluded:

> a famine must be unavoidable I'm sure, wheat the stuff of life has been very dear a long time and still continues to advance. Last Friday it sold in Wakefield market at £3 15s. per bushel! How is the labouring man to get bread?[4]

By the middle weeks of August, Magistrate Radcliffe reported: 'there is scarcely a night I do not hear of robbery's for arms, Lead, Gun powder, or money.'[5] Earl Fitzwilliam informed General Maitland that all the firearms in Rastrick had been taken, and the perpetrators had fired indiscriminately into numerous houses in the village who were 'very limited in numbers, but exceedingly wicked & attempting by violence (it being their only means) to present resistance to the authority'.[6] A shearing frame was broken in a mill near Rastrick on 16–17 August and a house attacked nearby, with Luddites searching for arms.[7]

With a bad harvest looming, famine seemed certain, and as the price of wheat rose, food riots broke out, as Tomlinson tells us, because 'bread which is now intolerably dear' was beyond the means of the working class.[8] Rioting broke out again on Tuesday, 18 August 1812, when 'Lady Ludd' led the protesters in Leeds. The property of a miller at Holbeck called Shackleton was attacked – windows were broken and the damage was later estimated at between £30 and £40. At Armley, on 19 August, a crowd threatened to storm the premises of a meal seller when he produced a gun loaded with shot and discharged it into the crowd. The reaction of the crowd and the resulting casualties go unrecorded. At Sheffield, similar disturbances took place the same day, as well as the following day: flour dealers were compelled to sell their stock for 3 shillings per stone, and oatmeal proportionally similar. The *Leeds Mercury* described the mob as being 'principally led on by women'. The same day, constables made twenty arrests during a similar riot in Sheffield.[9] Lady Ludd was in Leeds a few days later, on 20 August, and led a mob who seized potatoes in the market place, and shopkeepers were ordered to lower their prices. In Sheffield, fearful of what may follow, the local bourgeoisie organised a meeting at the Cutlers' Hall to arrange a subscription to relieve distress to those not already on Parish Relief. £700 was subscribed by the meeting. The *Leeds Mercury* said: 'The town is in much confusion, none knowing to what lengths these acts of insubordination, once begun may be carried.'[10] The solution for General Maitland was simple:

> I have no difficulty in saying, that I believe the only Thing that will give Security to this part of the Country in the long Nights that are approaching, will be, a most Active Use of the Troops, under proper Police Officers, for the Period we have antecedent to the Setting in of Winter.[11]

The scale of the threat was made clear when Thomas Broughton, a weaver from Barnsley, was interrogated and admitted that:

> there are about 200 persons twisted in in Barnsley ... the Committee at Barnsley do not admit Irishmen to be twisted in, for fear that they should betray the society ... last Monday morning at Barnsley, he heard a person, whose name he does not know, but whom he understood to come from Sheffield, declare to Joseph Isaacs, that there were 8,000 men nearly complete in arms, in and about Sheffield, and would be in a few days, and therefore they did not mind the soldiers – though they once thought the South Devon were good fellows, but now they thought them worse than the Huzzars. That since he has been upon the secret committee, the informant has been told by his fellow committee men, that delegates had been at Barnsley, from Manchester, and Stockport, (but he was not present), whose business it was, to collect numbers, and other information. That one Haigh now in York Castle for administering unlawful oaths, told the informant that there were 450 Luddites twisted in, at Holmfirth; the greater part of the neighbourhood of Huddersfield,

and a great number at Halifax, and that they met there as Dissenters under the cloak of religion, and also 7,000 or 8,000 in Leeds. The informant saith that a very great number of Luddites are local militia men. That the Luddites have in view ultimately to overturn the system of government, by revolutionising the country. That certain delegates at Ashton under Lyne, on the 4th of August inst. told the informant that the first measure to be adopted in bringing about a revolution, would be to send parties to the different houses of the members of both Houses of Parliament, and destroy them, and then the people in London belonging to that Society, would seize upon the Government. That the committee at Barnsley, and the informant for himself, thinks, and believes, that in case a revolution should take place, Sir Francis Burdett and Major Cartwright would join them. That James Haigh of Dukinfield, near Ashton, told the informant that there were persons of property concerned in the disturbances who did not actively appear, but who wrote orders and had them put under the doors of delegates. That voluntary contributions are collected from those who are twisted in from 1*d*. per head, to 1/- a week; and that the informant has received from the committee at Barnsley 10*s*. 10*d*. for going journies. That the Luddites at Barnsley have no arms, but believe when a rupture takes place, that they can seize the arms of the military unawares, viz. before they have time to collect them.[12]

The observations are important. They confirm wider links to Manchester and Stockport radicals – no doubt Colonel Hanson – and imply that Luddites had military experience in the Local Militia, and there was a secret underground army ready to topple the government. The Luddites were in essence the United Englishmen reborn. Indeed, one Luddite stated that Irishmen were not to be twisted in because the Irish had given away the secret: surely, this is a reference to the Despard conspiracy and the activities of William Putnam McCabe, as we explored in our companion volume, *Fighting Napoleon at Home*? The reference to religion makes us also think of the New Jerusalem and Ezekielite sects of the 1795–1805 period, or perhaps even to Unitarians. The reference to reformist politics is important, as it links Luddism with the reformist agenda then being pushed by Major Cartwright.

Harvest began in the middle of August but continuing bad weather impeded it. Tomlinson writes, on 27 August:

> the last week was not very favourable for harvest week, how ever we have done our best: my corn is not yet all cut … the police about this time are very active in taking the Luddites: one man was turned informer of the whole band of robbers who were all confederates in the late infernal

practice of plundering honest men's houses ... some of them are taken and committed to prison, others have fled their neighbourhood and left their families; heavens, I hope upon the whole that the practice is stopped for a season; I am quite of the opinion that if Government had not took it under hand, there would have scarcely been one householder who was passed over.[13]

J.A. Stuart Wortley, at the end of August, feared a bad harvest and war with America would trigger a new round of insurgency.[14] General Maitland wrote from Wakefield:

> I find it is their united Opinion, that the late occurrences at Sheffield, entirely arise from the high Price of Flour, & in this Opinion I am not only inclined to concur, but I own, I think this kind of tumultuous Proceeding is so far salutary, that it completely explains its Object, and End, and naturally leads one to suppose, there is nothing beyond what shews itself.
>
> On my arrival here last night, I understood there had been some symptoms of the same Spirit shewn here, & in seeing this Morning Coll. Campbell from Leeds, I have received from him a Report, of similar Proceedings having taken place there: All this however is in itself nothing, & it must be acknowledged, the Price of which the People complain, is unaccountably high, and I understand too, from every Enquiry, infinitely higher than in London.
>
> The unfortunate circumstance that took place in Sheffield of their not suffering Voluntarily, but tolerating without proceeding to Extremity the Sale of Flour at Three shillings, instead of Seven Shillings, has led considerably I believe to the appearances of Tumult at Leeds, and some trifling symptoms of it here: But all these have no relation to, or connexion with the System that is alone dangerous here 'To Wit', that of Secret Meetings, and treasonable Oaths.
>
> A Relief from the immediate high Price, will set all this to rest, and I should apprehend that Relief, is nearly at hand, for the Price of Wheat fell considerably in the Market here yesterday, though the Price of Flour kept up, and if I am not grossly misinformed, there was too yesterday a small Importation of Wheat from London, which in itself must produce an immediate fall.[15]

Maitland was correct in his assessment: starving people with little or nothing to lose were willing to risk it all for food, and found succour in the militant aims of the Luddites to overturn the Crown and existing government, which they blamed for the famine. Making matters worse, unseasonal heavy rain impeded the harvest.[16]

Magistrate Busfield reported that threats had been made to destroy all the standing corn at Heaton, and lamented that all the corn around Cleckheaton had already been burned, but reported he had 'no reason to suppose the evil is increasing in our district'.[17]

Busfield was wrong. Another new wave of arms raids and machine breaking was beginning.

In the early hours of Saturday, 22 August 1812, at least fifty armed men arrived at the house of Edward Hepworth, a farmer from Sheepridge. The group broke into the house and demanded he lower the price of the milk he sold and also to hand over any firearms he possessed. Hepworth replied he had no firearms: the Luddites disbelieved him, ransacked the house, destroying furniture including a valuable clock, and on finding no firearms, promptly left.[18] During the night of Saturday, 29 August 1812, the house of a man called Haigh at Skircoat, near Halifax, was visited by a group of Luddite arms raiders who took three weapons from him.[19]

Two days later, between 11 p.m. and midnight in the evening of Monday, 31 August, Luddites launched arm raids at Brighouse in the West Riding. Simultaneously at Thornhill, near Dewsbury, three houses were raided for arms by forty Luddites, and four guns taken away. The following day, about 2 a.m., shots from a blunderbuss and other weapons were fired into the home of a Mr Waddington, a corn miller living in Brighouse. Seven bullets were found lodged in his bedroom ceiling, with a musket having been discharged into his parlour. The Luddites had managed to avoid a patrol of soldiers that had just passed by.[20]

In retaliation, the Crown stepped up its efforts to eradicate the Luddite threat.[21] The goal of the Crown was to strike fear and terror into the Luddites through a show of strength:

> The numbers that have come in have been induced by Fear, and Fear alone, in fact whenever we seized any of their Heads that moment they begin to come in, and not till then, and of this I have the most clear and distinct Proof. It is very difficult to get at them from the Magistrates' Clerks, but the return of those coming in, who have already been sworn is fast increasing, in fact, in that part of the Country where there has been real Military Exertion the Thing is over, and if we can set it agoing here in the same Way we will soon get rid of it.
>
> Upon this Head I am happy to tell you that I think tomorrow or next day we will be able to commence at Barnsley, and I have at present great hopes we shall be able to lay hold of at least 6 or 8 of the Ringleaders, if we succeed in this, it will be a great Thing.[22]

Maitland sent out 'flying columns' to arrest suspect Luddites, who were held on no charge. So successful were the tactics, that barely a week later, at the start of September, Maitland was able to report:

> I went to Sheffield as I stated, and yesterday Morning four Men composing a Secret Committee at Barnsley, were seized by Warrant from the Magistrates of Sheffield, they were examined by Stuart Wortley, and committed to Sheffield, for further examination on Friday. He believes the truth of the original information which will attach capitally to two of them, I think it is the strongest I have seen, but what I want to see, is the effect it has in bringing in others, on this I shall be able to inform you in a day or two.—
>
> I am sorry to say at Huddersfield and in its Neighbourhood, there are still some instances of Nocturnal Plunder, particularly in the Arm Ways and that we get on very slow indeed for want of Information, a short time I hope will however let us into it, as we have got a good number of People now at Work.[23]

The Luddites would not be so easily cowed.

Some time on the evening of Thursday, 3 September 1812, the home of Mr Preston at Greenroyd, near Halifax, was raided by a party of between twelve and fifteen Luddites in search of arms. The Luddites demanded Preston's pistols: he protested that he had none, and offered them another type of gun instead. Preston tried to engage the Luddites in conversation, but they refused and left, telling him to lock up his home.[24] At Southowram, near Halifax, a mill containing gig-mills was burned down. In a simultaneous raid, the woollen manufactory of Messrs Richard Lindsey and Sons, Old Hall, Gildersome, was attacked. In a raid lasting little more than twelve minutes, seventeen shearing frames were destroyed and the machinery used for raising and dressing the cloth was 'greatly injured'.[25] Lindsey himself reported:

> I was awakened this morning about one O'clock by a dreadful noise has if a number of men were breaking into our premises but on looking out of the window I was convinced the Luddites were come upon us has I soon heard them very distinctly breaking the Shears and in about ten or fifteen minutes all were again silent I heard no shouting or firing of guns whatever consequently I concluded they were but few in number I soon got a light and walked out into the Mill and found our Shears and dressing Machinery very much broken apparently with hammers and pickaxes—we are now almost at a loss what to do as there are no Soldiers in this neighbourhood and it appears evident that nothing but force of arms will secure our property.[26]

A new wave of machine breaking appeared imminent. Indeed, a spy reported:

> The first attempt that it is now to be made is to [divert] of the Soldiers by false Alarms, until they can accomplish the destruction of Bradley Mills, & an old Soldier has Volunteer'd to blow them up with powder. They are only waiting for an opportunity to destroy the owner of the Mills, as also justice Ratcliffe. There have several places where they have a considerable quantity of arms & ammunition, & the Two men I have employ'd are in full expectation of seeing where they are concealed in a short time.
>
> The Luddites have met 5 or 6 times within these 14 days at a place about 2 Miles out of the Town [west] of Huddersfield at a place called Dungeon Wood at the foot of Taylor's hill—a meeting took place on Crosland Moor on Monday last to consult about some of their Society that had been taken up—
>
> These are the principal parts of the information obtain'd at present.
>
> An agent from Glasgow came down to Huddersfield about Ten days ago, & put up at the Packhorse. The people at Huddersfield would not receive him as he had not he is proper credentials, he staid 'till he sent a Glasgow for them (their own letters) he is now gone back—
>
> Disturbances to break out at Wakefield very soon.[27]

Despite the attack in Gildersome, Hugh Parker, the Sheffield magistrate, wrote to the Home Office that his district was quiet and he had no cause to put the Wath Wood and Rotherham troops of Yeomanry on standby. However, he did inform the Home Office that property was still being attacked in the West Riding, and added, with much self-promotion – he seems to have taken much pride in this – he at the head of a troop of cavalry had rounded up a party of twenty-two suspected Luddites and food protestors.[28]

Two days later, a spy reported to Fitzwilliam:

> abt 8 o'clock he heard several person in the Ship in Waterlane Sheffield talking abt purchasing all the powder in Sheffield. To send it to the neighbourhood of Huddersfield – these people said they were short of nothing but powder – they did not appear residents of Sheffield but strangers, hawkers &c.[29]

The magistrates met in Wakefield at the start of September, and felt confident that they were gaining the upper hand. The offer of pardon to all Luddites who took the Oath of Allegiance, they felt, had fatally undermined the Luddite cause. Maitland reported that 600 Luddites in Stockport had taken the Oath of Allegiance and hoped that with a strong military presence that a similar success could be achieved in Sheffield and Barnsley, amongst other places.[30] Writing from Wakefield, General Maitland remarked:

> I attended at a Meeting of the Lieutenancy yesterday, when they came to the Resolution, of enforcing the Ward and Watch Bill, where Voluntary Associations had not taken place, and this Measure is to be finally adopted Wednesday Sen' night at a Special Meeting to be called for the purpose.
>
> Several instances of the old System, of taking Arms, and destroying Machinery, have taken place within the last fortnight, and what makes this truly alarming is, that such is the State of Fear in the Country, that the People will not only, not come in, and tell, but even when you send to them they are afraid to state what has passed.—
>
> I cannot flatter you, with stating that I think the evil Spirit here is broke in upon in the smallest Degree, and an universal system of Terror prevails with regard to the result of the Long Nights, set originally agoing and sedulously supported by the Threats, and the Boasts, of the disaffected, of what they will then accomplish.—
>
> I have now got Parties out, all over the Country, but the result of this will not be known, or felt, for at least a time, no pains however shall be omitted on my part, in endeavouring to get rid of it.[31]

The same day that Maitland was flattering himself that the magistrates and the Crown were winning back control of the West Riding, a food riot broke out in Sheffield:

> On Tuesday morning the scenes of tumult were renewed with increased violence: carts loaded with potatoes were stopped in the streets and sold at reduced prices: a corn warehouse was attacked with great fury, as well as many bakers' shops, without any mischief being done, except the breaking of windows, and some other trifling affairs. What added to the tumult was, the bread served out to the soldiers was found to be short of weight; and many of them were, on Monday, seen active in the mob. A peace officer and a party of the West Kent Militia are now stationed in every house or warehouse considered in danger, while parties of Light Dragoons constantly parade the streets.[32]

The same day as the food riots, Francis Raynes, whose tactics were to send out flying columns of heavily armed men to isolated cottages houses to apprehend Luddites, which had been so successful in Lancashire, arrived in Wakefield. Part of the responsibilities of the troops garrisoned in the West Riding was:

to enforce the shutting up of the public houses at nine o'clock, and to see that no person remained there after that time. Too often were these houses made the place of resort of the Luddites, for the purpose of conducting their illegal plans; consequently, our appearance was not very agreeable to the landlords, and we frequently received much abusive language from them, which obliged me to make formal complaint to the magistrates, who generally punished them by suspending their licenses.[33]

As could be expected, the soldiers were hated by the working class of the West Riding for their actions in rounding up kith and kin and also for those who gave evidence against them, one being the Reverend Hammond Roberson, vicar of Liversedge, as Captain Raynes remarked: 'The People are violently enraged at us and swear vengeance against Robinson, and Ashworth, for giving information,' and added, 'the People exclaim against Soldiers going about, such a secret manner but say they will soon put a stop to it.'[34] Captain Raynes reported: 'In compliance with his Orders, I have sent the following Officers with Detachments from the West Suffolk and Stirlingshire to proceed by Rout and carry into effect the Instructions I had the Honor to receive.' He further transmitted intelligence that he had uncovered a plot to blow up Rawfolds Mill:

> A man of the name of Starkey of Mill bridge got acquainted with George Ashworth & James Robinson, he proposed to them a plan of blowing up Mr. Cartwrights Mill and took them down to the spot where they mean to commence their operations, he also shewd them some Houses where there are Arms, and wish'd they would engage with him to take them in consiquence of Starkey discovering Robinson and Ashworth I made known circumstance to Sir George Armytage. Sir George has examined Robinson and Ashworth, and issued a Warrant to apprehend Starkey. My Party with a Constable will secure him this night if possible, he will appear before Mr. Radcliffe tomorrow with the two evidences. They are a very turbulent set here, and speak their sentiments freely, even before the Soldiers. In all the Towns I since visited they have neither Associations, or Watch and Ward; I shall have the Honor Sir, of sending a Report of every Township, as soon as I have made the necessary enquiries. Sir George Armytage has beg'd I will always apply to him when I have occasion.[35]

Francis Raynes' flying columns of infantry and cavalry were backed by a citizens' militia or Armed Association, in imitation of those formed in 1798. The Militia and regular cavalry, supported by the Armed Associations, replicated the Luddite tactics of midnight surprise attacks on isolated houses and villages. So successful was Raynes' operation that on the 14th, John Lloyd, a solicitor from Stockport, reported:

> a man was taken up by patrol at Flockton for merely being found out of his House at an unreasonable hour — but as it was known he had been in the Company of a person of bad character Capt. Thornhill & myself went over to examine him – the result of which fixed some suspicion on this Companion & we examined him to good effect also — for he gave such Information as was sufficient to obtain a Warrant against two men the one for Burglary (in pursuit of the Ludding system) and the other for inciting the Informant to join in Burglary These men were taken before the Justice and the one of them *Earl Parkin guilty of the lesser offence impeached many others of capital offences 3 of whom had been taken and are this day committed to York and others are in custody here for further Examination.
>
> On Friday night Capt. Thornhill & myself set off to Halifax with 6 or 7 warrants agt persons charged with administering & aiding and assisting in administering an unlawful oath and with having stolen lead to make bullets for their use as Luddites—The warrants were agt 6 persons all of whom we succeeded in taking during the night, and sent them to Huddersfield from which they have been this day committed (all six) to York. The Exams are not by any means complete but as soon as taken shall be transmitted. It was my wish to have this done prior to commits taking place, but I was absent, and the Justice was satisfied of their guilt—and therefore committed them. I do hope we have been making a series impression, such as may induce a material change in the disposition of the people—Several have been taken up for words—I wish we could get at the knowledge of their deeds—A man of the name of James Starkie has been committed to York for endeavoring to incite two persons to felonious outrages & not being able to get bail was committed to York.[36]

The following day, John Allison, a solicitor in Huddersfield, informed Viscount Sidmouth that Magistrate Radcliffe had committed to gaol 'John Baines Senior John Baines Junr. Zachariah Baines George Duckworth Charles Milnes alias Gledhill & William Blakebrough all of Halifax' for illegal oath making, as well as three men for arms raids.[37]

Despite the arrests, at Sowerby on the 19th, William Barker, a tax collector, was the attention of Luddite arms raiders. They Luddites took away two firearms, ransacked his home and destroyed furniture. The men also made a pile on the floor from some of Barker's clothing and set it on fire, and stole £20 in Halifax bank notes and valuables such as silver plate.[38]

At the end of the month, Michael Hoyle, who lived at Rishworth, reported to the authorities that his home had been raided by

Luddites looking for arms. Sometime on the evening of Monday, 28 September, he tells us, the assailants arrived at his house and demanded entry otherwise they would break the door down. Hoyle admitted them to his house and noted that they were armed with blunderbusses. They demanded the shotgun he had hung over his fireplace, and after further threats, Hoyle gave the Luddites £40 in Bank of England notes and they took a silver watch of his from a drawer.[39]

As October began, arms raids continued: the Luddites were not yet defeated. Sometime between 2 and 3 a.m. on Monday, 5 October 1812, Luddites raided the home of a clothier, Benjamin Strickland, who lived in Kirkheaton. Strickland recalled that he was woken by banging on his front door and voices demanding entry, threatening to break the door open. In his sworn disposition, Strickland states that he heard someone calling out for 'Enoch'; in response he got up quickly and went to open the door. Upon doing so, three disguised men rushed into the house, and a fourth demanded he hand over any firearms he had on the premises. Strickland told the Luddites that his gun had been sent to the guardhouse and one of the men replied, 'Then we must have your money,' pushing a pistol into his chest. Someone called to others apparently outside: 'Number 13, come and plunder the house.' Strickland didn't hesitate and gave the men keys to his desk – upon which one of the Luddites unlocked his desk and took out thirty to forty shillings in silver and copper coins. The men demanded his silver pocket watch, which he handed over.[40]

Another raid took place two days later. Fifteen armed men assembled at Long Can, near Ovenden, and entered two houses, taking away in total £30. The same group – who were organised on military lines command by a sergeant – raided the home of John Ramsden and took away a double-barrelled shotgun, silver items and cash (sixty-four half guinea gold coins and £28 in notes) to the total value of £130. The same night, a raid took place by a smaller group on the home of Mr Greenwood; they took away a £1 note, silver cutlery and a damaged firearm, which the Luddites returned![41]

Luddism was not yet dead: these were the dying embers.

Days later, sometime before 9 p.m. on Sunday, 11 October, John Briggs, the miller at Balm Mill near Cleckheaton, found he was the attention of Luddites. Briggs was not at home, but his brother was. Three men demanded that he hand over any firearms that were in the house: Briggs being unable to provide a firearm, the Luddites robbed the house, obtaining sixty-three guineas in gold, and £10 in silver coins. Other property to the value of £80–90 was also taken.[42]

By the end of the month, Earl Fitzwilliam was concerned that the dark nights would afford further opportunities for machine breaking, and believed, contrary to General Maitland's confident assertions to Viscount Sidmouth that Luddism was a spent force, that 'the whole band of Luddites of our riding have escaped untouch'd; their system of Oaths & Terror apparently renders them intangible; an appearance much to be lamented.'[43] On 31 October, a solicitor in Huddersfield informed General Acland:

> Eight were committed last night and are gone off to York this morning — Three will be remanded for further Examination — and two more are taken up — Two have fled & I think they are gone to Dublin — Can you Sir or General Maitland assist me in having sought for and secured in Dublin, or must I send to Government?

We wonder if these men fleeing to Dublin were connected to the Ribbonmen.[44]

Chapter 19

DEATH AND BURIAL

By the middle weeks of November, Luddism was over. Why? Partly because of the famine, partly because of the bad weather and, as General Maitland put it succulently, 'It is through Fear I sincerely believe many were induced to take these Oaths, and it is by Fear, we will alone get them to come back.'[1] He noted to Viscount Sidmouth:

> I have seen and conversed with all the Agents whether Civil or Military, employed in the worst Parts of the Country, and they are perfectly unanimous in their Sentiments that confidence is reestablished on the part of the Loyal and that despondency is the prevailing principle among the Disaffected.
>
> The whole language of the Country is totally changed, and the Seditious have now the same dread of speaking to one another, that the Loyal formerly had of giving any Information … this Luddite System, as it is now breaking up here exactly as it broke up in Cheshire and Lancashire, when ever the Loyal found they were safe, and the Disaffected found they were in danger.[2]

He added quite correctly that Luddism was driven by famine, unemployment and endemic low wages:

> Had we been more fortunate in our Harvest, or had the American Ports been now open to us, I should not entertain a doubt that the whole of this unpleasant Scene was near a close, but undoubtedly so long as the Price of Manufacturing Labour is so low, and that of Provisions so high, we must still contemplate with a considerable degree of anxiety, to the result of the present Winter, and that I apprehend anything serious but the natural effect of such pressure must in prudence demand to be looked at with a cautious and jealous Eye.[3]

He concluded his letter:

> I think the Spirit of the late combinations will be completely broken. It will be necessary to be on our Guard all the Winter, but I am sure I do not go too far in stating distinctly to your Lordship that the whole of our Situation here is infinitely ameliorated.[4]

Playing the Luddites at their own game through fear, terror and intimidation was the order of the day. Captain Raynes reported that, thanks to his counter-terrorism raids, which owed a great deal to the Luddites' own tactics:

> I am happy to have it in my power to state, that a material alteration seems to be taking place amongst the people in the part of the Country where I am now stationed, for the reports made to me, and what I have myself observ'd of the turbulent spirit which so much prevailed on our first arrival, is greatly abated; the Public Houses are become tolerably orderly and the inhabitants in general are more inclined to be civil.[5]

Earl Fitzwilliam wrote to the Home Office that he considered Luddites to be terrorists:

> your Lordship is already apprized of the great number of Prisoners (nearly 50) in York Castle, on charges emanating from the combination & system, now commonly denominated Luddism: your Lordship is likewise aware what a great length of time, this description of crime has prevail'd, & gone uncheck'd, because unpunish'd. Not a week passes, but fresh instances of alarming outrage occur, committed by irresistible numbers, well arm'd, & organized under a system little short of military discipline. That this system should so long continue in such force & efficacy, must be imputed in a great degree to its having gone so long unpunish'd. This circumstance cannot fail to impress those engaged in the combination with a confidence in their own security under the system establish'd, affording thereby strong inducement to others to enlist into the Gang, whilst at the same time, it not only dumps all spirit of resistance in the peaceable Inhabitant, but it deters him from coming forward with evidence against the Criminals, which under present appearances he considers as unavailing for any good end, but as productive of increased danger to himself.
>
> These considerations have long made All, who are witnesses of what is passing, most anxious, that whenever any cases can be brought home against the persons charged, that they should be brought to trial as early as possible, every one considering the conviction of some of the Offenders, as positively necessary for the restoration of tranquillity in

> these parts, & for the safety of the peaceable Inhabitants—this is not the opinion of the last-mention'd description of person alone, but equally so the body of the Magistrates, & particularly of those most actively engaged in attempting to suppress this combination—I am empower'd to stick it likewise, as the decided opinion of Gen: Maitland, with whom I have most recently corresponded on this point, & who joins with the Magistrates in opinion, that it is most desirable that the Trial of these persons should not be delay'd a day, whenever any of them cannot be brought to conviction—
>
> Offenders under this system, may be class'd under four different heads— 1st Murderers & Terrorists — 2d — Destroyers of machinery — 3d Housebreakers for Arms, or mere plunder — 4th Twisters-in, or the administrators of Oaths—
>
> Under the first class, come the Murderers of Horsfall, against whom, I am given to understand, the evidence is most complete — likewise Schofield for attempting the life of Hinchliffe — evidence more doubtfull, but from what I have heard, likely to become much more strong, if confidence can be inspired into the witness.[6]

Eight men were in custody in September, and had been arrested by Magistrate Radcliffe for their involvement of the assassination of William Horsfall. General Maitland informed Earl Fitzwilliam that the evidence against the men was slight and he feared they stood 'little chance of being convicted'.[7] Viscount Sidmouth was conscious of the 'urgent expediency of accelerating as much as possible the trial of the prisoners' to make an example, and thus to cow the Luddites into submission.[8] Any notion of a fair trial was not even considered. Examples were to be made of all those who sought to challenge the Crown.

We note thirty-six men were held in Wakefield gaol and sixty-four were held in York for trespass and other charges, drawn from all parts of the woollen trade.[9] Two of the men placed at York gaol were charged with administering illegal oaths and were bailed; others had been charged with collecting and applying money for illegal purposes. A man called Shoefield was arrested for the attempted murder of George Hinchliffe.[10] Even as men were facing trial, Viscount Sidmouth issued orders to secure the arms depot in Halifax from a feared arms raid by Luddites.[11] The British government sought to suppress the Luddite movement with a mass trial at York in January 1813, following the attack on Cartwright's mill at Rawfolds, near Cleckheaton. The government charged more than sixty men, including Mellor and his companions, with various crimes in connection with Luddite activities. While some of those charged were actual Luddites, many had no connection to the movement. Although the proceedings were legitimate jury trials, many were abandoned due to lack of evidence, and thirty men were acquitted. These trials were certainly intended to act as show trials to deter other Luddites from continuing their activities. The harsh sentences of those found guilty, which included execution and penal transportation, quickly ended the movement, which understandably piqued interest across the Riding:

> I think it necessary to mention Sir, the immense number of people going from this part of the Country to York, even from out of Saddleworth I am inform'd by the Keepers of the Tollbar at Mills Bridge, and many others, they never saw the road so throng'd as on Saturday and yesterday, not only by foot passengers, but carts and carriages of almost every description fil'd with people.
>
> I am sorry Sir to be compel'd to state a petty depredation was committed in the neighbourhood of Clifton on Saturday night or Sunday morning, the villains only succeeded in robbing a house of some [illegible] I have reason to think they were disturb'd by the Patroles, but they escaped undiscover'd and even without alarming the owners of the house,—Last night the same neighbourhood was thrown into some commotion by the firing of a Gun two or three times; my Piquets being out in that direction, they ascertained it to proceed from a vessel laying at Brighouse which two of the North Lincoln went on Board but the Master denied having any Arms, however they look'd into the cabin and found a Gun which was still warm, they brought it away with them, and took the name of the owner, who I mean to summon before a Magistrate, he belongs to a Wakefield Trader.
>
> Major Hankin has just cal'd upon me, and mentioned the great numbers of people assembled in Huddersfield at the time Mr. Ratcliffe went through; Major H says one of his windows was broken by a stone thrown from the street.[12]

At 9 a.m. on Friday, 8 January 1813, George Mellor, William Thorpe and Thomas Smith, who had been convicted for the murder of William Horsfall, were executed at York Castle. Even before the trial had begun, the Crown had planned their execution:

> it appears to me very material to consider how their Bodies are to be afterwards to be disposed of so as to prevent their being triumphantly buried by their Friends. I lay gibbeting out of the question. The Alternative is, ordering the Bodies to be anatomized. But is there any Surgeon at or near Huddersfield, who would dare to dissect these Bodies? If not, I am very much disposed to think that an execution at

York should be preferred. As you are on the spot, you can form the best opinion upon the question I have asked.[13]

The trial was a stitch-up: the Crown wanted to make examples of these men, and made sure that they appointed a judge and jury who would find them guilty. This was a sham trial. The men were denied justice by the Crown, which wanted vengeance. The Luddites were convicted on felony charges that risked capital penalties, such as burglary, robbery, arson and 'endeavouring by threat' to obstruct justice. No charges were made at the Luddite trials for capital offences directly relevant to the revolutionary acts of treason and sedition: the Crown downplayed the seriousness of the threat from the Black Lamp and other groups. Even then, in order to obtain sufficient evidence to bring prosecution, the Crown relied upon numerous devices to obtain witness statements from accomplices and others, which included the use of violence and torture as well as kidnapping. The Crown endorsed the use of these devices as the consensus was that in all likelihood these activities would never be exposed in the public forum. Led by Viscount Sidmouth as Home Secretary, the perception of the ruling elite was that draconian sentencing was required to crush the spirit of the people to rebel against the elite. Sidmouth moved swiftly to 'inflict that extensive retribution which the heinousness of the offences, the necessity for a striking example, and the mistaken lenity manifested at a previous assize, had rendered indispensable' so as 'to inflict extensive retribution'. Thus, the trials at York were to proceed to execution without delay, leaving no possibility for mercy.[14]

As could be expected with men found guilty on flimsy charges and evidence obtained through torture, eight days later, fourteen Luddites who had been sentenced to death four days previously for the attacks at Rawfolds and Cartwright's mill were executed. At 11 a.m. on Saturday, 16 January 1813, the Under Sheriff brought out the first group of seven men who were to be executed: John Ogden, Nathan Hoyle, Joseph Crowther, John Hill, John Walker, Jonathan Dean and Thomas Brook. As the condemned men walked to the platform, they sang the Methodist hymn 'Behold the Saviour of Mankind', with John Walker leading the singing in a firm voice. The men prayed and some addressed the large crowd that had come to see them die. The *Leeds Mercury* of 23 January 1813 tells us:

> After sentence of death had been passed upon the persons convicted of making the attack on Mr. Cartwright's Mill, at Rawfolds, and of the Burglaries, fifteen in number, all of them except John Lumb, who

> was reprieved, were removed to the condemned-ward, and their behaviour in that place was very suitable to their unhappy situation. They confessed that they had offended against the laws of God and their Country, but on the subject of the offence, for which the sentence of death was passed upon them, they were very reserved; yet all of them except one, tacitly confessed that they were guilty of the crimes which they stood convicted, when they were asked if any of them could say they were not guilty, they all remain silent except James Haigh and Nathan Hoyle, the former of whom said, 'I am guilty,' and the latter, 'I am innocent;' this was the day before the execution; but Hoyle did not make any declaration to that effect when brought to the platform. Their minds for the most part had attained an extraordinary degree of composure; except the mind of John Ogden—he appeared some time to be much disturbed, but on the question being put to him whether his agitation arose from any discovery that he had to make, and with the weight of which his conscience was oppressed? he answered, no; his agitation arose from the terrors of his situation.[15]

The executioner caused the platform to drop, a shriek rose from watching crowd, and the bodies were left suspended until midday, when they were cut down and then removed. At 1.30 p.m., the second group of seven were led from their cells to the platform: John Swallow, John Batley, Joseph Fisher, William Hartley, James Haigh, James Hey and Job Hey. Again, the men sang as they walked to the platform before they were hanged.[16] The execution destroyed fourteen families: the men left behind them thirteen widows and fifty-seven fatherless children. It is undeniable that some of those executed at York were innocent of the specific charge and those most guilty may have escaped the penalty by being allowed to give evidence.

The funerals of the executed Luddites raised tensions across the West Riding. Captain Raynes reported:

> Three Carts & a Hearse with the Bodies of the unfortunate men that suffer'd yesterday are arrived at Birstall, the people are assembling in considerable numbers, but at present no disposition to riot appears, I shall take care to send persons to observe everything that passes on the road, and during the interment.[17]

Two days later, Raynes informed General Acland that a:

> Serjeant of the Greys and James Robertson, on Sunday detained a man at the Globe Inn, Mills Bridge for saying, as the Bodies of the Men executed at York were passing, that 'they should be reveng'd, Blood should have

Blood,' and using many other violent expressions, I sent him before Sir George Armytage the following morning who bound him in £100 and two Sureties of £50 each, to appear at the quarter Sessions.

many unguarded words of a similar nature have fallen from people drinking in Public Houses, but thought it better after making one example not needlessly to irritate them by too minute an observation of their expressions.[18]

One of the Luddites was interred in Elland, as Lieutenant Cooper reported:

The only Funeral in the neighbourhood of Elland was that of John Hill and no disturbance occurred but what was the consequence of the Methodist Parson refusing to read the service over the body, which was not of sufficient importance to notice.[19]

The Reverend Thomas Jackson, the local Wesleyan Methodist minister who officiated, called the burial 'an outrage' and urged Methodists to obey the law and not to take matters into their own hands to improve their lot. As in the 1790s with the expulsion of 'democrats' from the denomination by the Reverend Thomas Coke, the successor to John Wesley, to avoid the appellation of being disloyal subjects and interalia Jacobins, the Methodists were distancing themselves from the fact that members of their denomination were Luddites.

The executions, however, seem to have dampened the ardour of the Luddites and supporters; no doubt, the overwhelming military presence was also partly responsible for:

a material alteration is taking place in the sentiments and disposition of the People, from various conversations which have been held in Public Houses, and repeated to me by persons whose information I can rely upon, I find many of those who were known to be most active in the late disturbances have been heard to say, they are sensible of folly of their conduct, and are sorry they ever had any thing to do with such a bad concern—

I am told about twenty have taken the Oath of Allegiance before Mr. Scott, I applied to him for information on the subject, which he has declined giving me, as he conceives himself bound to secrecy. I have the Honor to enclose Mr. Scotts reply to me.[20]

As early winter 1813 progressed, Luddism was a spent force: the executions as much as the cold weather had cowed the Luddites and other revolutionaries, as General Acland reported:

> I went this morning to Huddersfield & fortunately met Mr. Radcliffe, Scott & Armytage the magistrates also Lloyd & Alison, they all agree the temper & feeling of the country is totally changed, & that there is every [reported] prospect & expectation of all continuing quiet.[21]

In February, a list of Luddites who took the Oath of Allegiance in Halifax was transmitted to Earl Fitzwilliam. In Elland, we find George Armitage, a coal miner, taking advantage of the pardon, as well as George Cooper, also a miner, croppers James Gregg, Stephen Dyson and John Hanson, clothiers Thomas Joanson and Joseph Cooper, and worsted spinner Abraham Hincliffe. Just forty-one men came forward, compared to the thousand or so in Manchester. We also note coal miners amongst the Luddites: George Armitage and George Cooper from Elland. We also find shoemakers like Thomas Schoefield.[22] Colliers had gone on strike in 1811 for higher wages. As had happened a decade earlier, as the economy shrank, demand for coal shrank, so men were laid off and wages fell. Luddism therefore cut across professional boundaries and represented a broad cross spectrum of the working class. This was not merely machine breaking, but class-consciousness, protesting at the price of food, lack of work, low wages and, above all, the desire for the workers to have their voices heard by a government that simply would not listen. This was a replay of 1799–1800. Luddism was not unique in 1812, but its scale of violence was.

By early March, Acland was able to inform General Maitland:

> have heard from good authority that very few of the Arms that have been stolen about Huddersfield remain in possession of the persons that took them away—such as [any] remain have been render'd useless from different causes but the far greater part have been either thrown into the Mill Dam near Sir George Armytages or a hole in the neighbourhood.[23]

By April, 'all was quiet' and the Militia and regular troops had been largely withdrawn from the West Riding. Luddism, it seems, faded away during the long, cold winter nights.

This did not mean that Luddism and revolution was over.

The 'modern and mechanised nineteenth century' was born in bloodshed: blood of both the working man, and also of the slave. Ironically, as slaves gained their freedom, English workers found themselves increasingly treated as slaves, with no rights, as 'things' to be exploited – resulting in the campaigns of Richard Oastler and others,[24] as well as the Ten Hours Act.[25] The failure of Luddism did not mean that the domestic system ended overnight. Thus, hand cropping of cloth staggered on into the 1820s, but was largely extinct by 1830, and it was not until the 1860s that the last of the independent master clothiers passed into history. This did not mean community anger withered away. On Wednesday, 25 and Friday, 27 September 1816, large demonstrations took place in Leeds, involving over 1,000 unemployed men, primarily croppers who had been displaced by mechanisation. On 2 December 1816, a great rally was held at Spa Fields, where an estimated crowd of 10,000 was addressed by the radical orator Henry Hunt. A small group of Spencean revolutionaries attempted to transform the meeting into an insurrection, which included an effort to enter the Tower of London. Rumours quickly spread to the provinces that Spa Fields was to trigger a revolution, and in Sheffield, John Blackwell, a local agitator who had been active in political outbursts since 1802, headed up a revolutionary movement that broke out into violence.[26] The croppers made a last stand in 1817 in presenting a final petition to Parliament to halt the gig-mill and shearing frame: the radical Whig Henry Brougham spoke to the house:

> the feeling which existed against machinery must be a ground of formidable alarm; for it showed that, instead of now being, as it lately was, a source of wealth, it was the cause of the most severe distress to a great body of the people, because the hands thrown out of work by the introduction of machines in one branch could not now find employment in other lines. This was a serious evil, well deserving the serious attention of parliament.[27]

Of the 3,625 croppers in the West Riding, just 860 were in work, and the number of shearing frames had increased from 100 to 1,462. Earl Fitzwilliam braced himself for a renewed wave of Luddism.[28] Parliament, as could be expected, again backed capitalism. With unemployment rising and starvation once more stalking the streets, 40,000 men were expected to rise in revolution in Huddersfield, 20,000 in Wakefield and over 60,000 in Nottingham, reported Wakefield solicitor John Pemberton Heywood to Earl Fitzwilliam: the working man sought to take matters into their own hands 'to re-dress their grievances'.[29] Nottingham was the scene of a fresh wave of machine breaking, culminating with the execution of Daniel Diggle on Wednesday, 2 April 1817. [30] In Leicestershire, 'Thomas Savage, Joshua Mitchell, John Amos, Wm. Towle, John Crowder and Wm. Withers, for entering Messrs. Heathcote and Co's factory, at Loughborough, and aiding and abetting the shooting at John Asher; Thomas Babington, for setting fire to a stack of oats belonging to Mr. John Moore, of Newbold

Verdon' were executed on 17 April.[31] Sir John Byng, hero of Waterloo, was sent north in March 1817 with troops to garrison the West Riding.[32] A concerned Earl Fitzwilliam informed Viscount Sidmouth, 'I thought it my duty to return immediately to Yorkshire' in order to 'endeavour to provide suitable means for overawing and suppressing that dangerous spirit' in Leeds and environs.[33]

Francis Edmunds of Worsborough, at the head of his troop of yeomanry, rounded up ten Luddites in Sheffield on 29 May.[34] On 6 June, thanks to information gained from the men arrested in Sheffield, delegates were arrested in Thornhill Lees, near Dewsbury, amongst whom were found Luddites: Horbury militant John Smaller and Benjamin Scholes from Wakefield were arrested on charges of sedition along with William Wolstenholme. All three stated that they were members of the United Englishmen, Wolstenholme confessing he was one of Despard's men and 'had been 28 years in the cause'.[35] Violence did break out on 8 and 9 June 1817: the men, armed with guns, pistols, and makeshift pikes, planned to march on Huddersfield when reinforcements arrived from the neighbouring villages. The men assembled at Folly Hall. The yeomanry had been on active service since the 8th, and the magistrates knew that 'the revolution was planned' for the 9th. The yeomanry had been alerted by '4 or 5 signal guns' at 4 a.m. on the 9th, heard between Honley and Huddersfield.[36] Folly Hall bridge was an obvious point of assembly for an attack on Huddersfield; the yeomanry opened fire about a half hour later. In the exchange of fire with the militants, a cavalryman's horse was wounded, and the 'Patrole found themselves compelled to retire to Huddersfield' for reinforcements. John Armitage, at the head of the Huddersfield Yeomanry, dispersed 'a few hundred persons' in the early hours of 9 June and made ten arrests. He was supported in the action by a detachment from the 33rd Regiment of Foot and a troop from the 13th Light Dragoons. A troop of the 13th were garrisoned in Wakefield, where the yeomanry was also called out.[37] Arms raids in Honley had taken place over the previous days to arm the 'disaffected persons'.[38] The Huddersfield Rising – which had been betrayed by a government spy – was echoed with similar scenes in Sheffield, and Pentrich, where riots were brutally put down. The Pentrich rebels of Derbyshire had strong links to Sheffield radicals and had sent their delegates to meet the Sheffield revolutionaries at the Blue Bell public house in March.[39] The Sheffield group, as with the Despard plotters and Luddites, had contacts in Wakefield, Huddersfield, Holmfirth, Barnsley and Leeds.[40] These connections had been nurtured by the Constitutional Society network in the 1790s and expanded subsequently through the radical

Hampden Club movement – both founded by Major John Cartwright – and the delegate system upon which it relied. When arrested, William Wolstenholme had Hampden Society publication number ten in his possession and, as we have seen, Hampden Society handbills were linked to Luddism.[41] About the arms raids, signal rockets and signal guns, Sir John Armitage remarked, 'seems to be exactly similar to that practiced at the time of the Luddites, but the plan seems to be more general', and added, 'the numbers more numerous, the persons engaged more cautious & desperate'.[42] Indeed, the Pentrich rising, Folly Hall, the March of the Blanketeers and the Spa Fields meeting all serve to indicate the breadth, diversity and widespread geographical scale of the demand for economic and political reform in 1816–20, which culminated in Peterloo, Cato Street and Grange Moor, which are largely outside the scope of this book.

The demands made in Sheffield or Leeds in 1792 would not come to reality in an imperfect state until 1831, and the working men and women would have to wait more than 100 years to get the vote. The pace of reform was slow – and reform is still needed. When the right to assemble and protest is being challenged, when a government can be elected to power by around 30 per cent of the population and government is controlled by big business, much is yet to be done to bring true democracy to this country. Many who had fought for reform since the 1790s were jubilant when it happened. One such veteran reformer was the Reverend Thomas Johnstone, who had been gaoled in 1793 for his vocal opposition to the policies of William Pitt, who in a public address expressed the view that reform was one:

> of the great struggles which have been made at different times to achieve this blessing, without feeling a glow of deepest veneration towards those who have distinguished themselves in this great cause. I recall, more especially, as belonging to Yorkshire, the names of Sir Geo Saville, that simple-minded warm-hearted patriot; the venerable Wyvill, of kindred soul to Major Cartwright and the eloquent Walter Fawkes, with many others who are deeply fixed in our memories. If I could call spirits from the vasty deep, or rather from a higher world, I would call them, and I do think, if they could, that they would come when they were called; but at any rate gentlemen, our imaginations can in some measure embody them, and as we think how such great and good men would cordially join in our triumph, so we can animate our hearts by the thought.[43]

Chapter 20

CONCLUSION

For the working class, the twenty-five years from 1790 to 1815 was a time of struggle and starvation. Bad harvests and the changing nature of the economy meant that unemployment, poverty and famine were the common themes of the era. The Industrial Revolution was as much a revolution as that in France: both were violent and witnessed the creation of a new world. Unlike France where the violence lasted a few years, in England, it was long and drawn out, starting in the 1770s and climaxing with the Pentrich Rising and Peterloo Massacre, which marked the end of the eighteenth century and the dawn of a new era. The Luddites, for many, had a just cause: they had been declared economically redundant in the name of progress and profit.

> How far they are commendable who wish to introduce Machinery at this time as a substitute for manual labour. And, secondly, How far they are justifiable who oppose it.
> As to the first, I think there can be no difference of opinion amongst men, tolerably informed, only as to the type of manner of introducing it; for it would be evidently absurd to employ men to perform that business which might be conveniently executed by a machine, unless, by throwing a number of men out of employment, the detriment to society would exceed the advantages; and that this is the case at present I think is pretty evident, for there are already a great deal more men than can find employment ... when we have all other nations to contend with, Machinery will prove an useful auxiliary enabling us to undersell them; but at the present juncture, when we have few other markets than our own settlements, it can make no difference to the Merchants whether their cloth be dressed by hand or machinery, provided they in this respect be unanimous ... I may add too, that the introduction of Machinery has been much too sudden and general; but there has not been time given to those who are injured by it to obtain employment in any other way; and

that, upon the whole, those who introduce Machinery at this time, are not entitled to that approbation they have generally received ... a man's trade is a kind of hereditary right which he has derived from his parents, it is a sort of property to him for which he has paid, and ought to be held as sacred as any other kind of property whatever; it is not reasonable that a man who has spent a long and laborious apprenticeship in order to learn a difficult business, in expectation that the public would employ him, should at once be deprived of all advantage from exercising it, and reduced to the rank of a common labourer. That this will be the case is evident, for by the general substitution of Machinery numbers will be obliged to seek for common labour, where their work will be much increased, and they will not receive above one-third of their former wages.

Now, Sir, if any other order of men, the Clergy or Military, for instance, was affected in so serious a manner, by increasing their duty and taking away two-thirds of their salary, would it not excite violent discontents among them? and would they not oppose, by every means in their power, a system so ruinous to their interests, however beneficial it might prove to the public?[1]

The woollen trade and its attendant community and traditions was being forcibly changed by market forces from the domestic system based on apprenticeships and specialised trades with a high degree of skill to a low-skill, low-wage industry. The stumbling blocks to deskilling the woollen industry, ending apprenticeships and maximising profit via mechanisation were the skilled tradesmen themselves, who quite reasonably objected. The Tories, since 1802, had sought to smash the power of the clothiers and croppers, especially after their political defeats in 1806 and 1807. In siding with capitalism, the government sowed the seeds of Luddism. The natural response to economic extinction by the croppers was resistance, by legal channels, when possible, but also by direct action. That this resistance to machinery went beyond the West Riding as is evident in the links with the West of England. This resistance also cut across trades since opposition to machinery and the factory system came not just from croppers, but also from the clothiers themselves as well as stocking frame weavers in Lancashire. We cannot overstate the sense of local feeling against the government and the war amongst the working classes of the West Riding and the country as a whole: when Spencer Perceval was assassinated, large swathes of the country cheered his death. Many of the Luddites and reformers' grievances were placed squarely with the Crown, yet in terms of political rhetoric and ideology, the Luddites, reformers and radicals did not have a single narrative or set of aims.

Local context for the Luddites in Yorkshire was more important than Westminster. The actions and attitudes of parsons, magistrates and landowners – often the same man! – in driving change, as a direct consequence of government policy in a highly visible manner, made these men targets for retribution. Magistrate Radcliffe had been a figure of hate in the West Riding since he joined the bench as a magistrate; the various assassination attempts against him demonstrated the settling of old parochial scores from the time of Despard. Class violence against Cartwright and Horsfall – again, a simpering community sore for a decade before 1812 – who had pushed forward renewed mechanisation with a change in government legislation, revealed they were targets for retribution. Horsfall had been a 'wanted man' ever since he had erected gig-mills and shearing frames a decade before. It is telling that of the mills in Horbury, just Foster's Mill was a target: Dudfleet Mill, completed in 1792, was not targeted, nor were the fulling and scribbling mills at Springhead and Ford at Horbury Bridge. Foster was targeted for his role in the enclosure of Horbury, which, as we noted, generated local anger as much as for his employment of machine finishing of his cloth. Tellingly, during the attack on his mill, the scribbling machines were left unscathed, while the shearing frames and gig-mills were smashed.

At its most basic, Luddism was a response to the changing nature of the economy: change brings poverty and hardship, as one commentator succinctly put it in 1816:

> About thirty years ago the carding-engine and spinning-jenny were introduced: this was the first serious encroachment on the labourer; up to this period the whole female population of a manufacturing district was constantly employed spinning, &c. and the male cultivated the land: there was not a cottage within twenty miles of a manufacturing town whose inhabitants were not furnished with labour, and consequently with bread. A reference to the parish books would enable any gentleman to trace its effect on the poor-rates. The next step of innovation that lessened labour was the use of the scribbling engine; this branch of the trade employing fewer persons, chiefly men and boys, and being introduced during the war, was less felt; then followed the various machines used to dressing cloths, called gigs and shearing frames, whose operation collectively has transferred the labour of the country to an immense pile of building called a Factory; the machinery of which is worked by water or steam, and managed by a few persons only, instead of giving employment and support to thousands, who would, in their turn, by the wages arising from labour, be enabled to purchase the

produce of the land, and other articles of support which yield a tax, and thereby contribute to take the burthen from the landed interest.²

Luddism in town and country represented two halves of the same struggle to protect community and tradition in the face of elite opposition. The relationships between place, property and customary rights were at the heart of these conflicts. Leeds Tory merchants summed up the plight of the croppers and clothiers as being:

> the unavoidable effect of the progressive improvement of society in general, which who would wish to put a stop to?... who opposes the improvement of machinery, aims a fatal blow at the commercial interests of his country, since it is our Machinery alone which enables us to manufacture at a cheaper rate than our continental rivals ... they must accommodate themselves to the changing circumstances of the times.³

In a shrinking economy, where were the unemployed to find work? What were masters of their trade to do when faced with extinction? The merchants failed to see the working class as people, and treated them as 'things to be used and exploited' to make money. The merchants put profit first and unapologetically put people second.

It is also worth remembering that the Luddism of 1812 was also closely associated with foods riots, in both Yorkshire and Manchester. Food and protest had been intimate bedfellows since the eighteenth century; this was now joined by industrial grievances and the language of universal rights as articulated by Thomas Paine, Major Cartwright and others. In this light Luddism was a continuance of the United Englishmen, and Folly Hall was almost the last gasp of England's abortive age of revolution; the last outburst of the forces unleashed by the French Revolution to bring about political reform that was enmeshed with workers' rights. The forces that led to the abortive revolution of Marcus Edward Despard re-emerged as Luddism and the rights-consciousness of Folly Hall and Cato Street. In this interpretation, Luddism was far more than simple machine breaking and mindless violence: it was a war between community and tradition; the haves and the have-nots. There can be no clear distinction for those who engaged in Luddism in a broader sense. Luddites were fighting against forced changes to their community and tradition, and were empowered by nascent conceptions of class and rights consciousness. Many – like John Banes the elder – had participated in underground radical movements a decade earlier, and others participated in legitimate constitutional reform movements, be they the activities of Major Cartwright or the wholesale politicisation of the woollen industry through the peace petitions and the 1806 and 1807 election campaigns. Indeed, 'underground' and 'legitimate' lines of protest were deeply interconnected. Luddism was an important moment in the development of the working class, and represented the tip of a wave that broke into violence as the expression of a wider and deeper sense of community outrage. In this sense the United Englishmen, Despard and Luddism all represented the same community anger, which had yet to coalesce into a formal labour movement.

It was a battle the possessing classes refused to lose. Luddism was:

1. An act of desperation by croppers, cloth dressers and those engaged in the woollen industry who had been made unemployed by the adoption of machinery. These men had no other means of fighting for their jobs and way of life other than with violence, when their voice had been consistently ignored by the government.
2. A reinvigorated revolutionary and republican sentiment inspired by Thomas Paine and Jean-Paul Marat in stating the people had the right to change the government, if that government failed to act on the will of the people.
3. Carried out by desperate men and women during a cost of living crisis.
4. An act of rebellion by hundreds of men after many had been made unemployed by the depression in manufacturing across the north by Spencer Perceval's bellicose attitude to America in signing the Orders in Council.
5. Driven by Ezekielite and Swedenborgian religious righteous indignation.
6. Part of the struggle for Irish independence.
7. Part of Napoleon's broader strategy to ferment chaos in England, to divert troops from the Peninsular War and British attention away from events in Europe.

Luddism was far more complex than machine breaking. As with the miners' strikes of the 1970s and 1980s, and the steelworkers in Sheffield, these were desperate men, who had lost everything through government policy: they had nothing left to lose other than their lives in a desperate gamble to protect their community and way of life. With God on their side, believing they had a religious mission to fulfil to tear down the monarchy as prophesied by Ezekiel and to bring a New Jerusalem, these men and women across the north of England set about their work, perhaps knowing all too well what their fate would be if they failed: hanging. Desperate people at desperate times took desperate measures to secure a future for themselves and their communities by attacking those who quite literally ignored their petitions and silenced their legitimate voice through electing MPs to represent them. When no other means of legitimate protest was left, what else could these people do? The stark choice was to fight for their community and way of life, or to meekly submit, and bend the knee to the merchant princes like Benjamin Gott and the hated factory system. Inspired by the words of the Old Testament, they chose to fight. This was anti-war and anti-government protest writ large, just as it had been since the heady days of 1799. The societal and economic stresses of the late 1790s never went away as the nineteenth century progressed, and indeed, are still found in our society today. Despite the Crown's best efforts, radical demands for political reform did not abate, and resulted in the Reform Act in 1831, and subsequent Acts, resulting in a democratic country being created in the years after the First World War. Justifiable working-class anger existed at the government's continued backing of capitalism against labour, failing to answer calls for peace with France and reform. The Industrial Revolution is more than just a name of an epoch: it was a total change in the nature of society; it was a revolution that was as real as that in America or France, with similar far-reaching consequences for those caught up in the struggle and very clear battle lines. Yet these battle lines are literally air-brushed from history to brand the Luddites simply as machine breakers, in a battle that was lost in a single year, and not viewed as half a century of conflict, with far more complex aims and objectives on the part of the radicals than has been considered by most historians. Luddism was not simply standing in the way of technology: it was the desperate cries of the working man who sought to have his voice heard, to get the vote, to have political representation, to preserve his way of life and community. Machine breaking was just one small facet of a broader working-class struggle, powered by the idealism of the French Republic, Thomas Paine and the Old Testament.

The failure of the English Jacobins to bring about radical change does not mean that the threat was not real: Despard and Luddism set the scene for over a hundred years of working-class struggle: Despard plotters never gave up their dream of universal suffrage. The ideals of Despard drove the explosion of radicalism that rocked the country from late 1811 into 1813. The English Revolution remained a 'might have been' because the middle class felt no cause to assume the role of Jacobins. The working-class radical movement was a product of grievances centred on economic, social and political spheres. It was nourished by the memory of the French Revolution, as much as by the political and economic repression of the British Crown. The English working-class *Enragés* failed because they could not harness the middle class to the cause. This does not mean that the threat was not real. The violent events of 1812 show how close revolution came. These social stresses remain today: has society really moved on in over 200 years? Millions rely on charity via food banks, just like the 1790s. Today, like 200 years ago, the rich get richer at the expense of the poor: predictably, conflict arose from the changing shape of society and community. The battle of unions against the government, or in simpler terms, capitol verses labour, is as much a part of life in 2023 as it was in 1812.

NOTES

Opening Words

1. Edward Royle (2000), *Revolutionary Britannia?*, Manchester University Press, Manchester, pp. 41–2.
2. Malcom Thomis (1972), *The Luddites: Machine-Breaking in Regency England*, Schocken Books, p. 91.
3. John Dinwiddy (1992), *Radicalism and Reform in Britain, 1780–1850*, Hambleden Press, London, p. 386.
4. John E. Cookson (1997), *The British Armed Nation*, Clarendon Press, Oxford, pp. 209–20.
5. Linda Colley (2005), *Britons: Forging the Nation 1707–1837*, Yale University Press, London.

Chapter 1: The Eighteenth-Century Woollen Industry

1. York City Library, Yorkshire Association papers, WYV/1/39/50, Letter from John Milnes of Wakefield, 18 April 1780.
2. John Goodchild, MSS notes, West Riding woollen trade.
3. John Goodchild, MSS notes, Westgate Chapel and the Wool Trade, 12/03/2017.
4. University of Leeds Special Collections, Account books of Jonathan Akroyd GB 206 MS 158.
5. York City Library, Yorkshire Association Papers, WYV/1/39/50, Letter from John Milnes of Wakefield, 18 April 1780.
6. Op. cit.
7. David Jenkins (1975), *The West Riding Wool Textile Industry 1770–1835*, Pascold Research Fund, Wiltshire pp. 3–4.
8. Gregory, Derek (1982), *Regional Transformation and Industrial Revolution: A Geography of the Yorkshire Woollen Industry*, The Macmillan Press, London, p. 46.
9. Jenkins, p. 4.
10. Ibid., p. 36.
11. Arthur Rose, 'Early cotton riots in Lancashire, 1769-1779', in *Lancashire and Cheshire Antiquarian Society* 73–74, 1963–1964, pp. 124–52.
12. Adrian Randall (1991), *Before the Luddites: Custom, Community and Machinery in the English Woollen Industry, 1776–1809*, Cambridge University Press, Cambridge, pp. 149–86.
13. Paul Lindsay Dawson (2020), *Wakefield at Work*, Amberley Publishing, Stroud.
14. Jenkins, p. 208.
15. W.B. Crump & G. Ghorbal, p. 12.

16. Jenkins, pp. 208–209.
17. *Leeds Mercury*, Monday, 13 June 1786. *See also Leeds Mercury*, Monday, 20 June 1786, ibid., 27 June 1786.
18. *Leeds Mercury*, Monday, 11 November 1783.
19. *Leeds Intelligencer*, Monday, 19 January 1795.
20. *Leeds Intelligencer*, Monday, 13 April 1795.
21. Herbert Heaton (1965), *The Yorkshire Woollen and Worsted Industries*, Clarendon Press, Oxford.
22. Jenkins, pp. 209–15.

Chapter 2: Community and Tradition

1. John Goodchild, pers comm, 12/04/2017.
2. Paul Murray Thompson (2015), *Matthew Murray 1765–1826 and the Firm of Fenton Murray and Co. 1795–1844*, privately printed, p. 80.
3. John Goodchild, pers comm, 1/10/2012.
4. York City Library, WYV/1/39/50, Letter from John Milnes of Wakefield, 18 April 1780.
5. https://www.geog.cam.ac.uk/research/projects/chambersofcommerce/leeds.pdf.
6. University of Leeds Special Collections, Account books of Jonathan Akroyd GB 206 MS 158.
7. *Leeds Mercury*, Monday, 26 January 1805. *See also* ibid., 21 September 1805.
8. John Goodchild, MSS notes, West Riding Woollen Industry.
9. *Leeds Intelligencer*, Monday, 10 March 1794.
10. Gregory, pp. 92–3.
11. Jenkins, p. 28.
12. Ibid., p. 84.

Chapter 3: Enclosure

1. University of Leeds Special Collections, Account books of Jonathan Akroyd GB 206 MS 158.
2. *York Herald*, Saturday, 14 February 1801.
3. Derek Gregory (1982), *Regional Transformation and Industrial Revolution: A geography of the Yorkshire Woollen Industry*, The Macmillan Press, London, pp. 84–5.
4. The National Archives [hereafter TNA], HO 42/91/256, Wilkinson, Eyre, and Ward to Dundas, 23 July 1791.
5. *Sheffield Register, Yorkshire, Derbyshire, & Nottinghamshire Universal Advertiser*, Friday, 29 July 1791.
6. Ibid., HO 42/19/256, Eyre to Dundas, 23 July 1791.
7. https://drive.google.com/file/d/1xErwxbyGo6qE-bmztCtKiF0DPxCF60apITz1t6vBYTEYJ8c85vV3P4VVTZRL/view.
8. TNA, Treasurer Solicitors' Papers [hereafter TS], 11/9523496ii.
9. Sheffield City Archives [hereafter SCA] WWM F44/1, H. Hunter to Earl Fitzwilliam, 12 December 1791.
10. Emma Vincent Macleod (1998), *A War of Ideas: British Attitudes to the War Against Revolutionary France 1792–1802*, Routledge, London, pp. 204–205.
11. *Hull Advertiser and Exchange Gazette*, Saturday, 9 February 1805.
12. Wells, Roger A.E. (1986), *Insurrection: The British Experience 1795–1803*, Sutton Books, Stroud, p. 200.

13. TNA Home Officer Papers [hereafter HO] HO 42/61/380. Letter from [the Rev William Atkinson], chaplain to the Bradford Volunteers [Yorkshire West Riding], to Home Office, 30 March 1801.
14. Ibid.
15. Rev James Bicheno (1810), *The Consequences of Unjust War*, J. Johnson, London, pp. 2–10.
16. *London Courier and Evening Gazette*, Saturday, 6 June 1801.
17. *Kentish Weekly Post or Canterbury Journal*, Tuesday, 07 April 1801.
18. *Carlisle Journal*, Saturday, 11 April 1801.

Chapter 4: First Stirrings of Discontent

1. W.B. Crump & G Ghorbal, pp. 92–3.
2. John Goodchild, MSS Notes, West Riding Woollen Trade.
3. Sheffield City Archives [hereafter SCA], Wentworth Woodhouse Munuments [hereafter WWM] F/65/69, Letter from John Milnes, Wakefield, to Fitzwilliam, 28 April 1791. *See also* ibid., F/65/7029, April 1791, Letter from Pemberton Milnes, Wakefield, to Fitzwilliam, 29 April 1791.
4. SCA WWM F/65/89–91, Note from Mr Ellison's mill at Birkenshaw concerning army clothing.
5. Gregory, p. 46.
6. W.B. Crump (1931), *The Leeds Woollen Industry 1780–1820*, Leeds, Thoresby Society, pp. 318–19.
7. Journals of the House of Commons (JHC), Vol. XLIV, 13 March 1794.
8. Adrian Randall (2006), *Riotous Assemblies: Popular Protest in Hanoverian England*, Oxford University Press, Oxford, p. 254.
9. Wells (1977), p. 4.
10. Paul Lindsay Dawson (2021), *A Potted History of Wakefield*, Amberley Publishing, Stroud.
11. *Leeds Intelligencer*, 19 May 1800.
12. *Sheffield Iris*, 15 May 1800.
13. *London Gazette*, May 1799, p. 507.
14. Ibid., p. 169.
15. Ibid., p. 507.
16. W.B. Crump & G Ghorbal, p. 46.
17. SCA WWM F/45/83 Letter from William Cookson (mayor), Leeds, to Fitzwilliam, 30 August 1802.
18. Wells (1986), pp. 234–5.
19. A.L. Dawson, pers comm.
20. Dawson (2020,) pp. 12–15.

Chapter 5: Combination

1. Roger A.E. Wells (1986), *Insurrection: The British Experience 1795–1803*, Sutton Books, Stroud, pp. 225–31.
2. Ibid.
3. Ibid., pp. 223–5.
4. John Rule (1986), *The Labouring Classes in Early Industrial England, 1750–1850*, Routledge, London, p. 374.
5. John E. Archer (2000), *Social Unrest and Popular Protest in England, 1780–1840*, Cambridge University Press, Cambridge, p. 53.
6. John Rule (2014), *Albion's People: English Society 1714–1815*, Routledge Educational, London.

7. TNA Privy Council (hereafter PC) 1/44/161, Barlow to Belgrave, 8 August 1799.
8. Ibid., PC 1/44/A161 Ford to Belgrave, 8 August 1799.
9. Ibid., Ford to Belgrave, no date, August 1799.
10. Edward Palmer Thompson (2013), *Making of the English Working Class*, Penguin Classics, London, p.310.
11. http://clok.uclan.ac.uk/17895/35/17895%20AAM.pdf.
12. TNA HO 42/47, Folio 355 to 357, Thomas Bancroft to Home Office, 11 April 1799.
13. Ibid., HO 42/65, Folio 442, Fletcher to Pelham, 3 April 1802.
14. SCA WWM/StwP/6/vi/54, Charles Bowns to Benjamin Hall, 29 May 1799.
15. PC 1/44/A161, Foxley to Belgrave, August 1799.
16. Ibid.
17. Ibid., Barlow to Richard Ford, 14 August.
18. Ibid., Barlow to Thomas Butterworth Bayley, 19 September 1799.
19. Ibid., Barlow to Richard Ford, 19 October 1799.
20. Ibid., Barlow to Richard Ford, 27 October 1799.
21. Ibid., George Orr to John King Under Secretary of State, 12 September 1799.
22. TNA PC 1/45/A 164 Thomas Butterworth Bayley to Duke to Portland, 4 December 1799.
23. Ibid., T.B. Bayley to John King, 27 November 1799.
24. John Bohstedt (1983), *Riots and Community Politics in England and Wales, 1790–1810*, Cambridge University Press, Cambridge, p. 140.
25. Ibid., p. 197.
26. William Wood (1801), *A Sermon preached at Mill-Hill Chapel, in Leeds, on the commencement of the Nineteenth Century*, Edward Baines, Leeds, p. 13.
27. J.E. Cookson (1982), *The Friends of Peace: Anti-war liberalism in England 1793–1815*, Cambridge University Press, Cambridge, p. 200.
28. Macleod, pp. 130–2.
29. SCA WWM, F45/13/b, J.A. Busfield to Earl Fitzwilliam, 14 April 1801.
30. TNA HO 42/49/137 Folios 295A–295B. Copy of an anonymous letter to Lord Eldon, 31 March 1800.
31. Ibid., HO 42/62/110 Folio(s) 310–311. Letter to John Vivian, 30 July 1801.

Chapter 6: Luddites Arise

1. Leeds City Library, Sales Ledger of William Lupton 1801–1805.
2. TNA HO 42/66/86, Folios 254–257, Copy of a letter from William Cookson.
3. SCA WWM, F45/e/115, Handbill, 14 October 1802.
4. Ibid., WWM F45/766, Joseph Beckett to Earl Fitzwilliam, 8 August 1801.
5. Ibid., WWM F45/d/53, Richard Walker to Earl Fitzwilliam, 13 June 1802.
6. TNA HO 42/65/212, Folio 468, J.A. Busfield to Home Office, 17 July 1802.
7. Ibid., HO 42/65/122, Folios 313–317, John Jones, 18 July 1802.
8. Ibid., HO 42/65/123, Folios 318–319, John Jones, 20 July 1802.
9. Ibid., HO 42/66/47, Folios 165–168, Letter from J. Read, 9 August 1802.
10. Wells (1986), p. 226.
11. TNA HO 42/65/173, Folios 398–399, John Jones to Mr King, 26 July 1802.
12. SCA WWM F45/79–1, William Cookson to Earl Fitzwilliam, 16 August 1802.
13. Ibid.
14. Ibid., WWM F45/d/80–1, William Cookson to Earl Fitzwilliam, 19 August 1802.
15. Ibid., WWM F45/d/83, Letter from William Cookson (mayor), Leeds, to Fitzwilliam, 30 August 1802.
16. TNA HO 42/66/29, Folio 130, Joseph Radcliffe to Home Office, 24 August 1802.
17. SCA WWM F45/83, Cookson to Fitzwilliam, 30 August 1802.

18. Ibid., WWM F45/d/85, Letter from Lord Pelham, Wimbledon, to Fitzwilliam, 2 September 1802.
19. Ibid., WWM F45/d/84, George Palmer to Mary Tucker, 27 August 1802.
20. Ibid., WWM F45/d/86, William Griffin, 5 September 1802.
21. Ibid., WWM F45/d/96, Whitehall to Earl Fitzwilliam, 27 September 1802.
22. TNA HO 42/66/118, Folios 337–341, Letter from James Read to John King, 3 October 1801.
23. Ibid., HO 42/66/173, Mary Tucker, 16 December 1802.
24. Ibid., HO 42/70, Folios 200–201, Hainsworth to Palmer, 20 May 1803.
25. TNA PC 1/43/A152, Observations on Combinations.
26. WWM F45/62, Cookson to Fitzwilliam, 27 July 1802.
27. TNA HO 42/70, Folio 200, Hainsworth to Palmer, 20 May 1803.
28. Ibid., HO 42/62, Cookson to Tugwell, Bath, no date, August 1802.
29. SCA WWM F45/83, Cookson to Fitzwilliam, 30 August 1802.
30. Ibid., WWM/F/45/116, Resolutions at a meeting of merchants and master cloth dressers, 6 January 1803.
31. Ibid., WWM F45/d/112, Letter from Fitzwilliam, Wentworth, to Lord Pelham, 27 September 1802.
32. Ibid., WWM F45/e/116, Resolutions at a meeting of merchants and master cloth dressers, 6 January 1803.
33. Ibid., WWMF/45e/117, John Beckett to Fitzwilliam, 28 January 1803.
34. Ibid., WWM F45/e/116, Rotation Office Leeds, 6 January 1803.
35. Ibid., WWF F45/d/112, Earl Fitzwilliam to Lord Pelham, 27 September 1803.
36. Ibid., WWM F45/d/112-2, Earl Fitzwilliam to Lord Pelham, 27 September 1802.
37. TNA HO 42/66, Cookson to Fitzwilliam, 18 August 1802.
38. SCA WWMF/45e/117, Beckett to Fitzwilliam, 28 January 1803.
39. Ibid., WWM F45/d/114, J.A. to George Palmer, Sheffield, 28 December 1802.
40. Ibid., WWM F/45/117, Beckett to Fitzwilliam, 28 January 1803.
41. TNA PC 1/43/A152, Observations on Combinations.
42. SCA WWMF/45e/117 Beckett to Fitzwilliam, 28 January 1803.
43. Ibid WWMF/45/79, Cookson to Fitzwilliam, 16 August 1802. *See also* ibid., WWM F45/80, Cookson to Fitzwilliam, 18 August 1802, WWM F/45/83, Cookson to Fitzwilliam, 8 September 1802.
44. TNA HO 42/66, Folios 226–227, James Read to Lord Pelham, 11 September 1802.
45. TNA PC 1/43/A152, Observations on Combinations.
46. TNA HO 42/66/86, Folios 254–257, Cookson to Fitzwilliam.
47. Ibid., HO 42/66, Folios 243–244, Pelham to Read, 2 September 1802.
48. Brook & Kipling (1993), *Liberty or Death*, Workers' History Publications, p. 12.
49. SCA WWM F/45/116, Cloth Dressers Case.
50. Brooke & Kipling, p. 13.
51. SCA WWM F/45/117, Beckett to Fitzwilliam, 28 January 1803.

Chapter 7: Political Agitation

1. TNA HO 42/83/9, Folios 27–44, Copy of an 1803 letter from John Read of Lincoln's Inn, 22 January 1803.
2. *Leeds Intelligencer*, Monday, 10 July 1803.
3. Thompson, p. 577.
4. Gregory, p. 124.
5. Ibid., p. 130.
6. *Leeds Mercury*, Monday, 26 January 1805. *See also* ibid., 21 September 1805.
7. Wells (1977), p. 45.

8. John Goodchild, MSS Notes West Riding Woollen Trade.
9. TNA HO 42/77/40, Dawson to Home Office, 15 October 1804.
10. *Leeds Mercury*, Monday, 26 January 1805.
11. Ibid., 18 January 1806.
12. Ibid., 8 August 1807.
13. TNA HO 42/83/3, Folios 5–14, Whitehall memorandum, 20 February 1806.
14. Ibid., HO 42/83/8, Folios 23–26, Unsigned note entitled 'Heads of a Bill proposed to be brought into Parliament by the Shearmen of Wiltshire, Somersetshire and Gloucestershire, with Observations upon it'.
15. Wilson, p. 169.
16. https://www.historyofparliamentonline.org/volume/1790-1820/constituencies/yorkshire.
17. *Leeds Intelligencer*, Monday, 22 June 1807.
18. *York Herald*, Saturday, 23 May 1807.
19. *Hull Packet*, Tuesday, 26 May 1807.
20. Crump, p.184.
21. *Leeds Intelligencer* – Monday, 25 May 1807.
22. *Hull Packet* – Tuesday, 26 May 1807.
23. *Leeds Intelligencer* – Monday, 22 June 1807.
24. Crump, W.B. (1931), *The Leeds Woollen Industry 1780–1820*, Thoresby Society, Leeds, p.184.
25. SCA Fitzwilliam MSS. E. 156/11, Thomas Lumb to Browns, 31 May 1807.
26. SCA Fitzwilliam MSS. E. 156/97, Thomas Lumb to Browns, 26 May 1807.
27. Ibid., E 156/92, Thomas Lumb to Brown, 23 May 1807.
28. Ibid., E. 156/102, John Milnes to Fitzwilliam, June 1807.
29. *Leeds Intelligencer*, 11 June 1807.
30. Ibid., Monday, 15 June 1807.

Chapter 8: Economic Warfare

1. Crump, p. 177.
2. Ibid., p. 178.
3. Gregory, p. 46.
4. Peter Maw (2010), 'Yorkshire and Lancashire ascendant: England's textile exports to New York and Philadelphia, 1750–1805', in *The Economic History Review*, 63(3), new series, 734–768, pp. 766–7.
5. John Goodchild, pers comm.
6. *Leeds Mercury*, Saturday, 17 October 1807.
7. Ibid., Saturday, 28 November 1807.
8. *Cowdray's Manchester Gazette* [hereafter *CMG*], 28 November 1807.
9. Chetham's Library, Hay mss, Mun. A. 3.10, Scrapbook 4, pp. 109–10.
10. Oldham Local Studies Library, MF/G19, Rowbottom Diaries, April 1808.
11. CMG, 5 December 1807.
12. Joseph Hanson (1808), *A Defence of the Petitions for Peace*, J. Ridgway, Manchester, pp. 15–16.
13. William Dawson (1807), *Stockport Flim-Flams*, Manchester.
14. TNA HO 42/91/963, Fletcher to Hawkesbury, 27 December 1807.
15. Ibid., HO 42/95/1, Fletcher to Hawkesbury, February 1808.
16. *CMG*, 27 February 1808.
17. Ibid., 20, 27 February, 12 March 1808.
18. *Leeds Mercury*, Saturday, 19 December 1807.
19. Chetham's Library, Hay MS, Mun A.3.10, Scrapbook 4, p. 110.

20. https://api.parliament.uk/historic-hansard/commons/1808/mar/18/petition-from-manchester-respecting-peace.
21. *Leeds Mercury*, Saturday, 8 August 1807.
22. Edward Parsons (1809), *The True Patriot, a Sermon preached at Salem Chapel Leeds on the Fast-Day. Wednesday, February 8, 1809*, E. Baines, Leeds, pp. 9–10.
23. Brooke & Kipling, p. 14.
24. *Bury and Norwich Post*, Wednesday, 27 January 1808.
25. *Leeds Mercury*, Saturday, 23 January 1808.
26. Cookson (1982), p285.
27. *Leeds Mercury*, Saturday, 19 December 1807.
28. Ibid.
29. Ibid., p. 204.
30. *CMG*, 12 March 1808.
31. Cookson (1982), p. 204.
32. Brooke & Kipling, p. 14.
33. J.L. & B. Hammond (1919), *The Skilled Labourer, 1760–1832*, Longmans, Green & Co., London, p. 85.
34. *Leeds Intelligencer*, Monday, 7 December 1807. *See also Leeds Intelligencer*, Monday, 14 December 1807.

Chapter 9: Fermenting Revolution

1. Leeds City Library, William Lupton Ledgers 1801–1815.
2. Crump, p. 80.
3. William Roscoe (1808), *Considerations on the Causes, Objects and Consequences of the Present War*, T. Cadell, London, p. 2.
4. Gregory, pp. 36–7.
5. *Nottingham Journal*, 16 November 1811.
6. TNA HO 42/117, Newcastle to Ryder, 16 November 1811.
7. *Nottingham Review*, 6 December 1811.
8. TNA HO 42/119, 'Declaration', 1 January 1812.
9. *Nottingham Journal*, 16 March 1811.
10. Ibid., 23 March 1811.
11. Ibid., HO 42/118, Letter from Ned Ludd.
12. *Nottingham Journal*, 16 November 1811. *See also Derby Mercury*, 21 November 1811, *Leeds Mercury*, 23 November 1811.
13. TNA HO 42/117, Newcastle to Ryder, 26 November 1812.
14. Ibid., HO 42/117, Folio 529, Letter dated Nottingham, 13 November 1811.
15. *Leeds Mercury*, Monday, 7 December 1811.
16. TNA HO 42/117, Folio 520, Letter John Pilkington, 12 November 1811.
17. Ibid., HO 42/117, Folios 607–609, John Byng to Home Office, 7 December 1811.
18. Ibid., HO 42/119.
19. *Leeds Mercury*, 29 February 1812.
20. TNA HO 42/118/54, Middleton to Home Office, 12 December 1811.
21. Thompson, p. 602.
22. Gregor,y pp. 146–8.
23. Ibid., pp. 143–5.
24. SCA WWM/G/83/37/1, Letter from Thomas William Tottie, Leeds, to Lord Milton, 17 April 1811.
25. Ibid., WWM/F/47/45, Joshua Beckett of Dewsbury to T.W. Tottie, 12 April 1812.
26. Marianne Elliott (1982), *Partners in revolution*, Yale University Press, New Haven, p. 354.

27. http://ludditebicentenary.blogspot.com/2012/01/historic-context-of-west-yorkshire.html.
28. Crump, p. 133.
29. Gregory, pp. 150–1.
30. *Leeds Mercury*, 4 January 1812.
31. Ibid., HO 42/117, Folio 520, Letter John Pilkington, 12 November 1811.
32. Ibid., HO 42/117, Folios 607–609, John Byng to Home Office, 7 December 1811.
33. Ibid., HO 42/119.
34. *Leeds Mercury*, 11 January 1812.
35. Ibid., 18 June 1812.
36. Oldham Local Studies Library, MF/G19, Rowbottom Diaries, January 1812.
37. Thompson, pp. 609–10.

Chapter 10: Yorkshire Machine Breaking

1. *Leeds Intelligencer*, 20 January 1812.
2. *Leeds Mercury*, 18 January 1812.
3. Ibid., 12 February 1812.
4. TNA HO 42/119.
5. *Nottingham Journal*, 1 February 1812.
6. *Wakefield and West Riding Advertiser*, 28 February 1812.
7. Brooke & Kipling, pp. 16–17.
8. *Leeds Mercury*, 29 February 1812.
9. TNA HO 40/1/7, Sworn Statement of William Hinchliffe, 28 February 1812.
10. Brooke & Kipling, pp. 16–17.
11. *Leeds Mercury*, 29 February 1812.
12. TNA HO 40/1, Folio 173, Radcliffe to Home Office, 26 February 1812.
13. *Nottingham Journal*, 21 March 1812.
14. Ibid., HO 42/121, to Joseph Radcliffe, 29 February 1812.
15. Ibid., HO 40/1/, Folio 1, Radcliffe to Beckett, 7 May 1812.
16. Ibid., HO 40/1, Folio 5, Sworn statement of John Sykes, 6 March 1812.
17. Ibid., HO 40/1, Folio 7, Sworn statement of Samuel Swallows, 6 March 1812.
18. Ibid., HO 40/1, Folio 9, Sworn statement of John Swallows, 6 March 1812.
19. Leeds University Manuscripts 193, Gott Papers, Vol. 3, 106, letter one.
20. Ibid., HO 401/1/11, Folios 35–36, Ralph Fletcher to Home Office, 15 May 1812.
21. Ibid., HO 40/1/11, Folios 32–32a, Major Clarke, 2nd Dragoons, Stockport, 2 May 1812, to W.R. Hay esq.
22. Ibid., HO 40/1, Folios 11–12, Sworn statement of George Roberts, 13 March 1812.
23. Ibid., HO 40/1, Folio 13, Sworn statement of John Garner, 13 March 1812.
24. Ibid., HO 40/1, Folio 14, Sworn statement of Hannah Dyson, 13 March 1812.
25. Ibid., HO 40/1, Folio 15, Sworn statement of David Crowther, 13 March 1812.
26. TNA HO 42/121, Joseph Radcliffe to Home Office, 17 March 1812.
27. *Leeds Mercury*, 21 March 1812.
28. West Yorkshire Archive Service [hereafter WYAS], Leeds, Radcliffe Papers 126/27, recto.
29. Ibid., verso.
30. *Nottingham Journal*, 4 April 1812.
31. Ibid., 28 April 1812.
32. Crump, p. 47.
33. *Leeds Mercury*, 25 March 1812.
34. WYAS Leeds, Radcliffe Papers 126/28, recto.

NOTES

35. The original writer says just ass, emphasis on ASS one feels being the correct reading.
36. WYAS Leeds, Radcliffe Papers, 126/28b.
37. Francis Raynes (1817), *An Appeal to the Public—containing an account of the services rendered during the disturbances in the north of England in the year 1812*, J. Richardson, London, p. 19.

Chapter 11: Yorkshire Climax

1. *Wakefield Herald and West Riding Advertiser*, 17 April 1812.
2. Ibid.
3. Raynes, p. 18.
4. Op. cit.
5. *Leeds Mercury*, 18 April 1812.
6. Wakefield Local Studies, 920: TOM, Journals of Matthew Tomlinson of Lupset Farm [hereafter Tomlinson], Vol. 1.
7. John Goodchild, pers comm, 1 July 1997, regarding Royal Wakefield Volunteers.
8. TNA HO 42/122, Colonel Campbell to H.C. Grey, 11 April 1812.
9. Ibid., HO 40/1/4, Hay to Home Office, 14 May 1812.
10. WYAS Leeds, Radcliffe Papers, 126/32.
11. *Wakefield Herald and West Riding Advertiser*, 17 April 1812.
12. Raynes, pp. 98–9.
13. Tomlinson, Vol. 1, p. 1175.
14. TNA HO 42/122, William Cartwright to Robert Rayner.
15. Ibid., HO 40/1/1, Huddersfield Petition, 29 April 1812.
16. *Leeds Mercury*, 18 April 1812.
17. David Glover, pers comm, 31 May 2012.
18. WYAS Leeds, Radcliffe Papers, 126/32.
19. Ibid., Radcliffe papers, 126/46.
20. *York Courant*, 20 April 1812.
21. Ibid., HO 40/1/1, Folio 20, Anonymous letter, 14 April 1812.
22. *Leeds Mercury*, 25 April 1812.
23. Frank Peel (1888), *The Risings of the Luddites, Chartists and Plug-drawers*, T.W. Senior, Heckmondwike, p. 129.
24. Tomlinson, Vol. 1, p. 1177.
25. Ibid.
26. TNA HO 40/1, Folio 18, Sworn statement of George Whitehead, 18 April 1812.
27. Ibid., HO 40/1, Folio 29, Sworn statement of Isaac Raynor, 25 April 1812.
28. Ibid., HO 40/1/4, Folio 34, Dyson to Radcliffe, 30 April 1812.
29. *Leeds Intelligencer*, 27 April 1812.
30. *Leeds Mercury*, 9 May 1812.
31. *Leeds Intelligencer*, 27 April 1812.
32. Thomas Howell (1823), *A Complete Collection of State Trials*, Vol. xxxi, Hansard, London, p. 1114.

Chapter 12: Cottonopolis

1. *Derby Mercury*, 13 February 1812.
2. TNA HO 40/1, Lloyd to Ryder, 21 March 1812.
3. Ibid., HO 42/121, Wood to Ryder, 25 March 1812.
4. *The Times*, 11 April 1812.
5. TNA HO 42/122/529, Whitelock to Ryder, 8 April 1812.
6. Oldham Local Studies Library, MF/G19, Rowbottom Diaries, 15 April 1812.

7. TNA HO 40/1, Lloyd to Ryder, 13 April 1812.
8. *Nottingham Journal*, 25 April 1812.
9. TNA HO 40/1/1, Lloyd to Ryder, 13 April 1812.
10. Ibid., HO 40/1/1, Lloyd to Ryder, 15 April 1812.
11. Ibid., HO 42/128, Clay to Home Office, 21 April.
12. *Nottingham Journal*, 2 May 1812.
13. *Leeds Mercury*, 2 May 1812.
14. TNA HO 40/1/3, Folios 100–102, Disposition of Bent to Fletcher, April 1812.
15. Bohstedt, p. 126.
16. Cookson (1982), pp. 225–7.
17. Gregory, p. 156.
18. SCA WWM/F/110/1, T.W. Tottie to Fitzwilliam, 24 March 1812.
19. Ibid., WWM/F/110/2, Letter from John Gant, Committee Room [Leeds], to Fitzwilliam, 24 March 1812.
20. *Leeds Mercury*, 28 March 1812.
21. SCA WWM/F/45/135, William Dawson to Fitzwilliam, 3 May 1812.

Chapter 13: Food Riots

1. Charles Creighton (1894), *A history of Epidemics in Britain*, Cambridge University Press, Cambridge, p. 162.
2. Tomlinson, Vol. 1, p. 1170.
3. Ibid., p. 1171.
4. Ibid., p. 1173.
5. SCA WWM/F45/127, Hugh Parker, Sheffield, to Earl Fitzwilliam, 15 April 1812.
6. *Leeds Mercury*, 18 April 1812.
7. SCA WWM/F45/127, Hugh Parker, Sheffield, to Earl Fitzwilliam, 15 April 1812.
8. TNA HO 42/122, Hugh Parker to Home Office, 15 April 1812.
9. SCA WWM F45/128, Thomas Fenton, to Earl Fitzwilliam, 16 April 1812.
10. Ibid., WWM F45/129, J.A. Stuart Wortley to Earl Fitzwilliam, 16 April 1812.
11. *Leeds Mercury*, Monday, 25 July 1812.
12. SCA WWM F45/130, Letter dated 18 April 1812.
13. *Wakefield Herald and West Riding Advertiser*, 17 April 1812.
14. TNA HO 40/1, Folio 18, Sworn statement of George Whitehead, 18 April 1812.
15. Ibid., HO 40/1, Folio 29, Sworn statement of Isaac Raynor, 25 April 1812.
16. *Leeds Mercury*, 18 April 1812.
17. Ibid., HO 42/19/296, Vincent Eyre to Portland, 30 July 1791.
18. *Wakefield Herald and West Riding Advertiser*, 24 April 1812.
19. Tomlinson, Vol. 1, p. 1174.
20. *Leeds Mercury*, 25 April 1812.
21. TNA HO 33/1/171, Hart to Freeling, 11 May 1812.
22. Malcolm Chase (1988), *The People's Farm: English Radical Agrarianism, 1775–1840*, Oxford University Press, Oxford.
23. Pat Hudson (2002), *The Genesis of Industrial Capital: A Study of West Riding Wool Textile Industry, c.1750–1850*, Cambridge University Press, Cambridge, p. 81.
24. *Farmer's Magazine*, 16 November 1812.
25. *Leeds Mercury*, 16 May 1812.
26. WYAS Wakefield, QS1/149/6, Bradford Quarter Sessions, July 1810; QS1/150/9, Wakefield Quarter Sessions, Oct 1811.
27. Nicholas Blomley, 'Making Private Property: Enclosure, Common Right and the Work of Hedges', in *Rural History*, XVIII (2007), pp. 1–22.

NOTES

28. Barnsley Local Studies and Archives, Spencer Stanhope Papers, 60554, piece 27, John Howson to Walter Spencer Stanhope, no date.
29. *Leeds Mercury*, 2 May 1812.
30. Op. cit.
31. *Leeds Mercury*, 16 May 1812.
32. *Manchester Mercury*, 21 April 1812.
33. SCA WWM F45/132, John Beckett to Earl Fitzwilliam, 19 April 1812.
34. Ibid., WWM F45/133, Sworn statement of William Clegg, 19 April 1812.
35. SCA WWM F45/135, William Dawson to Earl Fitzwilliam, 3 May 1812.
36. Tomlinson, Vol. 1, p. 1176.
37. TNA HO 40/1/2, Folio 28, Police Office Manchester, 6 May 1812.

Chapter 14: The Revolutionaries

1. Ibid., HO 40/124.
2. Ibid.
3. Ibid., HO 40/1/11, Folios 24–27, William R. Hay to Home Office, 1 May 1812.
4. Ibid., HO 401/1/11, Folios 28–28a, Letter from Eliza Ludd to Mr Simpson.
5. WYAS Leeds, Radcliffe Papers, 126/38.
6. A. Aspinall & E. Anthony Smith (eds., 1959), English Historical Documents, XI, 1783–1832, Oxford University Press, New York, pp. 533–5.
7. Kyle Hughes & Donald MacRaild (2018), *Ribbon Societies in Nineteenth-Century Ireland and Its Diaspora*, Liverpool University Press, Liverpool, pp. 46–7.
8. TNA HO 42/117, Folios 403–408, dated 31 October 1811.
9. Ibid., HO 42/117, Folios 409–412, dated 1 November 1811.
10. Ibid., HO 42/117, Folios 378–390 dated, 7 November 1811.
11. Correspondence Napoleon No. 18237, 7 Novembre 1811, au general Clarke.
12. Correspondence Napoleon No. 18123, 8 Septembre 1811 au general Clarke.
13. TNA HO 42/117, Folios 630–632.
14. Leeds University Manuscripts 193, Gott Papers, Vol. 3, 106, letter two.
15. *Chester Courant*, 2 June 1812.
16. TNA HO 42/125, Folios 3–8, Deposition of Joseph Barrawclough, 7 July 1812.
17. TNA HO 42/125, Folios 439–440, Letter dated Dyapool, near Hull, July 1812.
18. Paul Chamberlin, pers comm, 10/01/2222.

Chapter 15: The Revolution Begins

1. TNA HO 40/1/9, Folios 4–6, Ralph Fletcher to John Beckett, 6 April 1812.
2. Ibid., HO 40/1/8, Folios 40–45, Statement of H. Yarwood, 22 June 1812.
3. Raynes, p. 92.
4. SCA WWM F46/122, Deposition of Thomas Broughton, 26 August 1812.
5. TNA HO 40/1/3, Folios 90–92, Disposition of Bent to Fletcher, 17 April 1812.
6. Dawson, Paul L. (2023), *French Invasions of Britain and Ireland, 1797-1798: The Revolutionaries and Spies who Sought to Topple the Government of King George*, Frontline Books, Barnsley.
7. Ibid., HO 40/1/3, Folios 100–102, Disposition of Bent to Fletcher, April 1812.
8. TNA HO 42/126, Maitland to Sidmouth, 22 August 1812.
9. Oldham Local Studies Library, MF/G19, Rowbottom Diaries, 5 May 1812.
10. Ibid., HO 42/123.
11. Ibid., HO 40/1/5, Folios 27–28, Joseph Scott to John Beckett, 2 May 1812.
12. Ibid., HO 40/1/6, Folio 30, Joseph Radcliffe to John Beckett, 5 May 1812.
13. *Leeds Mercury*, 9 May 1812.
14. Ibid., 16 May 1812.

15. TNA HO 33/1/171, Hart to Freeling, 11 May 1812.
16. TNA HO 30/29/6/11, Folio 1607, Letter from Wolverhampton to Granville Leveson-Gower, 13 May 1812.
17. Tomlinson, Vol. 1, p. 1178.
18. TNA HO 40/1, Folios 115–116, Ralph Fletcher to Henry Hobhouse, 15 May 1812.
19. Ibid., HO 42/123, Geo Coldham Town Clerk to Home Office, 14 May 1812.
20. Ibid., HO 42/123 Folio 174, Anonymous to Prince Regent, 17 May 1812.
21. Ibid., HO 42/123, Folio 42, Examination of Thomas Clare, 15 May 1812.
22. Ibid., HO 42/123, Folio 428, Oswald Smith to Richard Ryder, 16 May 1812.
23. Ibid., HO 40/1/11, Folios 45–48, Report Citizen Bent, 12 May 1812.
24. Ibid., HO 40/1/11, Folios 45–48, Report Citizen Bent, 12 May 1812.
25. Ibid., HO 40/1/4, Folios 124–126, Report Citizen Bent, 12 May 1812.
26. *Hull Advertiser and Exchange Gazette*, Saturday, 8 May 1813.
27. Ibid., HO 40/1/3, Folios 100–102, Disposition of Bent to Fletcher, April 1812.
28. Ibid., HO 40/1/5, Folios 238–249, Francis Foljambe to Home Office, 29 April 1812.
29. *Leeds Mercury*, 16 May 1812.
30. SCA WWM F45/138, Earl Fitzwilliam to Richard Ryder, 16 May 1812.

Chapter 16: Arming the Revolution

1. SCA WWM F46/15, Francis Lindley Wood to Earl Fitzwilliam, 28 May 1812.
2. *Leeds Mercury*, 13 June 1812.
3. Ibid., 6 June 1812.
4. Ibid.
5. Ibid., 30 May 1812.
6. TNA HO 40/1, Folio 33a, Sworn statement, 5 June 1812.
7. Tomlinson, Vol. 1, p. 1179.
8. TNA HO 40/1, Folio 39, Statement, 11 June 1812.
9. Ibid., HO 40/1, Folios 40–41, Anonymous statement, 11 June 1812.
10. Ibid., HO 40/1/6, Folios 31–32, F.L. Wood to Home Office, 7 June 1812.
11. SCA WWM F46/17, Francis Lindley Wood to Earl Fitzwilliam, 13 June 1812.
12. Ibid., WWM F46/18, Francis Lindley Wood to Earl Fitzwilliam, 14 June 1812.
13. Ibid., WWM F46/19, Francis Lindley Wood to Earl Fitzwilliam, 17 June 1812.
14. Tomlinson, Vol. 1, pp. 1179–80.
15. SCA WWM F45 57, Disposition of Joseph Woodhead, 24 June 1812.
16. TNA HO 40/1/6, Folios 52–53, Disposition of Joseph Woodhead, J. Cartledge to Sir Francis Lindley Wood, 7 June 1812.
17. Tomlinson, Vol. 1, pp. 1180–1.
18. TNA HO 40/1/6, Folios 44–45, Sir Francis Lindley Wood to Earl Fitzwilliam, 17 June 1812.
19. Ibid.
20. TNA HO 42/125, Sir Francis Lindley Wood to Earl Fitzwilliam, 18 June 1812.
21. *Leeds Mercury*, 20 June 1812.
22. Ibid.
23. Ibid., 27 June 1812.
24. *Wakefield Herald and West Riding Advertiser*, 19 June 1812.
25. *Leeds Mercury*, 25 July 1812.
26. *Wakefield Herald and West Riding Advertiser*, 19 June 1812.
27. Ibid.
28. *Leeds Mercury*, 13 June 1812.
29. *The Gentleman's Magazine*, Vol. 111, p. 584.
30. Ibid., HO 40/1/4, Folios 127–129, Report Citizen Bent, 16 June 1812.

NOTES

31. Ibid., HO 40/1/4, Folio 137, Extract of Letter from R.W. Stockport.
32. Ibid., HO 40/1/4, Folio 138, Extract of Letter from R.W. Stockport, 17 June 1812.
33. Ibid,. HO 40/1/11, Folios 38–39, Thomas Paine to Richard Wood, 6 May 1812.
34. TNA HO 40/1, Folios 52–53, Disposition of Joseph Woodhead, J. Cartledge to Sir Francis Lindley Wood, 22 June 1812.
35. *Lancaster Gazette*, 18 July 1812.
36. Tomlinson, Vol. 1, pp. 1181–2.
37. TNA HO 40/1/4, Folios 154–155, Ralph Fletcher to John Beckett, 23 June 1812.
38. TNA HO 42/124, Stevenson to Sidmouth, 23 June 1812.
39. SCA WWM F46 68, Walker to Fitzwilliam, 9 July 1812. Emphasis in the original letter.
40. Tomlinson, Vol. 1, p. 1182.
41. SCA WWM F46/20, Francis Lindley Wood to Earl Fitzwilliam, 27 June 1812.
42. Cookson (1982), pp. 227–30.
43. *Leeds Mercury*, 18 June 1812.
44. TNA HO 40/1/1, Maitland to Lord Sidmouth, 19 June 1812.
45. SCA WWM F46/22, Francis Lindley Wood to Earl Fitzwilliam, 9 July 1812.

Chapter 17: Arms Raids Continue

1. Ibid., WWM F46 78.
2. Ibid., WWM F46/40, Francis Lindley Wood to Earl Fitzwilliam, 11 August 1812.
3. Ibid., WWM F46/34, Abstract of Returns, 9 July 1812.
4. *Leeds Mercury*, 11 July 1812.
5. SCA WWM F45/117, Walker to Fitzwilliam, 13 July 1812.
6. *The Times*, 12 July 1812.
7. SCA WWM F46/23, Francis Lindley Wood to Earl Fitzwilliam, 11 July 1812.
8. TNA HO 42/125, J.H. Seale to Sidmouth, 11 July 1812.
9. SCA WWM F46/35, Parish of Halifax, Report of the Sub-Committee, 16 August 1812.
10. *Leeds Intelligencer*, 20 July 1812.
11. SCA WWM F46 73, Disposition John Wilkinson, 18 July 1812.
12. Ibid., WWM F46 73, Disposition Joseph Goldthorpe, 18 July 1812.
13. *Leeds Intelligencer*, 20 July 1812.
14. SCA WWM F46 73, Disposition George Pratt, 18 July 1812.
15. *Leeds Intelligencer*, 20 July 1812.
16. *Wakefield Herald and West Riding Advertiser*, 17 July 1812.
17. SCA WWM F46 70, Walker to Fitzwilliam, 18 July 1812.
18. Ibid., WWM F46 71, Anonymous letter.
19. TNA HO 42/125, General Maitland to John Beckett, 18 July 1812.
20. SCA WWM F45/157, Earl Fitzwilliam to Addington, 25 July 1812.
21. Ibid.
22. Ibid.
23. Tomlinson, Vol. 1, p. 1185.
24. Raynes, p. 102.
25. TNA HO 42/126, Sworn statement of John Hincliff, 23 July 1812.
26. Ibid., HO 42/125, Maitland to Sidmouth, 27 July 1812.

Chapter 18: Lady Ludd

1. SCA WWM F46/45, Wood, Naylor, Smithson to Earl Fitzwilliam, 17 August 1812.
2. Tomlinson, Vol. 1, p. 1186.
3. *Leeds Mercury*, 2 August 1812.

4. Tomlinson, Vol. 1, pp. 1187–8.
5. TNA HO 42/126.
6. SCA WWM F46/44, Earl Fitzwilliam to General Maitland, 14 August 1812.
7. Ibid., WWM F46/51, John Smyth to Earl Fitzwilliam, 20 August 1812.
8. Tomlinson, Vol. 1, p. 1189.
9. *Leeds Mercury*, 22 August 1812.
10. Ibid.
11. TNA HO 42/126, Maitland to Beckett, 22 August 1812.
12. SCA WWM F45/122, Disposition of Thomas Broughton, 26 August 1812.
13. Tomlinson, Vol, 1, pp. 1192–3.
14. SCA WWWM F46/52, J.A.S. Wortley to Earl Fitzwilliam, 31 August 1812.
15. TNA HO 42/126, Maitland to Beckett, 22 August 1812.
16. Tomlinson, Vol. 1, p. 1194.
17. SCA WWM F46/49, Busfield to Earl Fitzwilliam, 18 August 1812.
18. *Leeds Mercury*, 29 August 1812.
19. *Leeds Intelligencer*, 7 September 1812.
20. Ibid.
21. *Leeds Mercury*, 22 August 1812.
22. TNA HO 42/127, Maitland to Beckett, 31 August 1812.
23. Ibid., HO 42/127, Maitland to Becket, Wakefield, 3 September 1812.
24. TNA HO 40/2/7, Acland to General Maitland.
25. *Leeds Mercury*, 12 September 1812.
26. TNA HO 40/2/3, Roberson to Acland, 7 September 1812.
27. TNA HO 42/2/3, Disposition Thomas Ewart and Robert Luma, 24 September 1812.
28. SCA WMM F46 81, Hugh Parker to Home Office, undated, Sheffield, 8 o'clock.
29. Ibid., WWM F46 82, undated report from spy.
30. TNA HO 42/126, Maitland to Beckett, 29 August 1812.
31. Ibid., HO 42/127, Maitland to Beckett, 8 September 1812.
32. *Morning Chronicle*, 11 September 1812.
33. Raynes, p. 41.
34. TNA HO 40/2/3, Raynes to Acland, 12 September 1812.
35. Ibid., HO 40/2/3, Raynes to Acland, 11 September 1812.
36. Ibid., HO 42/127, Lloyd to J. Beckett, 14 September 1812.
37. Ibid., HO 42/127, Allison to Sidmouth, 15 September 1812.
38. *Leeds Mercury*, 19 September 1812.
39. Ibid., 3 October 1812.
40. TNA HO 40/2/3, Disposition Benjamin Strickland.
41. Ibid., HO 40/2/3, James Greenwood and William Irving to Major Bruce of the Stirling Militia, 9 October 1812. *See also* ibid., Disposition of William Thornhill, 17 October 1812.
42. *Lancaster Gazette*, 24 October 1812.
43. WYAS Leeds, Radcliffe MSS 126-92, Radcliffe to Fitzwilliam, 26 October 1812.
44. TNA HO 40 40/2/3, John Allison to Acland, 31 October 1812.

Chapter 19: Death and Burial

1. Ibid., HO 42/126, Maitland to Sidmouth, 2 November 1812.
2. Ibid., HO 42/129, Maitland to Sidmouth, 4 November 1812.
3. Ibid.
4. Ibid.
5. TNA HI 40/2/3, Raynes to Acland, 7 November 1812.

6. SCA WWM F46/93, Fitzwilliam to Sidmouth, 4 November 1812.
7. Ibid., WWM F46/53, General Maitland to Earl Fitzwilliam, 6 September 1812.
8. Ibid., WMM F46/95, Sidmouth to Earl Fitzwilliam, 7 November 1812.
9. Gregory, p. 169.
10. SCA WWM F46/62, Lord Sidmouth to Earl Fitzwilliam, 10 September 1812.
11. Ibid., WWM F46/64/1, Lord Sidmouth to Earl Fitzwilliam, 8 September 1812. *See also* ibid., WWM F46/64/25, Lord Sidmouth to Earl Fitzwilliam, 14 September.
12. TNA HO 40/2/3, Raynes to Acland, 4 January 1813.
13. Ibid., HO 40/2/4, Hobhouse to Acland, 14 December 1812.
14. George Pellew (1847), *The Life and Correspondence of the Right Honourable Henry Addington, First Viscount Sidmouth*, Vol. 3, Spottiswoode & Shaw, London, pp. 79–97.
15. *Leeds Mercury*, 23 January 1813.
16. Ibid.
17. TNA HO 40/2/3, Raynes to Acland, 17 January 1813.
18. Ibid., HO 40/2/3, Raynes to Acland, 19 January 1813.
19. Ibid., HO 40/2/3, Cooper to Acland, 24 January 1813.
20. Ibid., HO 40/2/3, Raynes to Acland, 14 February 1813.
21. Ibid., HO 40/2/9, Acland to Maitland, 22 February 1813.
22. SCA WWM F46/127, A list of those Luddites who have taken the Oath of Allegiance.
23. TNA HO 40/2/9, Acland to Maitland, 1 March 1813.
24. John A. Hargreaves & Hilary Haigh (2012), *Slavery in Yorkshire: Richard Oastler and the campaign against child labour in the Industrial Revolution*, Huddersfield University Press, Huddersfield.
25. Wilson, pp. 179–82.
26. SCA WWM F45 K/181, Fitzwilliam to Sidmouth, 2 April 1817. *See also* HO 42/156, J.A.S. Wortle to Sidmouth, 7 December 1816; HO 42/156 Fitzwilliam to Sidmouth, 7 December 1816.
27. Hansard, 11 February 1817.
28. SCA WWM F45 K, Various papers re: disturbances in 1817.
29. Ibid., WWM F45/177, Sworn statement of John Dickenson, 16 June 1817.
30. *Leicester Journal*, 11 April 1817.
31. *Leicester Chronicle*, Friday, 18 April 1817.
32. SCA WWM F45 K/180, Prest to Fitzwilliam, 10 March 1817.
33. Ibid., WWM F45 K/181, Fitzwilliam to Sidmouth, 2 April 1817.
34. Ibid., WWM F45/173, F.L. Wood to Fitzwilliam, 6 June 1817.
35. Ibid., WWM F45/175, John Byng to Fitzwilliam, 8 June 1817.
36. Ibid., WWM F45 K/182, Disposition Henry Alexandre, 9 June 1817.
37. Ibid., WWM F45 K/182, F.L. Wood to Fitzwilliam, 9 June 1817.
38. Ibid., WWM F45 K/182, John Armitage to Fitzwilliam, 9 June 1817.
39. TNA HO 42/167, Examination of John Cope, 15 June 1817.
40. Ibid., HO 42/165, Information of 'GR', 29 January 1817.
41. Ibid., HO 42/165, Examination of Wolstenholme, 31 May 1817.
42. SCA WWM F45 K/186, Sir John Armitage to Fitzwilliam, 12 June 1817.
43. John Goodchild, MSS notes, Rev Thomas Johnstone.

Chapter 20: Conclusion

1. *Leeds Mercury*, Saturday, 23 May 1812.
2. Ibid., 9 November 1816.
3. Ibid., Saturday, 6 June 1812.

SOURCES AND BIBLIOGRAPHY

Archive sources
Barnsley Local Studies and Archives
Spencer Stanhope Papers, 60554

British Library newspaper collection
Cowdray's *Manchester Gazette*, *Chester Chronicle*, *Derby Mercury*, *Lancaster Gazette*, *Leicester Chronicle*, *Leicester Journal*, *Nottingham Journal*, *The Times*, *The Morning Chronicle*

Chetham's Library
Hay mss, Mun. A. 3.10, Scrapbook 4

John Goodchild Collection: formerly at Registry of Deeds Wakefield
MSS notes Clarkson's Mill
MSS notes Rev Thomas Johnstone
MSS notes West Riding Woollen Trade
Westgate Chapel Archive

Leeds City Library
Sales Ledger of William Lupton

North Yorkshire Record Office
Wyvill papers Folio 168

Oldham Local Studies Library
MF/G19, Rowbottom Diaries

Sheffield City Archives
Wentworth Woodhouse Munuments F45, F46, G83
Fitzwilliam MSS Elections

The National Archives
Home Office papers HO 30/29, HO 33/1, HO 40/1, HO 40/2, HO 40/3, 40/9, HO 42/47, HO 42/61, HO 42/65, HO 42/66, HO 42/74, HO 42/83, HO 42/117, HO 42/118, HO 42/119, HO 42/120, HO 42/121, HO 42/122, HO 42/123, HO 42/124, HO 42/125, HO 42/126, HO 42/127, HO 42/128, HO 42/129, HO 42/130, HO 42/131, HO 42/132
Privy Council 1/35, 1/43, 1/44/, 1/45
Treasurer Solicitor's Papers 11/9523496ii

University of Leeds Special Collections
MS 158 Account books of Jonathan Akroyd
MS 193 Gott Papers, vol. 3, 106

Wakefield Museum and Local Study Centre
Wakefield Herald and West Riding Advertiser
Leeds Mercury
Leeds Intelligencer
920:TOM, Journals of Matthew Tomlinson of Lupset Farm

West Yorkshire Archive Service
Radcliffe Papers
West Yorkshire, Land Tax, 1703–1932
Quarter Session Records, 1637–1914

York City Library
Yorkshire Association papers

Printed Sources
Archer, John E. Archer (2000), *Social Unrest and Popular Protest in England, 1780–1840*, Cambridge University Press, Cambridge.
Aspinall, A. & Smith, E. Anthony (eds.) (1959), English Historical Documents, XI, 1783–1832, Oxford University Press, New York.
Bicheno, Rev James (1810), *The Consequences of Unjust War*, J. Johnson, London.
Blomley, Nicholas, 'Making Private Property: Enclosure, Common Right and the Work of Hedges' in *Rural History*, XVIII (2007), pp. 1–22.
Bohstedt, John (1983), *Riots and Community Politics in England and Wales, 1790-1810*, Cambridge University Press, Cambridge.
Brooke and Kipling (1993), *Liberty or Death*, Workers' History Publications.
Burrowes, Peter (1812), *Speeches ... on the trials of Edward Sheridan, M.D. and Thomas Kirwan*, J.J. Nolan, Dublin.
Chase, Malcolm (1988), *The People's Farm: English Radical Agrarianism, 1775–1840*, Oxford University Press, Oxford.
Colley, Linda (2005), *Britons: Forging the Nation 1707–1837*, Yale University Press, London.
Cookson, John E. (1982), *The Friends of Peace: Anti-war liberalism in England 1793–1815*, Cambridge University Press, Cambridge.

SOURCES AND BIBLIOGRAPHY

Cookson, John E. (1997), *The British Armed Nation*, Clarendon Press, Oxford.

Creighton, Charles (1894), *A history of Epidemics in Britain*, Cambridge University Press, Cambridge.

Crump, W.B. (1931), *The Leeds Woollen Industry 1780–1820*, Thoresby Society, Leeds.

Crump, W.B. & Ghorbal, G. (1967), *History of the Huddersfield Woollen Industry*, S.R. Publishers, East Ardsley.

Dawson, Paul Lindsay (2020), *Wakefield at Work*, Amberley Publishing, Stroud.

Dawson, Paul Lindsay (2022), *A Potted History of Wakefield*, Amberley Publishing, Stroud.

Dawson, William (1807), *Stockport Flim-Flams*, Manchester.

Dinwiddy, John (1992), *Radicalism and Reform in Britain, 1780–1850*, Hambledon Press, London.

Elliott, Marianne (1982), *Partners in revolution*, Yale University Press, New Haven.

Graham, Jenny (2000), *The nation, the law and the king: reform politics in England, 1789–1799*, 2 vols., University Press of America.

Gregory, Derek (1982), *Regional Transformation and Industrial Revolution: A geography of the Yorkshire Woollen Industry*, The Macmillan Press, London.

Hammond, J.L. & B. (1919), *The Skilled Labourer, 1760–1832*, Longmans Green and Co., London.

Hanson, Joseph (1808), *A Defence of the Petitions for Peace*, J. Ridgway, Manchester.

Hargreaves, John A. & Haigh, Hilary (2012), *Slavery in Yorkshire: Richard Oastler and the campaign against child labour in the Industrial Revolution*, Huddersfield University Press, Huddersfield.

Heaton, Herbert (1965), *The Yorkshire Woollen and Worsted Industries*, Clarendon Press, Oxford.

Howell, Thomas (1823), *A Complete Collection of State Trials*, vol xxxi, Hansard, London.

Hudson, Pat (2002), *The Genesis of Industrial Capital: A Study of West Riding Wool Textile Industry, c.1750–1850*, Cambridge University Press, Cambridge.

Hughes, Kyle & MacRaild, Donald (2018), *Ribbon Societies in Nineteenth-Century Ireland and Its Diaspora*, Liverpool University Press, Liverpool.

Jenkins, David (1975), *The West Riding Wool Textile Industry 1770–1835*, Pascold Research Fund: Wiltshire, p. 208.

Macleod, Emma Vincent (1998), *A War of Ideas: British Attitudes to the War Against Revolutionary France 1792–1802*, Routledge, London.

Maw, Peter (2010), 'Yorkshire and Lancashire ascendant: England's textile exports to New York and Philadelphia, 1750–1805', in *The Economic History Review*, 63(3), new series, 734–68, pp. 766–7.

Parsons, Edward (1809), *The True Patriot, a Sermon preached at Salem Chapel Leeds on the Fast-Day. Wednesday, February 8, 1809*, E. Baines, Leeds.

Pellew, George (1847), *The Life and Correspondence of the Right Honourable Henry Addington, First Viscount Sidmouth*, vol. 3, Spottiswoode & Shaw, London.

Randall, Adrian (1991), *Before the Luddites: Custom, Community and Machinery in the English Woollen Industry, 1776–1809*, Cambridge University Press, Cambridge.

Randall, Adrian (2006), *Riotous Assemblies: Popular Protest in Hanoverian England*, Oxford University Press, Oxford.

Raynes, Francis (1817), *An Appeal to the Public – containing an account of the services rendered during the disturbances in the north of England in the year 1812*, J. Richardson, London.

Roscoe, William (1808), *Considerations on the Causes, Objects and Consequences of the Present War*, T. Cadell, London.

Rose, Arthur, 'Early cotton riots in Lancashire, 1769–1779', in *Lancashire and Cheshire Antiquarian Society* 73–74, 1963–1964.

Royle, Edward (2000), *Revolutionary Britannia?*, Manchester University Press, Manchester.

Rule, John (1986), *The Labouring Classes in Early Industrial England, 1750–1850*, Routledge, London.

Rule, John (2014), *Albion's People: English Society 1714–1815*, Routledge Educational, London.

Thomis, Malcom (1972), *The Luddites: Machine-Breaking in Regency England*, Schocken Books.

Thompson, Edward Palmer (2013), *Making of the English Working Class*, Penguin Classics, London.

Wells, Roger A.E. (1977), *Dearth and Distress in Yorkshire 1793–1802*, Borthwick institute, York.

Wells, Roger A.E. (1986), *Insurrection: The British Experience 1795–1803*, Sutton Books, Stroud.

Wilson, Richard George (1971), *Gentlemen Merchants: The Merchant Community in Leeds 1700–1830*, Manchester University Press, Manchester.

Wood, William (1801), *A Sermon preached at Mill-Hill Chapel, in Leeds, on the commencement of the Nineteenth Century*, Edward Baines, Leeds.

INDEX

Akroyd, Jonathan, 5, 14, 15, 22
Aldred, Ebenezer, 10, 11, 15
Almondbury, 14, 48, 89, 132
America, 2, 7, 16, 21, 22, 61, 62, 63, 68, 69, 70, 73, 79, 80, 105, 108, 110, 122, 150, 151, 164, 173, 188, 189
Anglican, 1, 18, 39, 60, 71, 72, 109
Armitage, George, 180
Armitage, Sir John, 146, 183
Armitage, William, 156
Atkinson, Joseph, 30
Atkinson, Law, 34, 53, 57, 93
Atkinson, Thomas, 93, 104, 122
Atkinson, Revd. William, 27

Baines, Edward, 66
Baines, John, 100, 170
Bakewell, Robert, 57, 58, 68, 69, 70
Barnsley, 5, 14, 114, 115, 117, 118, 123, 128, 152, 154, 162, 163, 165, 166, 168, 182
Barrowclough, Joseph, 126, 127
Batley, 59, 152
Beckett, John, 51, 86, 117
Beckett, Joseph, 45
Beeston, 57
Belfast, 79, 128
Belper, 64
Birkenshaw, 30
Birmingham, 24, 129, 157
Birstall, 48, 50, 85, 132, 136, 141, 178
Black Lamp, 88, 90, 110, 120, 122, 177
Bolton, 8, 40, 65, 66, 71, 77, 80, 106, 107, 121, 133, 147
Bradford, 27, 40, 79, 125, 152, 157
Bramley, 10, 73, 116
Bramley, Richard, 34, 58

Brighouse, 154, 165, 176
Bury, 40, 106
Busfield, Jonathan Atkinson, 27, 46, 165

Cartwright, Major John, 1, 72, 114, 146, 163, 183, 187, 188
Cartwright, William, 98, 99, 100, 101, 102, 135, 169, 175, 177, 186
Catholic, 1, 58, 71, 79, 124, 129, 133
'Citizen Bent', 92, 107, 128, 129, 133, 134, 135, 157
Cleckheaton, 86, 99, 103, 165, 171, 175
Clifton cum Hartshead, 154, 156, 157, 176
Combinations, 36, 38, 39, 40, 41, 47, 48, 50, 52, 53, 56, 114, 115, 157, 158, 174, 175
Cookson, William, 17, 18, 19, 20, 28, 33, 34, 36, 45, 47, 48, 50, 51, 52, 53, 54, 58, 62, 108, 123
Crigglestone, 144, 152
Crosland Moor, 14, 84, 86, 167
Crosland South, 88, 89
Cumberworth, 14

Darton, 118
Dawson, William, 56, 109, 118
Derby, 40, 64, 79, 80, 129
Derbyshire, 40, 43, 71, 77, 81, 182
Despard, Marcus Edward, 92, 120, 124, 129, 182, 186, 187, 188, 189
Dewsbury, 60, 96, 97, 138, 152, 157, 165, 182
Dodworth, 5, 14
Dragoons, 4th, 24
Dragoon Guards, 2nd, 46, 84, 131, 151
Dublin, 124, 128, 129, 172

211

Elland, 140, 143, 154, 179, 180
Enclosure, 3, 21, 22, 23, 24, 25, 39, 115, 116, 186
Ezekielite, 27, 28, 135, 163, 188

Fawkes, Walter Ramsden, 57, 58, 150, 183
Fitzwilliam, Earl, 31, 44, 45, 46, 47, 48, 49, 50, 51, 52, 53, 58, 60, 108, 109, 111, 112, 117, 118, 135, 136, 139, 141, 142, 148, 153, 157, 161, 167, 172, 174, 175, 180, 181, 182
Fletcher, Colonel Ralph, 40, 41, 65, 88, 92, 107, 128, 133, 147
Foster, Joseph, 95, 96, 97, 120, 186

Gig-mills, 28, 30, 31, 34, 35, 36, 39, 45, 47, 50, 51, 52, 53, 54, 55, 57, 58, 74, 78, 83, 85, 93, 95, 150, 161, 166, 181, 186
Gildersome, 96, 97, 166, 167
Glasgow, 91, 125, 128, 129, 167
Golcar, 14, 84
Gott, Benjamin, 3, 15, 16, 17, 18, 19, 20, 28, 30, 34, 36, 39, 45, 46, 49, 50, 51, 52, 53, 54, 55, 57, 78, 108, 110, 189

Halifax, 3, 5, 7, 13, 14, 15, 18, 34, 35, 45, 47, 50, 79, 100, 101, 102, 125, 148, 150, 152, 153, 157, 163, 165, 166, 170, 175, 180
Hanson, Colonel Joseph, 64, 65, 66, 98, 125, 163
Hay, Revd. William Robert, 97, 120, 121
Heckmondwike, 85, 86, 96, 97
Holmfirth, 92, 126, 145, 152, 159, 162, 182
Honley, 17, 67, 86, 88, 92, 94, 132, 182
Horbury, 14, 72, 95, 96, 97, 116, 136, 137, 138, 139, 143, 144, 145, 147, 152, 160, 182, 186
Horbury Bridge, 160, 186
Horsfall, 53, 57, 103, 122, 175, 176, 186
Huddersfield, 5, 7, 13, 17, 30, 34, 35, 39, 45, 47, 50, 52, 57, 67, 70, 83, 84, 85, 86, 89, 91, 92, 93, 94, 96, 97, 100, 101, 102, 103, 112, 114, 117, 118, 125, 130, 131, 134, 136, 141, 143, 145, 147, 150, 152, 153, 157, 162, 166, 167, 170, 172, 176, 180, 181, 182
Hull, 27, 48, 64, 127, 133, 152

Institution, The Cloth Workers, 28, 36, 38, 39, 49, 50, 51, 52, 53, 54, 55, 56, 57, 123
Ireland, 38, 79, 91, 123, 124, 125, 128, 129, 133, 134, 142, 149
Irish, 79, 123, 124, 128, 129, 130, 134, 145, 162, 163, 188

Jacobinism, 20, 25, 27, 43, 66, 123, 134
Jerusalem, New, 26, 27, 28, 163, 188
Johnstone, Revd. Thomas, 183

Kihlman, Revd. Alexander, 1, 71
Kirkburton, 143
Kirkheaton, 171

Leeds, 5, 7, 10, 12, 13, 14, 15, 16, 17, 18, 20, 23, 31, 33, 34, 35, 36, 39, 40, 42, 44, 45, 47, 48, 49, 50, 51, 52, 54, 55, 57, 58, 59, 61, 62, 64, 66, 67, 69, 71, 72, 73, 79, 81, 82, 83, 85, 86, 92, 108, 109, 110, 117, 123, 125, 132, 136, 150, 152, 153, 156, 161, 162, 163, 164, 181, 182, 183, 187
Leicester, 9, 133, 181
Lepton, 118
Light Dragoons, 13th, 182
Light Dragoons, 15th, 24, 112, 117, 141, 144, 152, 168, 182
Light Dragoons, 16th, 67
Linthwaite, 86
Liverpool, 64, 71, 79, 108, 124, 127, 150
Liverpool, Lord, 149, 150
Liversedge, 86, 169
Lockwood, 14, 71, 89, 131, 143
Lumb, Thomas, 5, 18, 57, 58, 59
Lupset, 96, 111, 116, 158

Macclesfield, 107, 111
Maitland, General, 129, 150, 151, 157, 159, 161, 162, 164, 166, 167, 168, 172, 173, 175, 180
Manchester, 9, 40, 41, 43, 48, 50, 64, 65, 66, 71, 73, 74, 77, 79, 81, 88, 100, 101, 105, 106, 107, 108, 111, 117, 121, 124, 125, 128, 130, 134, 146, 152, 157, 162, 163, 180, 187
Marsden, 88, 103, 132
Meltham, 132
Methodist, New Connexion, 1, 67

INDEX

Methodist, Wesleyan, 71, 72, 100, 156, 177, 179
Middleton, near Manchester, 107, 118
Milnes, John, 13, 14, 18, 57, 58, 60

Napoleon, 1, 41, 61, 77, 79, 80, 123, 124, 149, 188
Netherthong, 132, 156
Netherton, 136, 137, 139, 141
Nottingham, 39, 41, 43, 64, 74, 75, 76, 77, 80, 83, 85, 90, 91, 101, 110, 133, 157, 181

Oates, Samuel Hamer, 18, 42, 83
Oldham, 50, 66, 71, 81, 106, 111, 121, 130
Ossett, 14, 113, 136, 138, 145
Ottiwell, near Marsden, 53, 103

Paine, Thomas, 1, 25, 26, 27, 71, 72, 146, 187, 188, 189
Parker, Hugh, 112, 113, 167
Perceval, Spencer, 109, 128, 132, 133, 149, 150, 185, 188
Peterloo, 59, 120, 183, 184
Pontefract, 97, 113

Radcliffe, Joseph, 46, 48, 85, 86, 87, 90, 92, 93, 100, 103, 105, 114, 122, 130, 131, 150, 156, 161, 169, 170, 175, 180, 186
Rastrick, 147, 154, 161
Rawfolds Mill, 97–104, 120, 169, 175, 177
Roberttown, 50
Rochdale, 48
Rotherham, 111, 112, 167
Rowbottom, Joseph, 64–5, 81, 106, 130

Saddleworth, 5, 43, 71, 80, 101, 134, 176
Shearmen, 47, 49, 50, 53, 74, 79, 99, 134

Sheffield, 24, 25, 39, 40, 41, 52, 64, 84, 111, 112, 113, 117, 123, 125, 139, 145, 150, 152, 153, 162, 164, 166, 167, 168, 181, 182, 183, 188
Sidmouth, Viscount, 1, 67, 130, 147, 149, 170, 172, 173, 175, 177, 182
Skipton, 28
Slaithwaite, 100
Soothill, 116, 132, 139, 144, 145

Thornhill, 160, 165, 182
Threshing machines, 115, 116, 117, 132, 139
Tomlinson, Matthew, 96, 99, 111, 115, 116, 118, 138, 140, 141, 147, 149, 158, 160, 161, 163
Trowbridge, 9, 32, 35, 39, 47, 49, 53

Unitarian, 10, 11, 18, 26, 28, 32, 56, 58, 78–80, 83, 86, 87, 122
United Englishmen, 25, 43, 56, 88, 97, 114, 121, 123, 126, 127, 129, 134, 163, 182
United Irishmen, 41, 121, 123, 124, 127, 128, 130

Wakefield, 1, 4, 12, 14, 18, 42, 44, 64, 65, 66, 69, 71, 72, 73, 108, 163
Wilberforce, William, 58, 86, 150
Wood, Sir Francis Lindley, 113, 136, 141, 150, 151
Wortley, James Archibald Stuart, 112, 115, 163, 164, 166
Wyvill, Revd. Christopher, 72, 183

Yeomanry, 1st West Riding, 32, 48, 112, 115, 130, 167, 182
York, 48, 56, 58, 59, 69, 83, 84, 89, 112, 152, 162, 170, 172, 174, 175, 176, 177, 178